Proclaimed from the Rooftops

Proclaimed from the Rooftops

TOPICAL HOMILIES
(BASED ON THE
EASTER-PENTECOST
DAILY LITURGICAL READINGS)

Michael Manning, S.V.D.

ALBA · HOUSE   NEW · YORK

SOCIETY OF ST. PAUL, 2187 VICTORY BLVD., STATEN ISLAND, NEW YORK 10314

Library of Congress Cataloging in Publication Data

Manning, Michael, 1940-
  Proclaimed from the rooftops.

  "Based on the Easter-Pentecost daily liturgical readings."
    1. Church year sermons. 2. Catholic Church--Sermons
  3. Sermons, American. I. Catholic Church. Liturgy
  and ritual. Lectionary (1969). II. Title.
  BX1756.M2922P76   232'.6   77-23471
  ISBN 0-8189-0355-4

Nihil Obstat:

Daniel V. Flynn, J.C.D.
Censor Librorum

Imprimatur:

✠ James P. Mahoney, D.D.
Vicar General, Archdiocese of New York
May 21, 1977

Designed, printed and bound in the United States of
America by the Fathers and Brothers of the Society of St. Paul,
2187 Victory Boulevard, Staten Island, New York, 10314,
as part of their communications apostolate.

1 2 3 4 5 6 7 8 9 (Current Printing: first digit).

CONTENTS

VIII   PROCLAIMED FROM THE ROOFTOPS

INTRODUCTION

The Holy Spirit gives enthusiasm and ever deeper meaning to our life in Jesus. I want this enthusiasm and meaning. I don't want to spend the rest of my life as a Christian just getting along with minimum requirements. I want to be all the magnificent things that God has created me for. I want to be full of deep faith in Jesus when others tell me it's not fashionable. I want to hope in Jesus even in the midst of painful discouragement. I want to love Jesus so much that I have to tell as many people as possible about Him.

This book is aimed at bringing you closer to this fire and strength of the Holy Spirit. On the way we first savor the wonder of the Resurrection. Then with one hand in the Acts of the Apostles and the other in the Gospel of John, we're bound for the ever renewing wonder of Pentecost.

Although the meditations can be used for daily homilies from Easter to Pentecost, I would hope the book could be used at any time in the year by people seeking to be renewed with the Holy Spirit.

I'm deeply grateful to Father Pat Connor, S.V.D. and Father Don Skerry, S.V.D. for their invaluable direction in preparing the manuscript. Special thanks to Mrs. Ana Ellis for her cheerful patience in typing.

Proclaimed from the Rooftops

1

"Then the Disciple who had arrived first at the tomb went in. He saw and believed" (Jn 20:8).

EXPECTING MORE!

> Jesus, you're so good to me. You're like a never-ending source of refreshment, joy and strength. Thank you for the great celebration of life that is Easter. But thank you more for not stopping two thousand years ago, but letting Easter be the beginning of a bigger and fuller life now! Thank you for never letting me have enough!

Easter is a terrible place to start a book. Any writer knows you have to build to a climax if you want to hold people's attention. But look at me! I start with the biggest happening the world has ever seen. What more could you expect after Easter? Things went to the extreme of Jesus, The Son of God, dying. He was murdered. Hung up on a cross, His life slowly ebbed away. The crucifixion was the most ugly and traumatic thing that had ever happened to the twelve men who had been His close associates and friends for three years. The Friday and Saturday of that week were about the lowest days that any one person could ever imagine or experience. But this Jesus who was dead was so powerful, He came to life. Talk about a climax! A man who was dead came to life and there were people who saw Him in the flesh.

They touched Him and talked with Him and even ate with Him. I know it's a little like a fairy tale, but it's true. Now that's what I call a climax! And look at me! This is where I start! How could one possibly build from this height?

What's so amazing is that there's more! Who could improve on the Resurrection? Only God. He's always full of the most extraordinary surprises. We want to box the Lord in and say that His life, death and resurrection is a fitting and significant historical fact. But the Lord Jesus is always blowing down the walls which we want to confine Him. He isn't just an historical character. He's now, right now, giving us the constant surprise of more and more blessings and wonders.

The coming of the Holy Spirit on Pentecost is that something more. Not only are we assured of everlasting life thru Jesus' victory over death, in addition, that life is going to be filled with an unimaginable wonder and peace and understanding and joy and power and enthusiasm. The greatest miracle of Easter and then Pentecost is that we will experience a never-ending fount of their reward. We might think we have a fullness of God's gifts, but if we will continue to expectantly look up to Jesus there will always be more.

Imagine if you will that you are back in your mother's womb and in a few hours you are going to be born. Let's pretend that your mother in her excitement has a chance to talk with you about what you have to look forward to:

Mother: Oh, I'm so excited. I've carried you for nine months and I've so longed to see you.

Infant: See? What does it mean to see?

Mother: Oh, you know, with your eyes . . . Oh, I guess you don't know about eyes. Well, they're wonderful, and with them you'll be able to see the magnificence of a mountain.

Infant: A mountain?

Mother: Oh, and you'll be able to stand on the mountain and overlook a valley filled with rich green trees!

Infant: Green? Trees?

Mother: Oh, and I want to take you to the ocean where you can experience the smell of salt water and watch the swell of a wave and then thrill as it smashes itself against the rocks.

Infant: Rocks? Ocean?

Mother: Oh, and when you are born your father and I will hold you tenderly and caress you and you will drink milk from my breast.

Infant: Father? Hold?

In Jesus we have the assurance that our fondest hopes will come true. But He doesn't stop there. What Jesus has in store for us even now in this life is more than we could hope for in our dreams!

"My heart has been glad and my tongue has rejoiced, my body will live on in hope, for you will not abandon my soul to the nether world, nor will you suffer your faithful one to undergo corruption" (Ac 2:26-27).

JESUS CONQUERS OUR DEEPEST FEAR

Jesus, you have conquered our greatest fear— death. Death is the greatest unknown. Thank you, Jesus, because in taking away this fear you have made me free to have joy even in the face of the most discouraging circumstances. You are the greatest freeing power I have known.

The French philosopher Gabriel Marcel once asked himself a fundamental question. What would be the greatest expression of love he could give to someone he cared for very much? I took up the challenge in my mind and went through a list of material gifts such as a house, a fur coat or even a life-insurance policy. There were good things to be found there but certainly not the greatest expression of love. I went a step further and considered loving devotion, and acceptance, and I even thought of giving one's life. In Corinthians, Paul says that even that can be done without love. Somehow there seemed to be always more that could be given. After a long process I turned to Marcel's conclusion. The greatest gift someone could give to another that he loved would be the assurance that they would never die. "I think you are so special that I never want your love to come to an end." Think about this awhile! Death is such a basic insecurity for us. The reason for the frightening aspect of death is that it's unknown. It's strange. We've never had anyone tell just exactly what it's going to be like. We fear only those things that we don't know. Death is such an unmanageable unknown, that when we face it, we are forced to dismiss its presence as far away as possible. So death goes into the sub-conscious or the outer periphery of our life. We do various things in order to deal with this great fear. Jogging, eating, and giving up smoking are means of fending off the reality of death in our lives. We know that with a healthier body we'll be able to stave off the dreaded fear for a while. This is behind the great concern for pills. Every time I slip on my seat belt in my car I'm trying to make sure that if I have an accident, although my body might be pretty well knocked around and even maimed, there's a better chance I won't have to face death. I'm sure this death fear is why a delightful relative of mine refuses to set foot in a plane.

In the face of this conscious or unconscious fear of death, we can get a little of the force of what Jesus does for us when he says, "If you believe in me you will live forever!" Easter is a time of victory over the greatest enemy that we will ever face. Jesus, in His Resurrection from the dead and His promise that we too can live forever, enables us to be free from fear as no other person could. That's what salvation means. We hear the word often, but basically it means freedom. Jesus has saved us. He's made us free. We are free from the greatest burden imaginable—death.

The problem with the Resurrection and its pledge of our never ending life, is that it's too good to believe. Look at the reaction of the soldiers who were guarding the Tomb, and you will see much the same reaction in each of us. Here they were, guarding a tomb for three days, and then suddenly there is this piercing blast of light and Jesus comes out of the tomb. That certainly is something to be believed in. But what do they do? They go to the Jewish Leaders and want to know what they can do to ignore the whole situation. The Resurrection is too good to believe! It's that way with me. I have to again and again make sure that I'm not toning down the strong reality of the Resurrection. Jesus was dead and now He's alive and in that victory I will live forever in Him!

My disbelief is like the businessman who wants to clear his department store of a certain stock and is willing to do it even at a losing price. He can't bring the price too low because customers wouldn't believe in the quality of the product. So he keeps the prices up. In Jesus' Resurrection I have such a key to life, happiness and meaning, but, like the soldiers, I live as though Eternal life is too good to believe.

The most beautiful aspect about the "no death" promise of Jesus is that it's not just a "when I die" reality, but it's something that happens right now. This promise of life means that I can have a fullness of living that is far beyond the greatest Humanitarian dream. In Jesus' Resurrection I have a here and now fullness of peace and joy and victory and power and love.

No longer can Satan tie me down with the fears that can make life aimless. In the Resurrection I can fill my cup of life to the brim and face each moment with exciting freshness, because there's always more life just ahead. I don't have to worry about the finality of death! Jesus, thank you for giving me more love than I'll ever be able to comprehend!

"Mary stood weeping beside the tomb. Even as she wept, she stooped to peer inside, and there she saw two angels in dazzling robes. One was seated at the head and the other at the foot of the place where Jesus' body had lain" (Jn 20:11-12).

ANGELS AND DEVILS

Jesus, you're wonderful. Your personal care for me is much more than I can imagine. Angels are a personal gift to me. They seem a little difficult to fit into my life at times because I get so caught up in rationalism and materialism. Help me to be open to the wonder of Angels as a sign of your limitless love for me.

Once I'm able to accept the astounding wonder of Jesus' being raised from the dead and thus promising me a life that will never end, I can't stop there. Now that I'm open and full of Christ's love and admiration for His limitless love there's more, and we're reminded of that in today's readings telling of Angels.

Angels are difficult to get excited about when the only reality I'll admit in my life is what I can touch with my hands and understand with my mind. But angels certainly are a reality in the Scriptures and their presence calls me to a deeper faith in the wonder of God's limitless creation. God's love for me is without bounds, no matter how much my finite mind wars against this truth.

One of the strongest realities of Angels to me is their power. It's reassuring to know that although fellow human beings can build awesome sky scrapers, seemingly endless roads, and space vehicles that can maneuver on Mars, there's another power that's even greater than all these man-made wonders combined. Angels, we are told, are beings of superior intellectual power. Because they are spirits, they aren't tied down to our restrictions of one place. This would be wonderful enough if they were just some creation that I was able to admire from a distance. The mind-boggling reality of these powerful beings is that they have been commissioned to watch over me and exert positive influences in my life. All this power has been given to guide, protect and care for me. What astonishing security and peace this can have when I make myself conscious of it.

When we try to make Angels something concrete in our lives, we run into a problem. We need to pull the Angels from their non-material realms and make them more understandable to us. So artists try to tap "the other worldliness" of Angels, their power and superiority and innocence, and we come up with a picture that is so other-worldly and strange that we prefer to deal with the stock market or the difficult decision of which mouthwash to trust. Wings and haloes and cherubic faces are difficult to take. We continually have to break away from our human and limiting images of Angels.

Our prayers should also include communication with Angels. They are a vital part of our salvation. Our appreciation of Angels should be a vital part of our awareness of God's infinite love. As we join the Angels in giving their endless praise and glory to the Lord, we should also ask that they speak to God for us. Thus we'll be more aware of the power they exert in our lives.

One of the important aspects of Angels is that they do battle. It's also good for us not to put under the rug the person they do battle with: Satan, who is real. We're made more aware of his presence by movies like **"The Exorcist"** and **"The Omen."** Although there can be much to disagree with in movies about Satan, they have value in making us aware of Satan's strength. The specific nature of the battle that goes on between Angels and Devils over us and our world is difficult to pin down. But, if we are honest with ourselves, we have to admit there are forces, good and evil, that move in us as we try to follow Jesus.

Although I would be the last to deny extraordinary manifestations of the power of Satan, I don't think that these ugly and obvious presences are his main concern. To me, the greatest power of Satan is to be had in his very subtle dealings with "very good people." In a very quiet way all he has to do is plant tiny seeds of exaggerated concern about the past and the future. The Kingdom of Jesus is the Kingdom of Now. "I am who am." The Kingdom of Satan is whatever can move people out of the power of now into the anxious concern about five minutes ago or ten minutes from now. Satan doesn't have to work fantastic signs, when all he has to do is make a very good person move out of the power of Jesus at this present moment and move into the ulcer-generating concern with yesterday or tomorrow.

Possibly my greatest battle with Satan involves my making sure that I am open to the wonder of the present moment and knowing that this is the only time that Jesus can work. If I move from the present into anxiety for the past or future, I need the help of all the Angels I can get, because I'm in enemy territory.

4

" 'What are you discussing as you go on your way?' They
halted, in distress, and one of them, Cleophas by name,
asked him, 'Are you the only resident of Jerusalem who
doesn't know the things that went on these past few
days?' He said to them, 'What things?' They said, 'All
those that had to do with Jesus of Nazareth, a prophet,
powerful in word and deed in the eyes of God and all
the people; how our chief priests and leaders delivered
him up to be condemned to death, and crucified Him.
We were hoping that He was the one who would set
Israel free' " (Lk 24:17-21).

GOD WORKS IN HELPLESSNESS

Lord, sometimes it's so hard to hope. My ol' world
never seems to learn its lesson. I seem at times to
be on a terrible roller-coaster ride with evil.
Sometimes things are going well, but then that
inevitable downfall comes. Jesus, help me to have
hope in your almighty ever-present power. Help
me to live the victory over evil and lack of hope.
You paid such a big price for victory over evil.
Give me your gift of undying hope!

Try to put yourself in the situation of the two disciples
as they made their way to Emmaus. They had been
following Jesus and were riding high on the hope that
He was going to be the person who would take them

out of the discouraging Roman domination they were living in. Things had seemed to be going well. As a matter of fact they were getting better each day. The blind were seeing, the lame were walking, the dumb were talking and the deaf were hearing. And as if that weren't enough, just a couple of weeks back Jesus had used His power to raise to life a friend of His who had been dead for four days. The disciples were on top of the world!

They were associated with the sure power that would overthrow the Romans. Then, three days before, everything had turned upside down. Jesus was roughly captured and judged and sentenced to die on a cross outside the city. I can hear them muttering in their discouragement now. "We felt sure that Jesus was going to be able to change our fickle life which never seems secure. We thought we could break out of our discouragement into a permanent victory! No such luck. Guess we'll have to continue on with our illusions of hope, while all the time we know the tragedy of last Friday is inevitable."

Jesus' resurrection has changed the inevitability of losing. In Jesus' resurrection we have the hope that will never die. What does that mean? Let me explain.

One of the radio stations that I listen to frequently in my car carries nothing but news. I enjoy keeping abreast of what's going on in the world. But as I listen more and more to the news or read it in the daily papers, there's an underlying paganism that I continually have to confront with my new life in Jesus. The news reports that we receive convey the inevitability of evil. There are happy things that happen in the world, but underlying this news is a basic pessimism, and the conviction that evil will inevitably tarnish any good. "In the long run, does it matter which politician is in office?" "Will world organizations ever stop the inevitability of war?" There is a terrible cyclic resignation in our understanding of world or national affairs. We're in an inevitable wind-tunnel that keeps going round and round with no possible prospect of our shooting straight out of the circle into a hope that will never diminish. This feeling isn't new. It's the same one that the disciples felt as they went from the scene of the Crucifixion. Sure, good will come, but defeat is inevitable.

As followers of Jesus, we have to declare war on the inevitability of hopelessness. With the light of Christ's resurrection as ammunition, we have to show that Christ has won the victory and that we need not face problems without hope.

Now it would be foolish to say that once the reality of Christ comes into our lives we will not have to face problems, or that terrible tragedy may not befall us— perhaps on a regular basis. The key is that with Jesus' resurrection a reality in our lives right now, we no longer have to see tragedy and heartbreak as an end but rather as the natural death experience that will bring out of hopelessness victory and peace.

Jesus promises us peace, but, paradoxically, we find a life of persecution and trouble like His. Our peace is based on knowledge of victory. We have hope of change and sense of direction that won't allow pessimism. Through Jesus' resurrection, history and the material world have taken on the new meaning. All things are working together for good.

One Thanksgiving I was traveling home to California with a van-load of college prospects, after visiting the college I recruit for in Iowa. Six of us were being bounced around in a borrowed VW van. There was snow and cold. I was sacked out in one of the seats after having driven for nine hours through the icy mountain roads of Colorado. It was 10:00 p.m. and we were in the middle of nowhere. Suddenly, I was jolted out of my sleep by a thud as the van hit something. A deer had bolted in front of us, and we smashed right into the animal, demolishing the front of the van. There was $900.00 worth of damage. As the van skidded to a stop and the frightened yells subsided, the first words I heard were from some uncomfortably joyful Christian, "Thank you, Jesus!", and I knew someone had the hope necessary to change a fatalistic world! Jesus, help me break out of no-hope to new-life in you!

5

"Then they recounted what had happened on the road and how they had come to know Him in the breaking of bread. While they were still speaking about all this, He Himself stood in their midst and said to them, 'Peace to you' " (Lk 24:35-36).

PARTICIPATION IN THE EUCHARIST

Jesus, one of the most beautiful signs of your love for me is your continued giving in the Eucharist. The Eucharist is special in my life, but I have to admit that at times it becomes a matter of rote and so much of the rich meaning is lost. As a leader, help me encourage the participation of others.

As a priest one of the biggest complaints I hear from people is that the Mass is boring! So they have decided not to attend regularly. A person can have a better communion with God by going off to the mountains or into the woods for an hour on a Sunday than by being stuffed in a church shoulder to shoulder with 700 strangers, listening to a priest drone mechanically through a script, while all the time you're wondering if he cares, if anybody is listening to him. Many people, as they grow older, find their reasons for going to Mass have changed. With many it used to be to make sure that they didn't commit a mortal sin. But as they think more about this attitude they conclude there is probably a greater sin in being a hypocrite by attending something that doesn't mean what it's supposed to, and so, through a few twists of reason, it seems for them better not to go to Mass than to attend.

What do you say to this, as a priest? As a celebrant, I can pick up the non-plussed expression on the faces of so many at Church. I know too that I contribute to the problem by not being prepared for my homily the way I should. I need to put heartfelt meaning into the Eucharistic prayers, which if I'm not careful, can become just another function. The problem is all the more complicated when as a celebrant you are in your second or third Mass of the day and the heat and the repetition and the tiredness of your body work against freshness, let alone excitement.

There is a problem. But how can we get a handle on the solution? One of the key difficulties is television. The average American looks at TV three hours a day. That's a lot of time for a person to spend seeking to be entertained. TV is a passive medium. People spend so much time giving of themselves at work or with the children that TV is a welcome relief. On TV somebody does something for you and you don't have to respond. If things get too involving you merely have to switch the channel.

This passive attitude is on the increase in our society. Being entertained by others has become very important. And so it's quite natural that we should have these passive reactions when we attend Mass. So much of our time is spent wondering if the celebrant is going to be any good or if his sermon is going to be interesting. How many times have you wondered if the choir was going to be any good because when it's lively the whole liturgy becomes more bearable?

The key to an effective Celebration is not a Bishop Sheen for each homily or the reading of the prayers with outstanding techniques of oral interpretation. We have to turn upside down our understanding of attending Mass. Participation has to be more and more the watchword. If the Mass is going to be effective for us we have to come prepared to participate. There are several outstanding roles in the Celebration: reader, server, usher, member of the choir, cleaning the liturgical clothes, cleaning the Church, helping to count the collection, or being part of a team that helps prepare the liturgies in the parish. But what about the rest?

The key to effective worship is for one to come with an open mind and to want to hear God speaking today in a special way.

Here are some practical suggestions for all participants in the Eucharist. Come to church at least ten minutes before the celebration starts. Make a sincere effort to communicate with the Lord and then ask that the Lord respond through the readings and prayers and reflections of the priest. Then pull out the missalette and go through the readings of the day. It would be good to even start mulling over the readings a few days before. After the readings have been read, start to formulate your own homily. Pick a point that seems to be common to the first and third reading or concentrate on the second reading and see what has spoken to you strongly. Then start preaching a homily to yourself on the readings as they speak to you. Now, with this background you can listen with greater understanding to the often strange-sounding readings, which are especially strange if you are hearing them for the first time. This approach to listening to the Scriptures will have an encouraging effect on the lector. As he sees the attentive faces of those listening to him he'll be more concerned and excited while reading.

Then we must discipline ourselves to make sure that we don't sit passively and listen to the Eucharistic ritual, even if it's the thousandth time we've heard it. No, we must be attentive and listen as if this were the first time. We have to be open to the power of the Lord and admit that He's going to do something big in our lives right now. When this attentiveness is present in even one person, it will spread like wild-fire to the other participants in the Eucharist. I know that as a celebrant. I can be celebrating my third Mass on a Sunday. I'm tired. It's a late hour and everyone seems to be wishing that I cut the homily short and move through the prayers quickly so that the wife can get home to get dinner ready and the husband can catch the last quarter of the game on TV. Everyone seems dead, but still I want to share what the Lord's put into my heart. All can be going down-hill in my presentation when suddenly I pick up a face that's brimming with attentiveness and interest in the last row far over in the corner. That one person's attention can change the whole complexion of the congregation. If one person prays well and sings with meaning and listens with all his power, his presence becomes infectious and soon his participation spreads. Really, it works!

Please don't give up hope on a priest or parish that seems to have dull liturgies. Your participation can be the seed that transforms everyone. The change might not come overnight, but your participation will inevitably change a dead parish to one that has all the life and excitement of the upper room on Easter Sunday.

"Just after daybreak Jesus was standing on the shore, though none of the disciples knew it was Jesus. He said to them, 'Children, have you caught anything to eat?' 'Not a thing,' they answered. 'Cast your net off to the starboard side,' he suggested, 'and you will find something.' So they made a cast and took so many fish that they couldn't haul the net in" (Jn 21:4-6).

LEARNING TO TRUST JESUS

Jesus, what I need to do is trust in your power. So many times I forget that you have power. I get so caught up in my own efforts to do various things that again and again I need to experience great weakness and thus appreciate that only in you will I ever come to fill the great role you have for me. That has to come through your power and not my bull-headed efforts to do things my way.

I'm not much of a fisherman. Last summer though, I was up in the Sierras on vacation, trout-fishing in a breathtakingly beautiful spot about 9,000 feet high. I was being taught by a real master. In four days of fishing we caught 80 fish. I was rather high on fishing! When I got home I was anxious to try my hand at the sport again. I asked another friend who liked to fish to come with me and we set out to repeat the thrill of the 80 fish in the Sierras. We got up at 4:30 a.m. (the desire for fish can drive a man to even that madness), and drove to a near-by lake. The air was cold, but the initial excitement out-weighed any discomfort. The two of us stood by the edge of that lake for three and a half hours and all I had to show for it was three lost hooks and one nibble. Fishing is a fickle sport!

I'm reminded of this when I reflect on the frustrations of the apostles in today's reading. They had been fishing all night. Daylight had broken, and they had caught nothing. Then something significant happened. Jesus came on the scene, on the edge of the water. But he wasn't recognized by the apostles. He called out, "Children!" I don't know, but that seems a somewhat offensive way to address burly, frustrated fishermen. "Cast your nets on the other side of the boat." Now what is important is that the apostles took this stranger's advice. First of all, who was this stranger to tell them how they should fish after they had tried to do it all night? They weren't amateurs! Secondly, the job of casting nets on the other side of the boat was more involved than pulling in one's line on a reel and then casting in the other direction. There were big heavy nets that had to be gathered and then moved. I'm sure that I wouldn't have been as humble and spontaneous as the apostles. My gut reaction to a stranger would be to wish that he'd mind his own business. But if I did take his suggestion and try fishing on the other side and had success, I would be more galled than happy that this know-it-all could come along without effort and succeed so quickly. My pride would fester!

The apostles had been good students of Jesus in the years he'd been with them. Sure, they were slow to understand that Jesus wasn't going to be a temporal King, but they learned a very important lesson. They knew how to be trusting and open to suggestions.

This is the big lesson that Jesus wants to teach us

today: we have to trust in the power of the Lord in our lives. This might mean that we will be called upon to do something that is very difficult or uncomfortable or impractical in the eyes of the world. But as long as we trust in the power of the Lord Jesus and listen to the direction that he's giving us in our lives, we're going to have the key to successful power. With our trust in the Lord we're going to be able to perform wonders that are far beyond what we expect. In the apostles' weakness and openness and trust even in a stranger, they had more blessings than they could easily handle. The catch of fish was so big!

One of the most difficult aspects of relaxing in the power of God's love for us is that we have to drink deeply of weakness. The apostles made themselves weak as they followed the stranger's suggestions, even though they knew what fishing was all about.

The power of God sometimes works most effectively when we are weak, and this happens not only by our own choice as with the apostles today, but also in the weakness of the human situation we're forced to live in. The Apostles had caught "not a thing." When in weakness we have "not a thing" we can expect this to be the spring-board for miracles. This is where we get to the honesty of knowing that we need direction from a power greater than ourselves. When things are going wrong and you don't feel that you have any resources left, watch out, for you are on the verge of magnificence.

7

"Jesus rose from the dead early on the first day of the week. He first appeared to Mary Magdalene, out of whom He had cast seven demons. She went to announce the Good News to His followers, who were now grieving and weeping" (Mk 16:9-10).

WHAT WAS JESUS' ATTITUDE TOWARD WOMEN?

Jesus, you were always interested in people that were being put down by others. You wanted to help them to be free. Right now our society is going through a lot of growing pains to understand the place of women. Help me be concerned as you are with the proper place of women.

Freedom was something that concerned Jesus very much. Whenever He found someone that was enslaved in any way, He used all His power to free him or her. People's consciences were being enslaved by the regulations of the Scribes and Pharisees. Jesus confronted them with the harsh words, "You hypocrites!" The blind were enslaved by darkness, the cripples were enslaved by weak muscles, Samaritans were enslaved by prejudice, the deaf were enslaved by silence and the dead were enslaved by death. Jesus gave freedom to all. There was another type of enslavement. Women were given a very inferior position in society.

We get a clue about Jesus' concern for women in

today's Gospel, when it's to women that Jesus makes His first appearance. That was quite an honor. Jesus rocked a lot of boats with His attitudes toward women. We can pick this up in the story of the Samaritan woman at the well. Remember the reaction of the Apostles when they came back and found Him alone with the woman? Jesus was a teacher, and as such should never have been alone with a woman. Jesus broke through that custom and loved the woman for who she was. He knew that she needed personal attention and wasn't about to overlook her because of custom. Then there was the fact that Jesus was a friend of Martha and Mary. It was not with the tradition of the times for the evangelists to make note of the fact that a man like Jesus had close bonds of friendship with two women.

In Jesus' time women had no legal rights; they were things. A woman was regarded as the mere possession of her father or husband and at his disposal to do with as he liked. In the regular form of morning prayer the Jew thanked God that He had not made him a Gentile, a slave, or a woman. In light of this it's interesting that in Jesus' pedigree there are five women mentioned—and what women! Rachab was a harlot of Jericho, Ruth was not even a Jewess, Thamar was a deliberate seducer and an adulteress, Bathsheba was the woman whom David seduced away from Uriah, her husband, with unforgivable cruelty. At the very beginning of His Gospel we see that Jesus stands for the knocking down of all barriers that will hinder people, and we as Christians must continue Jesus' struggle for the liberation of women.

That's very fine, you may say, but if Jesus was so strong in bringing liberation to women, why does St. Paul seem so chauvinistic? Let me share with you some reflections on what I think about St. Paul and women. When Paul says, "Wives, be submissive to your husbands," I don't think that he is calling women back to the slavery they knew before Jesus. Rather he's calling them to the greatest liberation possible, the liberation of Jesus. When the apostles were arguing among themselves as to who had the highest rank, Jesus responded by washing their feet. "Let him who would be a leader be he who serves." Paul says it his way when he says, "When I'm weakest, that's when I'm strongest of all." To a Christian the real exertion of power that comes with liberation is not found in wielding a big stick but in being submissive to another. In Hebrews, chapter 5, we read that Jesus learned obedience to the Father through cries and supplication. Jesus was a man of great power, but that power was founded on submission to the will of the Father. This is the key to Christian liberation —submission. So when Paul says, "Wives, be submissive to your husbands," he's really saying, "In your submission you will have power." Woman's power is found in submission, and who would deny the power they've exerted by their submission in changing the world.

One very important ingredient in all this is that before you can submit and give yourself away, as Jesus did, you have to first know what you have and appreciate it. Women must grow in love and respect for themselves based on Jesus' love for them, and only then give themselves away with effective power. If we don't respect the self we're giving, then we're wasting what we give. And it can never redound to the power that comes from obedient weakness.

In women's submission we have the key to effecting the revolution of the Kingdom.

8

"The place where they were gathered shook as they prayed. They were filled with the Holy Spirit and continued to speak God's word with confidence" (Ac 4:31).

"Do not be surprised that I tell you you must all be begotten from above. The wind blows where it will. You hear the sound it makes, but you do not know where it comes from or where it goes. So it is with everyone begotten of the Spirit" (Jn 3:7-8).

THE BAPTISM OF THE HOLY SPIRIT

Jesus, you are calling me to a new life in your Holy Spirit. I am to be born again. I so want your freshness. I so want to live a life that is continually being renewed. Please come to me. Be like a strong wind that blows even in places I least expect and let me be surprised with your ever-renewing life!

What is there about a new baby that fills us with excitement? There's a quiet awe that touches us as we come into the presence of a new baby. Even though all babies look red and wrinkly, they bring a smile to our faces. Babies are special. Why? I think one of the main reasons for our special attraction to babies is that they are a beginning. We in our lives have been through so much, and there are times when the mistakes that we've made start to pile up and we wish that we could have gained experience in some other way than the inevitable hurting of ourselves and others. A baby touches in a concrete way what it means to start again. What a joyous challenge for parents to know that now they're going to be able to mould, through love and direction, the child that will be with them for some 20 years. In this image of their love they can start again. Yes, a baby is special because it is hope personified.

This is why I think I'm so attracted to the conversation Nicodemus and Jesus had. The words of Jesus are so beautiful and full of hope, "You must all be begotten from above." In the midst of a world that would like to press us into hopelessness, we have a vision of hope in the chance for a new birth. We can be begotten again even if we've been living for many years.

We are not so terribly unrelated to the idea of new life even after a person has been living for many years. We can experience it if we see a five-year-old girl who's been caught in a rip tide down at the beach and been washed out to sea. After the rescue and her lifeless body is stretched out on the sand we think there is no hope, but then the skilled lifeguard puts his mouth to the little girl's mouth and suddenly the purple of death is changed to the blush of life, and where there was death, there is a coughing red-eyed life. The same rebirth comes to the heroin addict who dies during the time called "cold turkey." For minutes, hours, and days he goes without the drug and every fiber of his body screams for the needed heroin. The addict resists and soon has a new life and freedom from the clutches of the drug.

The death we're living might be even more subtle. Perhaps a person who professes to be a Christian has slipped into the death of meaninglessness, boredom, and mediocrity in his relationship with Jesus. Christianity has become a legal obligation or a social nicety.

The birth we speak of today is really a new birth into

the life of the Holy Spirit. We are called to be born again into a fire of love for Jesus.

What we need is something more than sitting back and thinking that all that matters is being baptized, perhaps when only an infant. This was a Baptism in the Holy Spirit. This was real. But just as new life and re-birth are experienced every time we touch life in a new way—whether we're resuscitated, or able to die to an addiction, so the Baptism of our youth has ever to be renewed.

This Baptism is something that moves in all facets of our life—physical, mental, spiritual and social, in a continuing renewal of the Holy Spirit in our lives.

This is where the Baptism of the Holy Spirit comes in. In the midst of a life that could be quite satisfied that salvation is being worked out rather well with a minimum of output and a maximum of return, the Holy Spirit comes in like a wind that's moving in the most unpredictable way, an uprooting hurricane that's be-yond the power that we could generate. Our lives be-come as strong as the mighty wind and as intense as any moon-struck lover's and we're on fire with a new life that we can't stifle. We actually experience something that's real. We can feel it. We're driven to do things that we never thought we were capable of. Our zeal for the Lord has no bounds. We long to share His love with everyone we meet. The love of Jesus is so real I want this reality of wholeness and fundamental meaning to fill the lives of those I love.

One of the greatest attributes of life to me is total unpredictability. I love a movie or play where I can't predict the unfolding of the plot. This is the unpredict-ability of the Holy Spirit, who always comes with a new-ness and freshness of His love. He's exciting and alive and He makes life a challenge even in the bleakest corner into which we've painted ourselves.

The saddest thing about this rebirth is that it can die unless we're careful. Some people use the phrase "backslide." They revert to the life they had before Baptism. They leave the life they've experienced. A psychologist friend of mine told me of his experience with some of his patients. Even at the height of seeming physical and mental maturity, certain people fall back to what he calls, "a womb with a view." Only by the power of the Holy Spirit can we maintain our new life. It's so important that we work to keep our vitality and grow to be the people that God has called us to be, through the continuing death to ourselves and the rebirth of the Holy Spirit.

9

"The community of believers were of one heart and one mind. None of them ever claimed anything as his own; rather, everything was held in common. With power the Apostles bore witness to the resurrection of the Lord Jesus, and great respect was paid to them all. Nor was there anyone needy among them, for all who owned property or houses sold them and donated the proceedings. They used to lay them at the feet of the Apostles to be distributed to everyone according to his need" (Ac 4:32-34).

TRUST GOD TILL IT HURTS!

Jesus, you call me again and again to trust you. You want me to let go of the security I can generate and know deep in my heart that you are caring for me and that I shouldn't worry, for you won't let me go. Trusting in you, I can do great things. Please help me. Let me reach out and run the most powerful risk there is, trusting you in everything.

Trust is a word that comes up again and again in the Scriptures. It's what the Lord is calling us to continually. Think of Abraham who trusted until he was ninety that he would have a son. Moses trusted in the Lord even though any travel agent could have told him his trip through the desert should have taken four days instead of forty years. David trusted when he knew that the Lord would forgive his adultery with Bathsheba. Hosea trusted that God would work things out, even though his heart was broken by his wife's being a harlot and having three children by other men. And likeable Gideon trusted the Lord that he could conquer 40,000 Midianites with 300 Israelites armed only with horns, jars and torches. And they did it!

In our every-day lives God is asking again and again that He be the center. But to do that He wants us to use our free will and stop putting our trust in what material things we can make or what power we can achieve. What He wants us to do is tell Him that we are going to trust in Him even when things get to looking bleak. We will thank Him even in tragedy for we know that He will take care of us and we won't have to worry. This is very hard, and yet is the heart of what it means to be a real child of God.

One of the aspects of trust that is so difficult is that we have to take on the role of weakness. We have to be foolish in the eyes of that world that strives to be so secure in its material castles. We have to let all anxiety go and know that even when we're weak we're really strongest of all because we've opened ourselves to the power of the Lord Jesus, the creator of all that exists. With that power moving in me there is nothing that I can't do.

One of the greatest symbols of security in our materialistic and capitalistic world is money. So much of everything that we do is based on how much we have and how much more we can get. That's why today's Scripture reflections sound so almost out of this world. That people would be willing to share their money in common and trust another person to have some of their hard-earned money is difficult to understand. Such an act could happen only with the power of God working in people.

I recently did some work with a minister whom I admire very much and thank because he's been an instrument that brought me close to Jesus. One of the things that I found him making a lot of sense about was his attitude toward taking offerings at his prayer meetings. Rather than complain about all the expenses that had to be met, his main direction in asking for money was that our giving of money should be a strong sign of our faith in God.

We should have a cause that is really dedicated to the message of Jesus, and then our donation should make us uncomfortable when it comes to material security. We should reach out with a real offering of faith so that although we might not have enough of our hard-earned money after a donation, it's given with a real trust in the Lord that he'll not leave us alone but will return our trust with real security.

I remember I had an experience of trying this kind of trust in the Lord. I was in San Francisco doing my work of recruiting men for the missions. My funds were getting low. After helping out in our parish in the city, I had $40.00 to get back down to Southern California. At this time, a missionary from New Guinea came for a couple of days. He was on his first vacation in seven years. He was planning to take a bus back to New York on his way back to the missions. As he was about to leave, I thought about trusting the Lord with money and even dipping into the security that is so important to me. Well, I gave the missionary $30.00, and told the Lord that I'd trust in Him. I hoped I would make it down to Los Angeles on the $10.00 I had left. Well . . . things went all right. I got down South and I was able to get by with a good bit of insecurity for a couple of weeks.

I kept reminding the Lord I trusted Him, and then two and a half weeks later, just as a big bill for new tires and a major car repair was tapping ominously at my shoulder, I got a donation for $300.00 in the mail. The trust I'd shown rebounded to the tune of a ten-fold blessing.

If you are having financial problems, I would greatly suggest the greatest means of security is tapping that security and trusting in the Lord. Untold blessings both material and spiritual will be yours.

10

"The light came into the world, but men love darkness rather than light, because their deeds were wicked. Everyone who practices evil hates the light; he does not come near it for fear his deeds will be exposed. But he who acts in truth comes into the light, to make clear that he deeds are done in God" (Jn 3:18-21).

IN JESUS WE CAN LOWER OUR MASKS

Jesus, why is it that I spend so much time trying to keep people in the dark about the true me? I wear all kinds of masks so that people won't know me. I'm afraid of the light. Let your light shine in my life, so I don't have to be ashamed of who I am, since you accept me—and that's enough.

A few years back, I was studying drama at the Catholic University in Washington, D. C. One of the classes was in pantomime. The teacher was Claude Chagrin, an outstanding pupil of Marcel Marceau. An exercise with masks taught me a great lesson. At the end of one class she asked each of us to go home and to make a paper mask for the next day. It was supposed to be rather abstract. That sounded simple enough. I went home and tried to be creative, but the best I could come up with was a sheet of paper with two pieces of string attached and a place for my eyes, nose and mouth.

When we arrived at class the next day, she told us to lay the masks on the edge of the stage. We were working in an old theatre. Then she asked us to come up one at a time and pick a mask other than ours, study what the mask said to us, and then, in pantomime, act out what we thought a person with that face would do. Ouch! I started to get nervous. There were over twenty in the class and so far we hadn't gotten to know each other very well. I was nervous about acting in front of strangers, all by myself on the stage. I didn't know what they would think of me.

When my turn came, my heart started to beat fast. I awkwardly walked up to the masks. I picked one that looked rather clever, and then tried to think of what I would act out as I got on the stage. I looked at the mask, and then at the people and was bewildered. But then, the magic happened. I put on the mask and suddenly I had a new feeling. There I was in front of people who I thought would be judging me and finding fault with me, but suddenly, with the mask over my face, I found that the muscles in my face relaxed and then my whole body was calm. I even smiled behind the mask. There I was, secure behind my mask. I could stick my tongue out at them, and they wouldn't even know. I could twist up my face and do all kinds of things behind the mask and they couldn't tell what I was doing. With a little cough from the teacher, I broke out of my reverie and did some silly little actions. After I was home and got a chance to do a little meditation on the day's activity, I found what a deep lesson for my life that mask experience was. I realized that although I didn't have a paper mask to hide behind, I did have a lot of masks that I wore for the various occasions I was in. I had one mask for my close associates, one mask for my superiors, one mask for people that are in need, and one mask for people that want to have a good time. I realized how important masks were to me to be able to cope with the various occasions I stepped into each day.

The Holy Spirit is the source of my unmasking. He is the Spirit of truth. Today's reading reminds me of the masks, because Jesus calls us to a life that's free of masks. He asks that we be whole and children of the light, rather than mask-wearers who want to hide from the truth.

One of my biggest difficulties with masks is when it comes to the Sacrament of Confession. I am one priest who hates to go to Confession. You see, I go to Confession to one of the priests in my community, one of the men that I live and work with. We work together day in and day out, and when I come to Confession I have to peel off that mask and lay all the bad stuff before him. I have to tell Father Charlie that I'm not the person that I wish I were. I have to put down the mask. That is hard. I have this fantastic image of what I think people see when they see me. I've put on this mask that I present to the world. When I go to Confession I have to take it off. The truth hurts! But you know what's beautiful when you share Confession with someone that loves you? You soon learn that your mask is transparent. After I lay out all those things that I'm so nervous about revealing, Father says, "Yes, is there anything else?" and I know that he knows me and he loves me for who I am; and I don't have to pretend I'm someone else, because he loves me as I am. In that love he gives me, I experience the acceptance of God. To Him I can bring the truth of my sins and feelings from darkness into the light and He'll say, "I still love you."

Please don't go into the dark again because you look much better in the light. The true you is fantastic!

11

"He whom God has exalted at His right hand as ruler and savior is to bring repentance to Israel and forgiveness of sins" (Ac 5:31).

AM I REALLY REPENTING?

Jesus, so many times when I try to change my life, I concentrate on the wrong thing. I deal with sin only on the surface level rather than getting to the roots. I'm like an iceberg that has ten percent above water and the rest, the majority of me, is hidden. Help me to get down to the root issues in my attempts to change my life through repentance and to accept your forgiveness.

I spend a great deal of my life telling myself that I should change. I'm forever getting upset that I continually revert to sin. I hear Jesus call me today to repentance and forgiveness and I wonder if it's possible because I've tried so many times and I never seem to have the secret of effectively repenting of my sins so that I can take a complete about face in what I'm doing.

I know that I'm not fully conscious of much of what is going on in me. The source of many of my actions is due to my unconscious self. Since Jesus wants us to be whole people, I think He calls us in a special way to start to deal with the unconscious parts of our lives, so that we can effectively move to repentance in our conscious life.

Let me elaborate what I mean. One of the most important problems in my life is anger. The problem isn't that I'm a hot-head going around shouting and cursing and using physical violence. The contrary is true. I have a very difficult time letting anger be a part of my normal life. I taught high school for three years and this was one reason why I was poor in teaching. I wasn't able to get angry. Anger is something that we as Christians have a hard time seeing as a good thing. I am annoyed by the mothers of children who come to Confession to me and complain that they lost their tempers and committed the sin of anger. When I pursue the question a little bit, more times than not the anger toward their children was very justified. As a matter of fact, the anger was a very loving expression, and not to have expressed anger would have probably been the real sin, because the children needed a good confrontation to enable them to rectify their lives. For the mother who in the past week was frequently angry, I say three cheers! She has a freedom and honest love that can be admired.

For some reason we have labeled anger as a very unchristian reaction. Although anger is a natural reaction on certain occasions, we have picked up the belief that Jesus wants us to suppress that emotion and be more like the serene holy pictures of Him who never seemed to be flustered or angry.

Anger is bad only when it's the symptom of selfishness and imprudence. Anger is good when it's channeled through love, and is an honest expression of ourselves.

Jesus was angry when he confronted Scribes and Pharisees. He was angry with the sellers and money-changers in the Temple. He was angry with Peter when he wouldn't admit that suffering and death were integral parts of the Father's will. He was angry with the Apostles when they wouldn't understand that His Kingdom wasn't a Kingdom of physical force for the overthrow of the Romans. So what about us? Despite the example of Jesus, we persist in suppressing our feelings of justifiable anger and find terrible fault with ourselves when we don't live up to the emotionless serenity to which Jesus seems to be calling us.

The problem is that this sub-conscious suppression of anger leads to all kinds of problems and the more we suppress them, the more sub-conscious they become and the less we're able to deal with them and be the whole people Jesus is calling us to be. Our attempts at repentance are doomed to regularly recurring failure.

When we suppress our justified anger four different things happen to us: 1) Physical tensions and sicknesses start to show and we can't figure out where they come from. For example, our inability to honestly express our anger can lead to tension and such things as ulcers. We go to Confession to repent of being irritable and not at peace in our family, but we don't realize that the core problem is that we're not able to express our anger honestly and with love. 2) Sudden outbursts of anger for seemingly insignificant things are due to unexpressed anger. In Confession people tell of being mystified that they seem to be mentally unbalanced because some simple litle thing can set them in a rage. But this thing was perhaps a trigger to anger that had been building up and now is spilling over into something that seemed innocent enough. This anger is especially harmful to others because they feel that their insignificant actions are very bad, and self-esteem is hurt. 3) Another reaction that occurs when anger builds up is physical violence. Unless anger has a proper ventilation through honest expressions of displeasure and good doses of emotion, violence is a common result. 4) Finally, depression very often is nothing more than a state of being overburdened with unexpressed anger. One of the best means of getting out of depression is for the person to start to express pent-up anger in a loving way.

Let's be honest with ourselves as we try to repent. Let's deal with the whole of our persons and not try to cure a cancer with a band-aid. Let's make a radical decision to get in touch with our emotions and the subconscious drives that are militating against our dealing with the talents and goodness that the Lord has given to us. That way we can grow to become the great people Jesus has called us to be. Let's give the Lord something to be really forgiven.

12

"When Jesus looked up and caught sight of a vast crowd coming toward Him, He said to Phillip, 'Where shall we buy bread for these people to eat?' " (Jn 6:5).

CHRISTIANITY AND SOCIAL INVOLVEMENT

Jesus, help me remember that your message was one of service to the poor. Help me to be sensitive to the needs of my brothers and sisters who are less fortunate than I in the areas of justice and freedom. So many people are suffering under social injustice and inequality. Help me to be involved with the needy as you were.

From today's reading we know that Jesus was very concerned with the physical needs of the people to whom He ministered. He knew that the message of His Kingdom wouldn't be effective if people were without enough food to live on. And so He multiplied the bread and fish. As a follower of Jesus, I must continually struggle with myself to be sensitive to and work for the physical needs of others. It's easy to get so comfortable with the security of a roof over my head, enough food on my plate, and kind friends to support me, that I can insulate myself from those in need. Social involvement is an integral part of the role of a Christian. Many times when I'm confronted by those who are down and out or who are struggling under social injustice, I come up with all kinds of excuses for not helping them: "They can get Social Security,"; "If I give a quarter to this panhandler, he'll add it to the other quarters he's gotten and buy a fifth." "Why should I be concerned with people who are just too lazy to get a job?" "Who am I to try and effect a change in Legislation? What do we have politicians for?" Despite some of these arguments, and many of them are probably quite valid, I must not shirk my responsibility to care for those who are in physical need.

In line with my rationalizations, there are those who say that Jesus wasn't involved with social problems at all. These people say that we should keep Jesus out of social concerns because Jesus' exclusive preoccupation was with the soul. He taught a mystical piety. He was content to leave material conditions just as he found them. He deliberately refused to take cognizance of any aspects of the life of man in the world aside from the spiritual. He came, not to save the world as it was, but to save men out of the world. He was not concerned with the redress of social wrongs or the irradication of social injustice; His thoughts were moving on another plane . . . So I can sit back and relax, because in Christianity there is a complete divorce between religion and social duties.

Deep in my heart I know that this is wrong. This attitude has led to a Christianity that appears to those outside it as indifferent or even hostile to reform and even encouraging old abuses. This is totally wrong. Even a cursory examination of the Gospels shows how wide of the mark it is. Jesus came preaching a Kingdom, and the very use of that idea raised profound social issues. He proclaimed a Gospel of brotherhood. He gathered His first followers into a social unit with a real communal life. The sermon on the Mount is full of social teaching. His healing miracles sprang from His passionate desire to help men physically as well as spiritually.

The hardships of the poor were never a matter of indifference to Jesus. True He declared that man shall not live by bread alone, but neither shall man live without any bread at all—and Jesus always remembered that. In the heart of the great prayers which He taught His Disciples He found a place for: "Give us this day our daily bread." Man's material wants, so far from being matters of no moment, were actually written upon the heart of God. "Your heavenly Father knows that you have need of all these things."

Although this is very true we have to be careful that we don't take the opposite view and say that Jesus was primarily a social reformer. This view holds that the first step toward redeemed humanity must be a redeemed social order. Improve external conditions, and then the Spirit of God will have a chance. Eliminate poverty and ignorance, then it will be comparatively easy to eliminate sin. This was not Jesus' line of approach. For one thing, Jesus was quite clear that the Kingdom could never be built by human efforts; it was to be the action of God. Moreover, Jesus saw and openly declared that changed conditions were futile apart from changed hearts. Hence His refusal to take the short-cuts suggested by the Tempter in the Wilderness (Mt 4:1). Men would never be right with one another until they were first right with God. The real trouble with humanity was too deep-seated to be reached by any social remedy or improved conditions. If Jesus was a great reformer, it was because He was a Savior first.

Jesus is continually making us uncomfortable. Would that we could either relax in the comfort of isolation or be on fire for action. But no, Jesus calls us to keep personal involvement in the fight against social injustice, but with a deep reliance on the all-important power of His Father. Jesus came with a social message for his age and for every age. But the basis of that message was not social, but religious. He headed no social revolution, and He legislated for no current social problems; but He brought and imparted a Spirit that was bound to set men crusading against social injustice everywhere. It is in this way that Jesus has been the driving power of noble social service for nineteen centuries. The Spirit of Jesus touched and abolished the infamy of the gladitorial shows. The Spirit of Jesus touched the institution of slavery. His Spirit touched and abolished the appalling factory conditions of the nineteenth century. Jesus is speaking with force on the prejudice of today.

We must truly feed the multitudes with the bread of life, who is Jesus. And His bread satisfies all our needs.

13

"The twelve assembled the community of the Disciples and said, 'It is not right for us to neglect the Word of God in order to wait on tables. Look around among your own number, brothers, for seven men acknowledged to be keenly spiritual and prudent, and we shall appoint them to this task. This will permit us to concentrate on prayer and the ministry of the Word!' " (Ac 6:2-4).

THE CALL TO LEADERSHIP

Jesus, I'm excited about the prospects of your Kingdom becoming more of a reality in my lifetime. But I know that won't happen unless more people are willing to take on the role of leadership in the Church. Please help leaders to arise and let them be people who are deeply committed to growing in love for you and then on fire to minister your word to all the people they meet.

Because of Jesus' resurrection, victory over death itself, we Christians must be filled with a great deal of hope and faith that no matter how discouraging world events may seem or how difficult even our family relationship may get, we have won a victory in Jesus that can spell defeat to anyone and anything that goes contrary to the Good News of Jesus.

We have to start a revolution of love in a world that only seems to hanker after alienation. We have the key to this revolution of unity and that key is Jesus Christ. We must move with all the force of Jesus, who has conquered those powers of evil in the world that want to cause separation in ourselves, from others, and God. We must have the hope of transforming the world in a more radical way than Marx, Lenin, or Mao ever imagined. We have all the power to do this at our fingertips. As a matter of fact, the power is dwelling in our hearts. That power is Jesus Christ.

But to bring that vision about, today's reading reminds us that we have to have leaders. The Kingdom of God will be ushered in by men and women who will be alive with the love of Jesus and who will proclaim His presence to be as real as it was in the first century, when Jesus walked the earth.

Jesus knew that the bringing about of His Kingdom wasn't going to come by magical good wishes. Men and women had to be willing to take up the challenge.

What is the nature of this leadership? Today's reading is quite succinct. A leader must be one who serves, prays, and is alive with the desire to spread the Gospel to all people.

In the past, in the Church with our strong hierarchical structure, the role of spiritual leadership has been the priest! He was the man in the small villages who was educated and spoke for God, and so all came to him for the answers. Now the role of leadership in the parish is being shared. Today's Scripture speaks of the founding of the office of the Deacon. I'm excited by the new dimension of leadership that the Permanent Diaconate is offering to the Church. More and more men will be open to the possibility of this call from the Lord to be of service to the people of God. My contacts with Deacons have been encouraging. Since many of them are married the Church's hierarchy is gaining a clearer view of married life.

But leadership is also to be found among people who move into the roles of extraordinary ministers, teachers in schools, CCD teachers, financial consultants in the parish, lectors, ushers, and adult-education teachers.

Although the proliferation of offices is great, we must keep coming back again and again to the importance of today's three ingredients of leadership: prayers, service, and preaching the Word.

I'm sure that you will admit the need for leadership. But how do you know God is calling you? Isn't that the problem?

The answer is: "He is! You! Right now!" You who are alive in Christ through the Holy Spirit can bring Jesus to everyone you meet. You must ask them if they've heard of Jesus, and have they surrendered their whole self to Him? This is the answer to whether you are called to be a leader. Do it! The Lord will lead you into other forms of Church leadership. Once you realize that your basic role as a follower of Jesus is to lead others to Him, and you start doing it, you will be called to a more formal function in the Church. How do you discern what service-role the Holy Spirit is calling you to?

First ask Jesus in prayers for clarification as to whether you are being called to the priesthood, religious life, CCD teaching, the Lectorship, to be an extraordinary minister or whatever. Fasting should also be joined with prayer. If after you have prayed and fasted, the possibility of service seems to be calling, take the next step. Talk to someone who knows about this sort of calling. Get a better picture of what will be involved in it. Be honest sharing your background of talents and weaknesses, and then, after prayer with your adviser, if the possibility is there, go on to the next step. Give what you're attracted to a chance! Go ahead and enter the Seminary. Apply for the Permanent Diaconate. Ask the pastor to appoint you extra-ordinary minister. Commit yourself to teach CCD for a semester. Then, give the work all that you have with prayer and dedication to Jesus and observe how thing go. You and those in authority will now be able to make a clearer decision as to what the Lord wants you to do. This is how to discern the movement of the Holy Spirit in your life. If the Lord is calling you, don't let His call slip by with the cop-out of unworthiness or by vacillating too long with the thought that maybe you should try something else more to your liking. Step out in faith and the Lord will bless you and give you His direction.

Do these three things: pray, consult and act, and you'll experience what being a Christian is all about! Remember above all else that we must trust in the power of Jesus. He's the source of all effective leadership!

14

"Stephen, filled with grace and power, worked great wonders and signs among the people. Certain members of the so-called Synagogue of Roman Freedmen would undertake to engage Stephen in debate, but they proved no match for the wisdom and spirit with which he spoke. They persuaded some men to make the charge that they had heard him speaking blasphemies against Moses and God. In this way they incited the people, the Elders, and the Scribes" (Ac 6:8-12).

DO WE DARE TO BE DIFFERENT?

Jesus, today we see Stephen having the courage to stand up for what he believes in: You. He even goes to the extreme of being persecuted. Lord, please give me the courage to be different. Lord, if I can live your Good News in my life, I will be different. It's so easy to just go along with whatever the majority of people are thinking. Don't let me rationalize myself out of standing up for my commitment to you. Help me to live the difference you make.

I spend a great deal of time worrying about what other people think of me. I have a great hunger to be accepted. I use all the talents of my personality to be accepted by as many people as I can. I guess this is natural, but when it goes to extremes, I think it's unhealthy. One of the many little sayings that I've pasted on the wall just above my desk is one by the philosopher, Gabriel Marcel, "From the moment that I become pre-occupied about the effect that I want to produce on the other person, my every act, word and attitude loses its authenticity." I really need not be so concerned with whether others will accept me.

This is why I find today's reading so powerful. I marvel that Stephen can be so indifferent to the acceptance of others. Stephen has the same commitment to truth that others picked up in Jesus when they said, "We know that you are a respecter of no man." I marvel at the dedication and strength required to be so different, and vulnerable to the flood of abuse anyone may receive when he goes against the majority. To be different runs the risk of being like Hans Christian Anderson's "Ugly Duckling," ostracized because he's not like everyone else.

The secret of how to live the difference that Jesus is in our lives is simply that of being willing to accept God's acceptance of us. We have to be willing to listen to and believe in Jesus when He says to us that He loves us right now, just as we are, with our weaknesses and strengths. We have to believe that He's telling us that we've been created because we are pleasing to our Creator and He's willing to support and stand behind all we endeavor to do to grow into the people that He's created us to be. God is saying, "I love you and I'm willing to go to any extremes to make you know this." With this knowledge deep in our hearts we can have the strength, like Stephen, to be different from the majority of the people in our world who would want us to just go along and not make waves.

You know as well as I that there are many things that are moving in the world as gigantic influences that are contrary to the love, the pouring-out of love, of

Jesus. We are called upon to take a stand against a spirit that is contrary to Jesus. Abortion certainly is something like that. If you take a stand against it as an immoral elimination of love and life you get all kinds of abuse from those who argue that freedom of choice is more important than the life and love of people. Then there is the large social acceptance of pre-marital sex and of the security of the pill. To take a stand means that you run the risk of being called a follower of some insensitive Italian in Rome who doesn't know what life is all about. The more we know and love Jesus, the clearer is the distinction between us and the majority in the world. But again, unless our non-conformity is founded on our acceptance by Jesus, who is God, we'll never be able to stand up against the majority and be different.

The strength to stand up for Jesus is something that we have to come back to continually just as we come back to the dinner table to get the strength to carry out our work. The Holy Spirit must be continually on our mind as we call upon Him to renew us in His Strength. The strongest ingredient in the courage to be different from others will be our faith. In a logical and materialistic world, my placing my faith in something as seemingly intangible as the constant care and love of God will make me stand out.

15

"Those who listened to his (Stephen's) words were stung to the heart. They ground their teeth in anger at him. Stephen meanwhile, filled with the Holy Spirit, looked to the sky above and saw the glory of God, and Jesus standing at God's right hand. 'Look!' he exclaimed, 'I see an opening in the sky, and the Son of Man standing at God's right hand.' The onlookers were shouting aloud, holding their hands over their ears as they did so. Then they rushed at him as one man, dragged him out of the city, and began to stone him" (Ac 7:54-58).

GOD'S CREATIVE COMMUNICATION

Jesus, I like to think that I'm a good listener. But I know that I have so much to learn about hearing others, especially you. I'm such a dreamer. I would like to box you in and tell you how you can communicate with me. But you are the Creator of the world. You are not satisfied with my puny means of communicating. You do it in unimaginable and loving ways. Help me to realize that you are talking with me and continually telling me that you love me.

Stephen was a wonderful man to behold. He was all afire with his dedication to the Lord and he was even working all kinds of miracles that strengthened his words about the Lord Jesus. Isn't it strange that certain people could be "stung to the heart," as Luke puts it in today's reading, but were still able to turn a deaf ear to all that the Lord was doing through Stephen? The picture of the onlookers shouting at the top of their lungs and holding their hands over their ears is interesting.

I wish that I could say that I am out of their category, but I'm not. Perhaps I'm not so blunt in my turning off what the Lord is trying to say to me, but I still go to great efforts to miss what He wants to say to me.

Recently I visited Yosemite for the first time. Seeing the vastness of this beautiful masterpiece of God's creations was something that I'll never forget. I was giving a retreat to about 15 high school students. One day after celebrating Mass by a stream, I suggested that we each get by ourselves and let the Lord talk to us. I went into an out-of-the-way spot and stretched out on my back. From where I was, I could see Bridal Veil Falls—a breath-taking drop of 200 yards, or more. As the water comes down it moves into never-to-be-duplicated patterns. When it hits the ground with a smash, it breaks into three meandering creeks. I was by one of the creeks. It was then that the Lord spoke to me through the rocks in the stream. There must have been millions of rocks and boulders in that stream. But magnificently each of the rocks was different. Of course, I knew that before, but at this moment it made a strong impression on me and I'll never forget it. If God can have so much creativity in making millions of rocks each so very different, yet all the same, how much more do I need to be open to the magnificence of God's creative communication and see God talking to me in unimaginably different ways.

If God is the creator of the universe with all its diversity, I have to blow my mind and be open to all kinds of new ways of communication. God can speak through a voice, through the Bible, through a water-fall, through a rock singer, through an exciting movie, through a magnificent mountain, and through death. There is no limit to God's creation.

My job is to be as open as I can to the diversity of God's creative ways of saying that He loves me.

The problem is that I know my limited means of communicating and think that they are all that God can use. We're like the admirer of a famous artist who came to him, interested in getting an original painting. He knew that to ask the master for one of his compositions would be a little too presumptuous, so what he did was draw the outline of a little rabbit. Then he put numbers in spots where different colors might go. He wanted to make things simple and not take up too much of the artist's time, so he kept the colors down to five. The eyes would be one color, the ears another, the tail a third, the feet a fourth, and the body a fifth. Nervously he came up to the master when he seemed to be a little free and told him how much he would like to have an original, but he knew that it would take a long time, so, if the master wouldn't mind, the rabbit was already outlined and all he had to do was to color in the spots numbered one, and so on. You can imagine the reaction of the artist! "You want to see a rabbit, I'll paint you a rabbit! Don't give me this simple-looking scribbling. I'm a great artist and I can't be tied down to filling in colors in numbered-off areas. I'm too creative for that. Please don't insult my genius by treating me as someone who has no creative talent." And the master would be justified.

That's the way we so often come to the Lord with expectations of how He can communicate with us. We must remind ourselves of the limitless creative power of God and be open to Him. We long for the experience of being knocked off our horse on the way to Damascus and having the Lord shout to us directions, loud and clear. He's continually shouting His communications to us, but in ways that are so simple and loving that we can't hear Him. In the next five minutes hear God speaking His love to you as the birds sing, the typewriter breaks down, the baby needs to be changed, a mountain is capped with a cloud, a sunset rolls with thousands of shades of colors before your eyes. The Lord also speaks through the person who says, "I love you," or the person who tells us that we're full of baloney. The Lord speaks to us when we read Scripture, when we are attending a boring Mass or as we are wondering what vocation we should follow in life. Allow the Lord to talk to you in ways you never imagined. How strange it must be for the Lord to continually be saying, "I love you," and no one seems to care.

The art of listening to God's communication in our lives is as simple as being attuned to now, and being conscious of all that's being said in love and returning that love with words of thanks. The more we live in the fullness of now, the more we can grow through the magnificence of God's creative communication.

16

". . . It is not to do my own will that I have come down from Heaven, but to do the Will of Him who sent me" (Jn 6:37).

THE OBEDIENCE OF JESUS

Jesus, you are God, but at the same time a human being, a complete and total human being. That means that you are in touch with one of the greatest difficulties we humans have: submitting our will to that of another. I'm so proud. I like to do things the way I think that they should be done. Sorry to say, Lord, I still have a hard time doing things as you would have them be done. Help me to submit my will to you and thus be able to really learn what freedom is!

I hadn't had my hand on a kite string since I was in grade school. To be exact, it was when I was in the fifth grade and living in Denver, Colorado. Funny how I remember that first time I attempted to fly a kite. I enjoyed it so much, I wonder now why I hadn't tried it again after so many years. I can remember the park on the east side of Denver. I can see now just where I stood. I remember it was a Sunday afternoon when I started, and I went at it until dusk. My brother had to come and call me home. It seemed to take me forever to pull in the kite. It had a good tail and I used two lengths of string. That was a glorious day. There's something so liberating about a kite! That was almost 25 years ago, but the thrill came back to me recently.

I was up in the mountains of Southern California giving a retreat to a Parish Youth group. After Mass, Sunday morning was set aside for free time and the moderators brought up about seven or eight kites to fill up the time. I was a kid again. I was the first one out into the open field on the side of the mountain in the gusty air. I'm afraid that the excitement in my laughter was a bit too booming, because before very long there were many others around me jabbering about the size of the tail or the proper tension in the bow of the kite. Sad to say my first efforts met with failure. I couldn't get the kite more than ten feet off the ground. It was beyond me how I could have lost my touch even though it had been some 25 years since I'd done it before. I was growing livid with envy as some young whipper-snapper pulled and tugged and nursed his kite up, up and away. I just couldn't do it. It was amazing how this fellow got his kite up so high. Soon his kite was just a speck as it climbed even higher than the mountain. I was hungry for his success. Finally, utterly frustrated, I asked him to see what he could do to get mine into the air. He had a magic touch. Soon my kite was bobbing and dancing higher and higher. Unfortunately, his kite by this time had gotten a little carried by the wind and glided into the mountain to be snatched up by the kite-hungry trees.

As I took command of my kite, I was king of the skies, totally thrilled. In the meantime the boy with the magic touch with kites had climbed up the mountain to retrieve his downed kite. The best he could do was release the string. He suggested I tie that string to my kite and get two added lengths of height. I did and the kite performed perfectly. It was going up into the clouds. I had to get a glove to ward off burns as the string came down the hill and through my hands. I was as free as that boy in the fifth grade in Denver. I was so proud and the kite was so proud. I figure that with things going so well, we might as well get more string and shoot for the moon. Then tragedy struck. In all the excitement of watching my soaring hawk and trying not to get string-burns, I didn't notice that the end of the string from the mountain was moving toward me. Before I knew it, the end came shooting through my hands and up and out of my grasp. I ran for it, jumping and leaping, but all in vain, for the end was soon up to the tree tops. I looked up to the flying kite and for five or ten seconds it shot upward like a propelled rocket. It was free. Then, without the home base support and control it began to sputter and wave in a futile attempt to gain altitude. I didn't see it go down. It was so high that its resting place was somewhere over the gigantic mountain it had been climbing. There was initial disappointment, but then the glory of the memory and the flow of the adrenalin that I still felt made up for the loss. I'd touched one of those peak experiences, and I knew that I would never forget my victory, and the freedom and pride and height of the little kite.

As I went back to giving the retreat, I was too full of the excitement of the kite to talk about anything else. In the kite the Lord spoke to me loud and clear in His beautiful creative way. "Michael, if you hold onto me, I will let you fly high and straight and free and joyfully. But remember that unless you come back to me for the source of your freedom, you'll start to flutter and dive and not know the freedom and salvation that I alone can give."

The message the Lord taught me through the kite was one of obedience. Unless I'm obedient to the will of my Father in my life, unless I have the hand of the Lord holding the strings of my kite, I'll never be able to soar

like the kite in my experience. I must continually con-
form my will to that of Jesus and then reach my fullness.
  The lesson is a hard one. It's so difficult to give my
will to that of the Father. I have to struggle just like
Jesus did when the author of Hebrews said of Him:
"With cries and supplications He learned obedience to
the will of His Father." Should my struggle to be submissive to the will of Jesus be any easier? If we have
the courage to trust and give our wills to the God of our
life, we'll have a foundation and source of freedom that
will be higher and deeper than any two bit freedom
material possessions can offer.

17

"I myself am the bread of life. No one who comes to me shall ever hunger. No one who believes in me shall ever thirst" (Jn 6:35).

REAL HUNGER

Jesus, I can be so comfortable in all the security you've given me in my work, my food and my shelter. I find my dependence on you weakening. What I hunger and thirst for, Jesus, is to experience your acceptance more and more. Your love for me is my food and drink. I need you.

I am at present participating in the greatest American pastime. No, it's not baseball. I've joined the ranks of those who are trying to lose weight. Now if you're really honest you'll have to admit that more time is spent talking about calories and cholesterol than about the batting average of the hottest rookie. Today's readings talk about food and hunger and I feel that I understand Scripture all the more now, because I've taken the plunge and have gone through the agony of having to pass up the sweets I long for and take only one helping at dinner rather than the two or three I'm used to.

It's with a bit of shame that I say that in our comfortable and blessed country I have to generate hunger through my will power. We can talk about thirst in the Scripture and relate that to a strong desire for a glass of iced tea after an hour of mowing the yard. I can relate to that TV commercial of the hot and sweaty man taking a sip of Lipton tea and falling into a cool swimming pool. But this hunger and thirst is self-generated and doesn't take on that much gravity because we always know that there's a cool drink in the icebox and McDonald's is just around the corner.

Our hunger and our thirst are quite shallow when compared to the hunger and thirst of people who live in conditions where there just isn't food and drink. To them Jesus' words, "I am the bread of life," or "When you drink the water I will give you, you will never thirst," have much more meaning. The power of Jesus' words is lost on me.

There's a problem with needing Jesus as the bread of life when my concern for bread is so secondary. I've asked myself, if food is not really a problem, where is my hunger? Quite honestly the big word that comes up is **acceptance**. This is something that I can't buy at the store. Yet most of my waking hours are spent in the real hunger for acceptance.

For me this acceptance has three divisions. First, I hunger to have a positive acceptance of myself. I need very much to see myself as good. I need to accept myself with all my strengths and weaknesses. I need to be able to see the dreams, the secret dreams that I have of myself, as attainable and good. I need to see my talents, although they are limited, especially when I compare them to others, as worthy of nurturing and growth.

Then too, I need to be accepted by others. I find this so often in my trying to curry the favor of others so that they will like me. How much of my spare time is spent in laying strategy as to how to get other people to agree with what I want, in a way that will not alienate them from me. I need so much to be able to bridge the separation that I feel from others whom I dislike or whom I have consciously or unconsciously moved out of my life. How can I communicate with people who don't trust me or whom I can't trust? How can I be accepted by a person with whom I seem to have a real personality clash and ordinary means of communication just don't seem to work? Oh, I hunger all right. I hunger to be united and loved and accepted by others.

Finally there is the acceptance that I receive from God. This is not something that I can earn. It's a gift. God comes to me and says, "You are really a goof-off. You have all these faults and failings and there is this long list of sins, like a broken record you keep playing again and again. But you know, there's something about you that I like. As a matter of fact, I like you very much. I accept you for all that you have, and I now want you to relax in the power of my love for you. I'm the one that can bring you together with yourself and make you like who you are and able to grow with the talents you have. I'm the key that can open the door to the lack of acceptance that you experience from other people. Because of my love, you can be accepted, and in the shadow of my strong hand you no longer have to be concerned with the things that others think important. You don't have to have a lot of money or power or influence. My love is enough for you. I give you a peace and a strength that is more than everything the world can give. You can accept yourself. You can love even people who formerly bothered you greatly. And finally you will have a driving hunger for me which I will satisfy in ever more satisfying ways!"

18

"Saul, breathing murderous threats against the Lord's Disciples, went to the high priest and asked him for letters to the Synagogues in Damascus which would empower him to arrest and bring to Jerusalem anyone he might find, man or woman, living according to the new way. As he traveled along, and was approaching Damascus, a light from the sky suddenly flashed about him. He fell to the ground and at the same time heard a voice saying, 'Saul, Saul, why do you persecute me?' 'Who are you, sir?' he asked. The voice answered, 'I am Jesus, the one you are persecuting' " (Ac 9:1-3).

A STUDY IN DOING AN ABOUT-FACE

Jesus, so many times my understanding of your power in my life is weak. When I hear today's reading of the conversion of St. Paul, I'm reminded of your power even over the people that you would least expect could be moved by you. Thank you for being full of power and wonder and thank you for making this available to me. Help me to widen my expectations of what you can do in my life and in the lives of others.

Who would have ever imagined the turn-about that happened in Paul's life? Look at him before he hit the road to Damascus. He was the plague of all Christians. He was dragging them out of prayer-meetings and homes, men and women, and throwing them into jail. Talk about a man to be feared. And then you stepped right in, Jesus, and turned everything upside down and completely changed Paul's direction. In this I'm reminded of how much I need to be full of expectant hope that you can move in the lives of people that are the most unlikely to be changed.

One of the most upsetting things that I ever say to myself or hear others say is, "You just can't change that person." I've said it so many times and I'm so ashamed when I compare that feeling with the power of the Lord as seen in today's reading. Many times we run into dead-end streets in our relationships with others. I'm thinking of married couples ready to give up on each other because the wife or husband has been acting in one way for so long it's impossible to expect him or her to change. How many times we have heard of the hopelessness of expecting change when we're dealing with a pastor, a boss, a fellow-religious, or a child. When you come to think about it, closing a person off like that can be very sinful. Sure there are frustrations. It isn't that we haven't tried. We have, but we've got to watch out when we don't see any hope because then we lose sight of the real power to transform even the impossible into a miracle of freshness and enthusiasm in the opposite direction.

Many times the basis of another person's not changing is not so much in the person as it is in us. I'm not much of an artist, but every now and then I like to dabble in some oils. It is a good way to relax and get my mind concentrating on something different. I'm a little proud of one of my paintings. Over a simple design I wrote the words, "I am what you see. Please see good." In so many cases I think that this is true. We are only as good and as great as the expectations that others have of us. Putting our faith in Jesus opens up all kinds of vistas for us because we know that Jesus is God and has seemingly limitless expectations of us. Would that we could have a little bit more of Jesus' view of ourselves and others we find unchangeable.

In our prayers for others we should start to exercise our faith and hope and concentrate on those people who seem to be furthest away from that to which Jesus is calling them. I'm thinking of public sinners who seem to spend their whole lives using people and propagating the Kingdom of fear and slavery and hate through the mass media and politics. Let's turn the world upside down and get these people moving in the direction of Jesus' peace, joy, freedom and love.

I admire St. Paul and wish that I could get some of his fire. Would that I loved Jesus enough to go to the extremes he went to. To travel and preach and run into so much opposition but to consider that as nothing because of the love of Jesus that was in his heart, that's what I strive for.

As I stop and pray for this, I wonder how I can open myself to the power of God to effect this transformation similar to that of St. Paul. Paul was fertile ground for his conversion because he sought the truth and, when he thought he saw it, he went in that direction with all that he had. I'm reminded of the words from the Book of Revelation: "How I wish you were one or the other— hot or cold! But because you are lukewarm, neither hot nor cold, I will spew you out of my mouth!" (3:15-16). Paul certainly wasn't pleasing God with his persecution of Christians, but He preferred this to comfortable mediocrity. Perhaps the greatest hindrance to the transforming power of the Holy Spirit in my life is my "getting by" mediocrity and my unwillingness to act one way or the other with vigor.

Paul was not afraid to love and be dedicated to something deeply. He had to risk. This is the most frightening thing the Lord is calling me to. I want to be sure and have all the facts laid out before I take even the smallest step. I'm so afraid of getting a bad reaction from others. Oh, to have Paul's love and dedication to the Lord so that I would be able to consider God's will before all else.

The road to Damascus seems so enviable at times when I'm not sure which way I should go in life. I would like to think that if the Lord came to me with a strong booming voice, as He came to Paul, then I'd know for sure what He wants me to do.

I have my problems with believing that Paul's call from the Lord was as simple as a flash of light and a booming voice which said things so unmistakably. I think the communications that God can give me are just as startling and wonder-filled as those he gave Paul. I too can have Paul's experience. Unless I am open to listening for the Lord like Paul, I won't hear the earth-shattering message that God is sending me right now, when he asks me to turn my life upside down for Him. Paul's change can be my change right now, if I listen.

19

"Many of the disciples of Jesus remarked, 'This sort of talk is hard to endure! How can anyone take it seriously?'. . . From this time on, many of His disciples broke away and would not remain in His company any longer. Jesus then said to the Twelve, 'Do you want to leave me too?' " (Jn 6:60; 66-67).

THE TRUTH AT ALL COSTS

Jesus, you know that there comes a time when I have to come out with the truth even though it might cause others to be alienated from me. Help me to have your courage to speak the truth when it's called for, knowing that you are backing me and won't let me down. Help me find my support in you.

How strong Jesus is in today's reading. No one likes to see close and dear friends leave His life, but Jesus wanted to make sure that this relationship with His friends and followers was based on the truth. So he had the courage to lay His cards on the table. His brand of love went to extremes. He wanted to be so intimate in His love that He would run the risk of being taken for granted. His intimacy and total giving were frightening in their implications, because those who would follow Him would have to run the risk of similar total love.

My problem with the truth isn't that I'm an overt

liar. My problem is with levels of the truth. I have developed a diplomatic ability to water down the truth. It's more that I'm obsessed with the search to come out with the truth, the whole truth, in a way that will put myself in the best light and not alienate others from me. Now, this attitude isn't totally bad. You don't get on a truthful kick and embarrass a person you've met with the truth about his bad traits. I guess the struggle is between prudence and truth. I sometimes find my prudence getting a little out of hand, especially when stacked up against Jesus' speaking the truth today.

The basic problem is my addiction to the pleasure pain principle. If something causes pleasure it's good; but if it causes pain it's bad. This is a natural reaction of a child. But now that I'm striving for maturity, I have to be careful I'm not always being led by feelings. Often to be truthful will cause a great deal of pain, and so I'll sidle away from confronting myself or others and opt for the greater pleasure of putting it off and wait for a more opportune moment. The problem is that the more I put off the moment of truth, the more remote comes the moment of confrontation. Then I become part of a vicious circle. I get into a situation which causes great pain and confusion, but I get deeper and deeper in this because the only way to break out is to go through the pain of truth-confrontation. If only I could be more spontaneous in dealing with the pain of truth I wouldn't be allowing the pain to fester and in the long run cause more pain.

We say that the truth hurts, and somehow we've made an image of a sweet Jesus totally unable to hurt people. So we don't tell people the truth. We know that Jesus wouldn't hurt people's feelings. Foolishness! Jesus was forever hurting people's feelings with the truth. The Scribes and Pharisees must have had their feelings hurt just a wee bit when they were called, "Hypocrites!"

The lawyers had their feelings hurt. Peter must have been hurt when Jesus called him Satan.

Hurting others' feelings with the truth is much more loving than maintaining the **status quo** to have a favorable press. Speaking the truth can be a very selfless act.

Hegel once said, "Love is separation and reunion." I have found this to be true in my love relationships with others and Jesus. Love is a process, a giving process, and as I grow I come more deeply into the truth of another person. This truth moves me from something I was comfortable with to a new level. Then leaving the old and coming to the new means a separation from what I knew and this causes pain. Although truth can cause this pain, the separation is the threshold of a greater union, closer because it's founded on a deeper level of the truth. When a married couple experience separation from an initial idealism and find the truth of their partner is different, the separation doesn't mean that love is lost. Rather after the clarification, this separation brings deeper love through a confronting of the truth. Love can now have a greater union and depth.

He who speaks the truth is often lonely, as Jesus knew when His disciples left. Our hope must be high that as we struggle to be people of truth, Jesus will not leave us, no matter how desolate our feelings. Jesus has asked that we follow Him in His quest for truth, and He will not abandon those He has accepted as His own.

20

"The apostles and the brothers heard that Gentiles, too, had accepted the Word of God. As a result, when Peter went up to Jerusalem some among the circumcised took issue with him, saying, 'You entered the house of un-circumcised men and ate with them.' 'I (Peter) remembered what the Lord had said, 'John baptized with water but you will be baptized with the Holy Spirit.' 'If God was giving them the same gift he gave us when we first believed in the Lord Jesus Christ, who was I to interfere with Him?' " (Ac 11:1-2; 16-17).

BEING OPEN TO CHANGE

Jesus, so many times I'm such a stick-in-the-mud! I don't want to change! Make me want to grow, even though moving to what is new and unfamiliar can be a painful process. Help me to trust in your loving care for me so that I'll be able to risk change.

When we think of the low opinion Jews had for Gentiles, we can understand how difficult it must have been for Peter to have so much contact with the uncircumcised Cornelius. Peter had to go completely against the grain when he spoke with him, and even went so far as to enter his house. The apostles and brothers couldn't understand how Peter could act so contrary to an age-old tradition.

The strict Jew believed that God had no use for the Gentiles. God's favor extended to the Jews and to the Jews alone. Sometimes they even went to the length of saying that help must not be given to a Gentile woman in the time of child-birth, because that would only be to bring another Gentile into the world. The really strict Jew would have no contact with a Gentile or even a Jew who did not observe the Law. Two things in particular the strict Jew would not do. He would never have as a guest, nor would he ever be the guest of, a man who did not observe the Law.

Even though he knew that the Lord was calling him to have this contact with a Gentile, Peter must have had a great struggle going on inside himself. Sometimes, when God calls us to do something, we can make the choice in our head to follow Him, but something at the pit of our stomach is telling us that moving into the world of newness and change is not what we should be doing. This action of having contact with Gentiles must have caused all kinds of trouble for Peter. How could such a sacred tradition be put away so easily? Following Jesus was hard because He was demanding so many changes. I can also imagine how difficult an openness to Gentiles must have been for St. Paul. He was such a dyed-in-the-wool Pharisee, with all his legalistic outlook, that to become the Apostle of the Gentiles must have involved great internal conflict, despite his openness to the will of the Lord.

Being a Christian is never a very secure thing if we see security as not having to change. We are constantly called upon to grow, to see new and better ways of loving the Lord and getting His message to as many people as possible.

On one level there are the changes that have rocked and are continuing to rock the Church. We can learn much from the openness of St. Peter as we see him moving away from a custom that had been handed down for centuries. There is struggle in each of us, in varied degrees, to resist change. I must admit that I still delight in hearing a recording of some Gregorian Chant. The way things were at Mass had many positive values. Although I find the new form of the Rite of Reconciliation more meaningful and effective, there's something in me that doesn't want to move away from things as they have been for so many years. But Christ through the Church calls for growth.

Liturgy aside, there's an openness to change in moral decisions that is needed in our life as we try to follow Jesus. We might be convinced of the value of abortion because we've only been open to what the mass media have said about it. But as we grow in our love of Jesus we will have to be open to a personal change of view.

On a more personal level, our life in Jesus should make us open to repentance. We must continually be open to the fact that sin can be a factor in our lives, and we must be ready to do an about-face. Habits of sin can seem to be very satisfying, and it is a struggle to break out of them. But following the direction of the Holy Spirit as Peter did in his relationships with the Gentiles, we can see that we can be called to just about anything.

One of the best examples of this openness to change through the direction of the Holy Spirit is the Blessed Mother. Mary was a woman who experienced great struggles in her desire to be open to the changes demanded of her. Before she was asked to be the mother of Jesus, she probably had a plan as to how she would like to have her life go. She was looking forward to a life with St. Joseph and perhaps some of the quiet pleasure that went with life in Nazareth. Then, with the word of God coming to her through the angel, her plans were turned upside down. She had to be open to change. When she said, "Your will be done," it was a difficult commitment, because she was leaving herself open for things she wasn't sure of. Then at the end of Jesus' life, the crucifixion must have forced a struggle to make herself open to the will of the Lord in her life.

God is never going to let up on us. We shall be continually faced with the challenge of growing. We shall have to repeatedly be open to moving from what is comfortable and secure to new things which seem nebulous, unsure and untried. But through it all we need a great deal of faith and hope in the Lord and in His undying confidence in us. He is never going to let us down, no matter how awkward we feel as we reach out in trust to His call.

21

"We gave you strict orders not to teach about that name, yet you have filled Jerusalem with your teaching and are determined to make us responsible for the man's blood" (Ac 5:29).

ALL IN A NAME

Jesus! Oh, Lord, I use that name so often and at times in such a non-thinking manner. Forgive me. Help me to grow in greater respect for your name. Help me to hold it in awe and wonder. Help me to realize that when I use your name, I'm using great power. In your name I can do all things. Don't let me forget that.

Have you ever thought about the word "name?" We use the word in many different contexts.

A name is the thing parents struggle with as the wife is carrying the baby. There are several reasons why a name may be chosen. A name can be chosen by parents because of its appealing sound. I remember a friend of mine baptized a baby with a Swahilli name, and although the name had no meaning for me, it did have a musical sound. Sometimes a name is picked because it belongs to a person the parents love and admire and whom they hope this new bundle of life, their child, will be like. I remember how honored I was when someone named her child, Michael, after me. That is a deep and sincere compliment, and I feel a strong urge to work at being worthy of that honor.

Without our name we feel cold and naked. This happens when, in prison, someone's referred to as such and such number or as we are known by our social security number. "Security number" is a contradiction in terms, because we are very insecure without our name. Without a name, we have a hard time handling others. We want to know a person's name. This even applies to animals. A child gets a new pet and what is one of the first and most vital questions? "What's its name?" So the little kitten becomes Fido and big-pawed Great Dane pup becomes Kitty. One of the cleverest names for a cat was one my niece came up with—Polly. Why so cute, you ask? The last name was Esther.

Names are important. Even nick-names are special because they say something about who a person is in the eyes of others. How pleased I am if someone remembers my name not having seen me for a long time. How I wish I could go beyond just remembering faces and be able to remember names! I should take the time to remember a person's name. Names are important.

Reminded in my everyday actions of the importance of a name, today's reading takes on a new freshness. The religious leaders are upset with the apostles because they are working wonders and telling of the salvation brought about by "that name."

When we say the name "Jesus," we are calling on more than just a symbol of something that reminds us of something else. We are saying God's name, and evoking all His reality. For the Jewish leaders to say Jesus would have meant dealing with more power than they could handle. So they sidle away from the powder-keg and deal with "His name."

When I hear discussion of the power of the name Jesus, I'm reminded of a story told me by a very un-

likely person. Mike Delahunty is a motorcycle police-
man in my home town. He's good-looking, six-foot-three
and at least 230 pounds. Mike was raised a Catholic and
was proud of serving as an altar boy. But as he grew
older he moved away from the Church and from Jesus
as the center of his life. He put his heart and soul into
being a cop and getting married. That was all that mat-
tered. He put so much heart and soul into being a cop
that his fellow officers gave him the name of "Mad Dog"
because of his fearlessness in maintaining peace in the
midst of a riot. This rough, tough peace-officer was one
day cruising the streets when he came upon a van that
seemed to have run out of gas. But the driver had been
so foolish as to leave the van in a ditch where it also
blocked part of the street. Traffic was piling up. As Mike
was surveying the van and the trouble it was causing,
a short, skinny hippy walked up with a can of gas. He
had a scrawny beard and a bad odor. Mike's temper
flared at the inconsiderateness of this anti-establishment
human being and started cutting loose with a stream of
cuss words that seriously called into question the up-
rightness of this young hippy's parentage. He ended
with "And I don't care what you say, I'm going to take
you in." The hippy turned to the towering officer and
with a smile that was as bright and true as possible said,
"But Jesus cares for me." Today, Mike still doesn't know
what happened, but at the sound of the name Jesus,
he found himself on his rear-end in the bushes, bowled
over by the power of Jesus' name. That word began a
trip back to the Lord for Mike that has reached interesting proportions. Mike has now given his life completely over to Jesus. If you're coming through my town
and you are stopped for speeding don't be amazed if,
along with your ticket, you get a little tract telling you
of the power of Jesus' name to transform your life.

The name of Jesus is a power that we should start

to utilize more and more. When we come across a sickness of body or a relationship that is falling apart, the power of Jesus' name can really work miracles. We see that power clearly when we hear that, "No other name in Heaven is given by which men can be saved."

22

"I have come to the world as its light to keep anyone who believes in me from remaining in the dark" (Jn 12:46).

JESUS AND THE KINGDOM WITHIN

Jesus, I'm a contradiction to myself. I'm so confused with myself at times. I read Scripture and know of the greatness to which you are calling me. I hear other people praise me for many of the gifts that you have given me. But Lord, again and again I fall short of what I know I can and should be. But my falling short is really not vicious. There seems to be some hidden force pulling at me in the dark. Be the light to show me who I am.

I wish I really knew who I was. The more I try and understand myself through reading, prayers, reflection and interaction with others, the more I'm continually surprised. Oh, I'm proud of how much I know myself. I feel that I know what my strengths and weaknesses are. I know too what I'm aspiring to do. But as I grow, I'm amazed at how much more there is to me. I feel like I'm that iceberg with only a tenth of myself on the surface and nine-tenths still to be discovered. I've got a bigger and more exciting adventure than any Columbus in my search to know myself.

I think I touch the mystery of myself most when I
fall into sin. As a priest, I have very high expectations
of myself, and I know that others also are banking on
me too. But when I get caught up in a bad habit of sin
that seems so hard to break, I'm frightened by something that's almost directing me against my will. There's
an unlit area of my life that's a mystery to me. I'm not
a vicious person. When I do something wrong I rationalize that good is somehow part of the aim of my action.
But still, I feel that my freedom is being impinged upon
and want to be set free. I know that Jesus, who came
to bring my salvation, which is another word for freedom, is the answer. Sometimes it gets discouraging.
I reiterate the sentiments of frustration that Paul felt
when he said, "I do, not the good I will to do, but the
evil I do not intend" (Rm 7:19).

Our reading today gives me much hope for I know
that in the darkness of not knowing who I am, I can
rely on Jesus to bring the fire of His love to enlighten
the dark corners of myself. But a serious question is
how do I deal effectively with something I know so little
about? The solution seems terribly difficult.

I've gained insight into the solution from two men
who are both priests and psychologists and who have
studied deeply the writings of Carl Jung. They use
Jung's insights to help know and love Jesus better. The
two men are John Sanford and Morton Kelsey.

As we move through Scripture, again and again we
find that Jesus is calling us to wholeness. He says that
the Kingdom of Heaven is like a hidden treasure. To
reach the fullness of His Kingdom we have to dig up
the treasure; we have to bring it out and then hold it.
There is a dark buried treasure in my sub-conscious
that must be brought out so that it can lead to my
wholeness. If it doesn't come out, it will remain unused
talent, and, more than that, it will start to become detri-

mental to me because it will be something confusing and lead me to evil through ignorance. Only when this "dark, buried treasure" is brought out will I be able to grow to the wholeness Jesus desires.

The word "wholeness" comes up again and again when we try to understand the message of Jesus. He wants us to be who we are completely. He wants us to be perfected, and we can only do that by bringing to our consciousness that which is dark and unused in our unconscious. We see Jesus saying this again when he compares the Kingdom of Heaven to a merchant looking for a fine pearl. Or when He says: "the Kingdom of God is within you."

Searching to find out who I am and uncovering all the unknown parts of me is not something that I can just read about and then choose not to do. It has to be a life-consuming job. I can't give up. This quest is intimately tied into my growth in love of Jesus. For to know myself is to know Jesus, who is the ground of my being and my life.

Jung found that an important key to this search was our dreams. We run into a mental block when it comes to being serious about dreams. They seem to be so fantastic and confusing and irrational. We want to put them away or not worry about them and just claim they're due to too much pepperoni on our pizza. I'm inclined to think that dreams are more than that. What is interesting is that when I go to Scripture, I find that dreams are a vital part of God's communication with man. Think of all the directions that Joseph received from the Lord in his dreams about how he should deal with Mary and her child. But dreams are also, as Jung holds, a real communication to our conscious life of what's going on in our subconscious. The real trick is understanding these communications. What dreams do is communicate in a symbolic way. We must try to read the signs. I've started keeping a journal and writing down what my dreams have said. Already I'm having to face things in the light of day that have helped me understand some of the unconscious truths in my life.

Be aware of the Kingdom within you, and pray often that the light of Christ will shine on you and let you know more and more of the fullness and richness of the treasure that the Lord in His fantastic creative powers has given you. Know that this search is an integral part in our search for Jesus.

23

"I solemnly assure you, he who accepts anyone I send, accepts me, and in accepting me accepts Him who sent me" (Jn 13:20).

ARE MISSIONARIES NEEDED?

Jesus, how I wish that I had the fire and zeal of the Disciples on the morning of Pentecost. I see them so excited with their love for you that they can't contain it. They have to go out and tell as many people as they can about the wonders of your salvation. Please give to your Church a new enthusiasm for the missions. Let it spring from an ever-deepening love for you that just can't be contained.

Jesus speaks today about sending His followers to make Him known to others. This brings to mind the vital importance of the missionary effort in the Church today. Let me share with you some of my yearnings for the missions, for this apostolate is very close to my heart. My job for the past four years has been to search out and foster the vocation in young men in the western part of the United States. I love the job for it has brought me closer to Jesus and helped me to do just what He did to organize leaders who would be educated in His Good News. They then went out and revolution-ized the world. We have to have this revolutionary atti-

tude in our life in Jesus. We should be so in love with
Jesus and want to share Him with others that we search
for more and more ways of getting His message to as
many people as possible. This is the key to the Pentecost
experience that is such a model for missionary enthusiasm. Becoming afire with the love of Jesus, we'll want
others to share the good things that we have. There are
many things going on in the world today that have
harmed the missionary image. As many of the world's
poorer countries, which for centuries had been living
under Western Colonialist power, are now becoming
independent, there is a strong negative feeling among
them for anything that smacks of non-native influence.
The novel **The Ugly American** was a book that told of
the frightening insensitivity of foreign diplomats in
Asia. The paternalism of the foreign do-gooder made
one wish for the day when all Americans would get out
of other countries. The war in Vietnam with its strong
home-land protests echoed a feeling in many Americans'
hearts that we have no right as Americans to have anything to do with giving directions to Orientals. All this
negative feeling has brushed off onto the idea of going
to the foreign missions to share the Gospel. "Why not
stay at home where you are with people that you know,
and Heaven knows there is enough missionary work
right here in our own country." Although we know that
it's good to share the Gospel with others, in our hearts
we're very suspicious of being influential in foreign
cultures.

Despite our fear of being an interferring foreign
power, there is still a vital need for missionary work.
I hear of exciting and fresh approaches to mission work
from many of the missionaries I've talked to. There is
at present a strong emphasis on the role of the missionary as one who serves.

This is in line with the teaching of Jesus. There is

more stress on teaching Jesus rather than on trying to establish a western culture and Liturgy. This means that the missionary today is a man who spends a great deal of time waiting and listening. He comes to the missions in love with Jesus and wanting to love people of a different language and culture. You can seldom move a person to listen to you if you are paternalistically rushing him to listen to your truth, to the exclusion of his. The modern missionary is one who has learned to listen and absorb the wisdom of the people with whom he works, and in that honest searching and growing he can convincingly teach the salvation won by Jesus' life, death, and resurrection. A missionary has to be an outstanding person. He has to be so in love with Jesus that he's able to expose himself to the strong faith of others, to hear the truth that they speak, and to complete their search for meaning with the ultimate meaning and happiness—Jesus.

What an exciting person a missionary is! He has to have this deep, committed love for Jesus that can stand against other beliefs. He has to be willing to take upon himself a new language and culture.

A missionary is exciting because he's open to tapping his rich potential to an extreme degree. That is what I call a truly rich man, because he hungers to always expect more in life. Paul expressed this quality of a missionary when he spoke of his being a Jew to the Jews and a Greek to the Greeks. How hard that principle is for the middle-aged person trying to understand a teenager and his blasting stereo. It's an ever deeper understanding that a missionary always has to reach.

What I'm encouraging you to do is, first, grow deeper and deeper in your love of Jesus. Then be open to the possibilities of your sharing that love even to the far reaches of the world, whether it's as a priest, a religious, or a lay-person. Consider growing to the greatness the Lord has created you for by being a missionary.

But what about the questions of the needs of the Church right here in your home town? I would be foolish to say there isn't a need. What we have to do is listen to what the Lord is saying in our lives. The Lord is calling His servants to cover both needs. But don't close out the more difficult call. If you are attracted to the missions, don't let the desire die. Give it a try!

If going to the foreign missions can't be worked out, but you are still on fire, you face the same problem as the Little Flower who longed for the missions from within her cloister walls. Do these things: pray often for the missionaries and the people they work with, support missionaries with correspondence and donations. Join organizations that can support missionaries. But don't be too quick in putting off the idea of your personally going to the missions. Your interest, impossible though it may seem, may be the act of trust that Jesus wants you to make to ensure the perfection of your love for Him!

24

"I am the way, and the truth and the life" (Jn 14:6).

THE WAY, TRUTH AND LIFE

Jesus, when I don't know where to go, you become for me the Way. When I'm confused as to just where the truth lies, you cut through all the confusion. When I wonder why life is so humdrum and monotonous, you come to me with the real meaning of life. Jesus, these things are so important: Way, Truth, and Life. Help me to always have you as the foundation of everything that I do. Thank you for doing that!

In three words, Jesus sums up what can be the foundation of our whole life. Jesus tells us that His love for us is all-encompassing. He is willing to meet our every need. All we have to do is turn to Him and realize that He has given us all that we need to find peace in our lives. Let's look at each of these words and see how deeply they speak of the meaning of His love.

I AM THE WAY:

I was listening to the radio the other day and heard a statistic which at first I doubted, but on reflection I thought it contained a lot of truth. The announcer said that 85 percent of America's working force is not satisfied with the work that they are doing. This means that

85 percent of the workers in our country are willing to work at a job they don't like in order to have two weeks' vacation a year. That's frightening. But then, if this is true, perhaps we have an insight into why there are so many people today who don't know what they should major in in college. Why should they strive to get a good-paying job when all the money they'll get won't bring them the satisfaction of creativity that they want out of the eight hours a day they spend on a job?

In the midst of this discouraging situation, Jesus comes in and says, "I am the way. I know how to give you the direction in your life that will show you how you can be the person that you were created to be." Perhaps you are going to have to change your job. Perhaps you are going to have to move out of a situation of high competition and be satisfied with making less money. Perhaps you are going to have to continue with a job that you don't like, but now take on the fire of Jesus' love and start making Jesus present in the world of your work. Perhaps you are tied into a marriage that seems to have deteriorated into a cold "putting-up with" each other in order to give some semblance of security to the children. You've gotten so stuck that you don't think that your marriage partner can change. Jesus says: "In this discouragement, you can come to me and I will show you the way that can totally transform your marriage into a growing and vital new experience of love."

In a world that is in sore need of a leader, we can turn to Jesus with all confidence and know that He can take us to the full use of our potential!

I AM THE TRUTH:

With all the cheap truth that comes to us on the commercials on TV, we wonder just what is truth? Everyone is trying to sell the "truth" that their product is better than the other, but everybody is filled with such saccharine sincerity the truth is made to appear cheap. After a good dose of these conflicting pressures, you begin to wonder if there is anyone that is truthful at all. Then there's the cheapening of truth that we hear from politicians. They tell us about all the good things they are going to do for us, but in doing so they undermine the credibility of those that oppose them. Are people really speaking the truth or are they saying anything that will appeal to our fancy so that we will vote for them? There seem to be so many conflicting "true" statements. How can you know what the truth is?

In the midst of this, Jesus comes to us with great singleminded stability and tells us that **He** is truth. If we will be faithful to Him, Jesus will give us the truth we need. If we study the Scriptures we will see that Jesus is speaking to us right now about the direction His truth will take us in.

I AM THE LIFE:

There are many inhibitions that keep being placed upon us by our society and culture, holding us back from being people that are free to live life to the hilt. In very subtle ways we are told that we are dwelling in an evil body that is really our enemy. We have been told possibly to restrain our emotions, to keep everything under a strong mental control.

Jesus wants us to live our life right here on this earth to the fullest. That's important. Jesus cares that what He's given us in our bodies is something that we must develop to our fullest capabilities and in so doing give Him the glory that He deserves as the Creator. Jesus wants us to tap the fullness of our emotions. He wants us to use our bodies to give Him all the glory that they can. He wants us to use our minds. He wants them to grow through study and being open to experiences. In Jesus, we have a pledge that if we follow His direction, He will bring us to the fullness that is ourselves. To me this means many things. I find Jesus when I move my body to the joy and rhythm of music. I find the life of Jesus when I can relax after an exhausting job or thrill to smashing a handball out of my opponent's reach. I touch the life of Jesus when I go through the intellectual excitement of being engrossed in a novel that I just can't put down or when I view a movie that makes me laugh or squirm with anticipation. Jesus is my life when I drive to the mountains or bake in the desert or feel the adrenalin flow as I walk among the bright lights of a big city at night.

Jesus has put me into this life for a purpose and He doesn't want me to just bide my time, but give Him all the glory I can by pushing all that I have to the highest peak possible.

This is Jesus: The Way, the Truth and the Life.

25

"But some of the Jews stirred up the influential women of the town, and in that way got a persecution started against Paul and Barnabas. The Jews finally expelled them from their territory. So the two shook the dust from their feet in protest, and went on to Iconium. The disciples could not but be filled with joy and the Holy Spirit" (Ac 13:50-32).

"I solemnly assure you, the man who has faith in me will do the works I do, and greater far than these" (Jn 14:12).

POWER TO OVERCOME THE UNLIKELY

Jesus, so many times I paint myself into a corner. I try to handle all the things that go on in my life, and I end up with so much frustration. Help me to learn once and for all that you are the real power in my life and if there is anything that I'll ever do effectively it will have to be done with your strength, founded on submission of my will to you. Help me. I'm so afraid of letting go and yet it seems to be just in this risk that I'll be able to grow in the strength that you promise.

Isn't that reading unbelievable? Look at all the rejection the disciples get and what is their reaction? They were filled with joy and the Holy Spirit. I think of how often when I deal with things on the natural plane, I want to give up everything, because of the negative feelings, not to mention physical assault. Look at the disciples in the same situation, full of joy.

This kind of crazy reaction is just what happens when you open yourself to the power of the Holy Spirit. Things happen that formerly would have turned into tragedy and sent you into a tail-spin of depression. Now, with the Holy Spirit, impossible situations turn into celebrations of joy, as in today's reading.

When we start to move in the power of the Holy Spirit, we can overcome some of the most unlikely situations. Right away we tend to think of some of the physical healings that the Lord can work and we resolve that we should trust the Lord to be able to heal some sickness. This is very important. But you know, I think there is a more serious kind of difficulty than physical sickness. What that is, is the broken or breaking down relationships among people who should be loving each other but who have moved into a petrified relationship. I think that if people were asked what is easier to cure, cancer would be easier than the healing of a broken relationship between a husband and wife. But as we trust more and more in the power of the Holy Spirit, we can even expect that the most damaged relationships can be healed, and exciting growth can happen. These relationships aren't restricted to the married. What about the daughter who is convinced that her parents are all wrong and has closed herself off, just waiting for the chance to get out of school and be free of her parents' oppression?

Who would ever think that Jesus could effect a change in the girl's heart? But this is just what we should expect. The Lord is full of love for us and wants us to trust in His miracles. The same thing holds for a rectory, where there can be cold impasses between pastor and assistant. So many times there is a real estrangement that seems to be cured only by the most extreme miracle or a transfer. As a member of a religious community I know of the deep discouragement that can set in when members become solidified in their thinking and are sure that others are diametrically opposed to their notion of what it means to be a religious, committed to Jesus. What about the boss you have been working under for so many years? Wouldn't a change in him or her be something on the order of Jesus' raising a person from the dead? And yet we so easily become discouraged and fail to see that with our hope in Jesus, we can overcome even these most unlikely obstacles. When you look at the Gospels you find that Jesus was much more successful in effecting physical changes in people than He was in bringing unity among the people He loved. The Gospels abound with healings of eyes, limbs and dead bodies. But again we hear Jesus' cry of anguish at the hate between Samaritans and Jews, or Jews and Romans, not to mention the Twelve contending with each other as to who was the greatest. Jesus knows our frustrations.

Jesus says in today's Gospel that with faith we can do the works that He has done "and greater far than these." Isn't that remarkable! All the wonders that Jesus did can be ours now, today.

I was forcibly struck by His words and decided to take Him up on His promise! I was set to revolutionize the world. I asked for the gift of healing. Then I started to exercise that gift with real faith. You know, the Lord started to work on people that I laid my hands on.

There was a girl who was told that she had two days to live because of a bleeding ulcer and cancer complications. She's doing quite well now several months after the crisis. Then there was the man who had cancer of the skin. His life seemed to be ebbing away. I prayed for a healing and the cancer started to recede and clear up. I was really riding high. Then I ran into obstacles. There was 22-year-old Steve who was in a car accident four years ago. He'd been in a deep coma for four years. For over half a year I went to Steve and asked that the Lord heal him. But Steve still was in a coma. My heart was wrenched. I saw the struggle of Steve's mom, dad, and sisters, as with great courage they longed for Steve to wake up.

One time I was overcome by the thought the Lord didn't seem to be true to His word. I was looking like a fool as I came again and again to pray that Steve wake up. The Lord didn't seem to remember His words that if we have faith, we can do even greater things than He did. Why was it that He was dragging His feet? Was He some kind of a cruel God that enjoyed seeing people suffer and not know why? My adrenalin started to flow, and I let out all the anguish I felt. After I had gone through this experience, when the blood started to cool in my veins, I felt bad that I had been almost blasphemous with the Lord. I didn't feel that I had done wrong, for the Lord wants me to be honest with my feelings. I knew He had greater love than I could ever experience or imagine. I felt bad because I couldn't understand. Then I understood that the Lord was listening to my prayers and effecting a miracle far greater than the waking up of Steve. My prayers were bringing about the miracle of unity. God was working a far more beautiful miracle than I had ever imagined in drawing people together through what was happening with Steve.

I still haven't given up on the healing of Steve, but I thank the Lord for the miracle that He's worked in me and Steve's family already. Yes, I feel deeply now that the Lord has been true to His word and that now, through us, He's working miracles that are far greater than the wonders of the Gospels. How much hope we should have in Jesus because He cares now!

26

"Anyone who loves me will be true to my Word, and my Father will love him; We will come to him and make our dwelling place with him" (Jn 14:23).

THE FABLE OF THE THINKER

Jesus, sometimes I am touched with the wonder of the fact that I've been created by you. Why me? I didn't have to be. But for some reason you came up with the idea of me and you liked it. You think that I'm special. Thank you. I appreciate that. I should be worthy of your trust. Help me. I want to be the magnificent creation that you had in mind when you made me. Thank you again.

Metal is something that you find all over the earth. When there is so much of it we tend to take it for granted. As for treating it with some special respect, well, that would be a little foolish. But there are some people who think that there is more to metal. There are some people who want to touch metal and make it real. Real? Yes. These people are called artists. They have the talents of taking the earth that God has given us and with their hands moulding that earth into something that puts real life into that which seems dead!

There was once an artist who began to touch and mold some ugly, heavy metal and make it real. The artist's name was Rodin. He saw a big piece of metal and wanted to transform it into a statue of a man. He wanted to make a statue of a man that he would call **The Thinker.** So he set to work and after much time, that big lump of bronze began to take definite shape and you could tell that it was of a man who was sitting down with his fist to his chin thinking deeply. The man wasn't wearing any clothes so that the beauty of his body could be seen unimpaired. Well, the statue was done so well by Rodin, that before too long the statue wasn't just a big blob of bronze but was now something that was able to think and feel. There was a special dignity given to it by the artist. The statue was very proud of himself and began looking down on the other pieces of bronze that were in the artist's room because he was by far the most attractive. Then one day, the thinker got religion. He had been taken to an art gallery and all kinds of people came by to look at him and say what a beautiful statue he was. He looked just like a real person. It was a French priest who came to look at him that got him thinking about religion. The priest felt that The Thinker should have been made differently. The priest spoke to the friend that was with him and said that it was a shame that The Thinker didn't have any clothes on, because the body is a temple of the Holy Spirit and should be respected and not left for all kinds of people to gape at. Then the priest thought that the statue would be so much better if it was in another position, rather than having its head bent toward the ground and looking as if the whole world had no answers to its questions. Wouldn't it be better if the head could be turned up looking to the wonder of God's heaven? And as for that fist that was all clenched at the chin, wouldn't it be more fitting if it could be opened wide and lifted to the Lord? That would be a statue that would give glory to the Lord.

The Thinker had a lot of time to ponder what the

priest said as he sat during the evenings alone in the art gallery. The more he thought, the more he felt that the priest made sense. He was more and more excited about giving praise to the Lord with all his being. Finally he decided that he was going to do just what the priest said as a sign that he wanted to give his life to the Lord. That night he resolved that he was going to change his posture so as to give greater glory to God. He started by picking up a dusting rag that the cleaning lady had left behind him and placed it modestly in his lap. Then with all the grace he could muster he turned his head into the air to look in the direction of his God. Rather than frown with a question, he smiled a broad toothy grin. That showed he knew God was the answer. Then just as the priest suggested, he opened his clenched fist and stretched his palms up as if open to the mercy of God. Then with all his strength, he held it there.

Well, the next morning, it didn't take long before people noticed his new look. But rather than admire him as he hoped they would, people began scurrying around shaking their heads. As a matter of fact, several people, instead of being happy, began to cry and sob. The Thinker was very confused, but thought that after a while people would get over the shock and would grow to like the way he looked. Then out of the corner of his eye he saw that the one that had created him, Rodin, was coming in. He was excited because he loved Rodin and felt sure that the creator would like the new creation. But that was far from the case. The manager of the art museum was very nervous and Rodin had a very angry look on his face. The manager of the museum said, "We don't know how it could have happened. We had guards at the entrance all evening. There was even a special light detector guarding the statue so that if anyone had come within three feet of the statue an alarm would have sounded. We've questioned the maid who did the dusting. She saw no one and certainly wouldn't have been strong enough to do all that damage." "Damage?" thought The Thinker. "What damage?" "I know what the problem is," said Rodin. "I'll have to ask that all of you step out of the room, for I want to be alone with the statue for a few moments." When all were gone, Rodin turned to the statue and said, "I know what's been going on. I made you out of a lump of bronze. You were nothing, and when I gave you something, you tried to be something you're not. I am your creator, and I've made you just as I want you to be. And it's only when you are what I've made you that you can be correct. Don't ever try to be anything other than what I've made you." And with that he reached up with his strong hands and pulled away the cloth at his waist, and brought the statue's arm down to the knees. The open hand became a fist. And with many grunts he pulled the head down to where it was gazing at the earth and resting on the fist. "And now you are what you're supposed to be, and you are never going to be any good unless you're what I've made you."

And the sculptor was right because The Thinker never changed his position and people just kept raving about how great he was. The statue remained very happy and decided that he had the wrong idea when it came to being religious.

27

"They stoned Paul and dragged him out of the town, leaving him there for dead. His disciples quickly formed a circle about him and before long he got up and went back into the town. The next day he left with Barnabas for Derbe. After they had proclaimed the Good News in that town and made numerous Disciples, they retraced their steps to Lystra and Iconium first, then to Antioch" (Ac 14:19-21).

SUCCESSFUL PREACHING

Jesus, I have to be on fire to get your Good News to others. Sometimes, though, I can become so much a slave of doing things over and over again, I lose the freshness of the revolution that your Good News calls me to. Help me to spread your Good News to everyone that I come in contact with and let my actions be always for your glory.

Being pelted with stones isn't exactly fun. When I try to picture what Paul's experience must have been like I'm astonished. Paul is stoned in Lystra. So bad is the situation that he is left for dead. But Paul just doesn't seem to make any sense at all; before you know it, he's on his feet and, rather than getting away from an attempted murder, he goes back into the town to be in the midst of those who hate him. I'm sure the people of the town didn't know how to handle a person they had just tried to murder, who came back to re-emphasize the points he had made.

As I enter the pulpit or begin to talk to a group of CCD students or to some college people, I can't help feeling the contrast between my feeble efforts and the fire and dedication of St. Paul. What gave him that dogged determination to preach the Gospel no matter how difficult the situation? Now there's a real missionary.

Clearly, Paul was filled with the fire of the Holy Spirit. There were no limits to his enthusiasm. This Holy Spirit so filled Paul with the love of Jesus that he moved to extremes of almost total disregard for his safety.

As a preacher of the Word, I feel that I must again and again risk my security in an act of love so that the Lord can be glorified through me. That is not easy! There is still that strong pulling away from anything that might in the least hurt me and threaten my security. I'm sure Paul had the same fears I have, but what makes us different is, he was able to accept the gift of the Holy Spirit which allowed him to let go of himself. He was assured that the Lord would stand by him. Even as the stones were smashing into his body, he knew he was being a channel of the Holy Spirit.

He had reached a degree of perfection that allowed him to see God's message coming across even in a situation like this. By his submission to the will of the Father, even with injustice, we see that Paul was a person who lived just what he said.

Unless we preach the truth, not only as something we've discovered in the Bible, but the truth of Christ's life, death and resurrection in our lives, then we're not really speaking the truth that's going to move the lives of the people we talk with.

Now who are we considering when we talk about

preachers? Only those in pulpits? No, also lectors, deacons, CCD teachers, grade school teachers and all Christians on fire with the love of Jesus. We must all be aware of the key to effectiveness in preaching. We must all give ourselves totally to Jesus as Paul did. No matter how well we may have the techniques of preaching and teaching down, unless we're expressing the truth of an experience with the Lord Jesus, we're going to be ineffective.

This personal expression of what the Lord is doing in our lives will be a source of excitement for us and at the same time a source of excitement for all those who come in contact with our searching for ways to love the Lord Jesus more and more.

The way to the power and authority of Paul is as close as the turning over of our lives to Jesus right now, and knowing that He accepts us. With the foundation of this acceptance we can preach Jesus no matter how precarious the situation.

28

"I am the true vine and my Father is the vine-grower. He prunes away every barren branch, but the fruitful ones He trims clean to increase their yield" (Jn 15:1-2).

THE IMPORTANCE OF GROWING

Jesus, growing is so difficult at times. I so want to just let things go and coast. To grow demands the energy of reaching out from what I know to what I don't know. I don't want to. Help me. Help me not be shy of the pruning that's an inevitable part of growing. Unless I take up this challenge, I'll never be whole—and I want wholeness very much, especially in you!

The words of Jesus are very hard today. In order to be a part of Him, I have to be a person who is continually open to growth. Off the top of my head, I can say that I like the idea of growth. Everyone wants to grow. But I'm afraid that many times that's just a pious platitude in my life that I'm not willing to make real. There are many facets of growth. There is intellectual growth. I know that I should read more. I know that I should give up my favorite who-done-it on TV, because there's a better show on the Educational Channel. I know that I should go and listen to that speaker who's in town tonight. But I don't. Then there are other areas of growth. There's the growth of my emotions. So many times I'm obsessed with the control of my emotions that I don't allow laughter, crying, exuberance, deep grief, dancing or quiet. I let my body go to pot by not participating regularly in strenuous exercise, be it sports or manual labor. I'm guilty of not being a person who's attuned to the importance of growth.

Jesus is such a wise person. He knows what it takes for me to develop into the person He created me to be. What wisdom when He says that unless I'm pruned I'll never grow in Him. It's the pain of pruning that's continually impeding me from being a growing person.

Trimming is a very interesting reality. We know that unless a tree is trimmed, it'll never be able to grow the way it should. The fruit a tree is supposed to produce will be very inferior without a trimming. Trimming is interesting when we apply it to ourselves. When a tree is trimmed it's naked. It can have all kinds of leaves and its shoots can be long and beautiful. But when the saw comes into the branches of our lives we are like people forced to stand naked before strangers. That is frightening. There isn't any hiding. There isn't any mask that we can slip behind. There isn't any clothing that we can put on to enhance our beauty or cover up scars. That which we hold as most private is exposed to insensitive eyes. When we are trimmed by God we are very much like that. We want to draw back. We seem so defenseless. We seem so weak. Most of all, we seem so alone and rejected. What do we have to look forward to? A long cold winter in a naked situation. Is growing worth it all? Wouldn't it be better to go back to the way things were and take baby steps rather than endure a drastic trimming. On top of this there's the pain of the amputated limbs. What if they don't grow back? Why did God do this to me? Why does He have to make a world with a pattern of growth that demands the pain of trimming?

In the awkwardness of not being able to answer many

of these questions, we stand alone with doubts. We are asked to be patient as we wait for answers that may never come. This is patience to the nth degree. This is the threshold of magnificence. This is the weakness that in the perspective of the Cross means resurrection. This is what Paul means when he says that when he's weakest, that's when he's strongest of all.

What's frightening is to know that a tree doesn't grow while being trimmed. In all our desolation and pain and nakedness we could endure, if there were something to hold onto, like a springing bud or a flow of sap, but all is cold and quiet. This is the pattern of a faith that will grow and blossom and live forever.

But we must wait. Growing doesn't happen until there is warmth and moisture and food. In this tender experience, we are in touch with growth. Sometimes when we're in a situation that seems to have perpetuated a denuding and stagnating trimming, our only hope is being assured that God works in us, as He does in nature.

God's love is not a thing that we can snatch into a bag and say, "Now I have it!" No. God's love is a growing thing. It can't be put into our definitions. It's moving and alive. Even when it seems to be dormant and we stand all alone and wonder where He's gone and why a lover would seem so distant, we are surprised by freshness and the unexpected. God hasn't gone, but the smothering power of His embrace has blinded us to His magnificence, and as we come up for air we see that His love has been surging and growing at a rate that we never even imagined. Love does not die in the trimming. Love is continually purified and we are called upon to move from what we are comfortable with to that which is new and awkward and unsure but, with time, all the more beautiful.

With God the aim is ever to have our yield increase.

29

"All this I tell you that my joy may be yours and your joy may be complete" (Jn 15:11).

JOY IS THE SIGN OF A CHRISTIAN

Jesus, I love to laugh. I love to be so filled with joy that I just bubble over into my terribly undignified laugh. I know you are the source of this happiness. Because when I have joy, I'm in touch with the wholeness that you are demanding of me. Help me to continually have this joy, even when things tend to get a bit out of hand and I wonder if I'll make it. With you and your joy, we can embarrass the world with happiness.

There is so much insecurity going around, insecurity with ourselves, others, and God. First, there are some who are insecure with themselves from the angle of either weaknesses or strengths. There are people who have great weaknesses and these weaknesses have come to full blossom through many failures. Insecure people don't want to face weaknesses and so they pretend they aren't there. But all the while those weaknesses are eating away like a cancer. On the other hand, there are people who are insecure in their strengths. These people have talents that are going unused because to step out means running the risk of being rejected or misunderstood. These respond to compliments with blushes and all kinds of negative retorts. Better to be insecure with talents than develop them and thus have to take on the burden of responsibility.

Secondly, there are people who are insecure with others. These spend a great part of their lives trying to figure out if other people really like them or, "are they just putting up with me?" When a person can't accept another person it's because he can't accept himself.

Finally, there is the greatest insecurity of all, the insecurity we feel with God. There are people who are so concerned with the judgmental power of God that they can't relax in their insecurity with Him nor develop a personal relationship. God can become so much "The Other" that intimacy is next to impossible. It's hard to move from a formal type of prayer to a more personal way when you have such feelings of insecurity with God.

All of these situations are obstacles to joy. Insecurity causes such tension and self-centeredness that we don't have time to lift our heads and see that the Lord has more to offer us if we but see the joy in the offing. How can we cut through the insecurity that is so much a part of our lives, so that we can live the life of joy, complete joy that the Lord is calling us to?

The answer is as simple as getting in touch with the real power that can overcome the crippling insecurity in our lives. You know who that power is? It's Jesus Christ! We have to come to Him and get from Him the greatest power that there is—the same power that could create heaven and earth and all creation in between. That power is ours today for the asking. If we turn to Jesus, He will help us to accept ourselves. We can relax with what others might think of us. We can bask in the knowledge, the true knowledge, that we have been accepted by God and He's never going to let us go, because we are His.

Joy happens in freedom and freedom is just what Jesus won for us when He died on the Cross and washed our sins away in His blood. He made us no longer unsure, but people of driving conviction who are able to assume authority in any situation, the authority of the power of Jesus, and help bring to completion the work of the Lord.

I must continually accept that freedom by reaching out in trust to the Lord, knowing that He'll be there to support me even if things tend to get a bit ambiguous and I might want to return to the womb of my insecurities. But with the power of the Holy Spirit, I'm able to reach out again and again for all the power that I need.

What words come to your mind when you think of the word joy? I come up with: new, fresh, uplifting, mellow, exciting, together, celebration, peace, bright, yellow, laughter and smiles. No fear.

Let's make sure that we are a strong sign of Jesus' joy to everyone that we meet. This will be the means of getting more people excited about Jesus. Who is the Jesus we preach? If there isn't joy in us who are members of His body, then that might be the reason He's not attracting more people to Himself! Courage is needed to be a joyful people. It's hard to reach out and accept the joy of Jesus when we know that we're going against the grain of what the majority of the world wants. Even this fear can be overcome in the security of Jesus' power and lasting joy.

30

"It is the decision of the Holy Spirit, and ours too, not to lay on you any burden beyond that which is strictly necessary. Namely, to abstain from meat sacrificed to idols, from blood, from the meat of strangled animals, and from illicit sexual union. You will be well advised to avoid these things. Farewell" (Ac 15:28-29).

PUTTING MORE TIME IN DOING THAN IN NOT DOING!

Jesus, sometimes I fail to see that you want more of me than just a lot of things not done. I try to prove myself to you by not doing the things that you ask me not to do. That is so short of the growing love that you want me to be on fire with. Help me to reach out in love to you by being anxious to risk doing things rather than by just treading the safe path of negative security.

That reading is interesting, isn't it? I don't know how many times I've gone through the New Testament, but for some reason I've never been struck by that sentence. I want to know what's happened to Jesus' Church since such simplicity was the rule back during the time of the Acts. The Church wasn't very big on making a lot of regulations about what you weren't supposed to do. The key to being an effective follower of Jesus was rather what you did out of the wellspring of your heart, which was in love with Jesus. I can't help thinking of the contrast of this with my youth, when I would be in Church on Saturday evenings to go to Confession and would pore over the list of sins at the back of my Saint Joseph's Daily Missal. I had the added problem of suffering from an acute case of scrupulosity, so the burden and the terror of the exhaustive examination was very real. Of course illicit sexual union was on the list, but to the best of my memory I didn't have to spend a great deal of time wondering if I had had any blood soup nor did my scrupulosity bother me as to whether the fried chicken I had two nights before had been decapitated or strangled. Sure is funny how our relationship with the Lord can get all tied up with long lists of "don'ts." I can spend the better part, if not all, of my life wondering if I have avoided wrong actions and never get a chance to develop a deep personal active relationship with Jesus.

This is possible through a total surrender of our lives to Jesus and the power of His Holy Spirit. As we hunger to know Jesus better and to have Him be a more vital part of our lives, we don't ignore the regulations that we hear from the Church and the Holy Spirit speaking to us in our hearts. But we can be quite single-minded in loving God more. This becomes a positive relationship, a consuming drive that takes so much positive energy that the scrupulous concern with what we're not supposed to do takes a back seat to the more important growth of our love relationship with the Lord. This desire for deeper love means that we're going to start to risk using the talents we have, in order that they may grow.

One of the outstanding characteristics of this hunger for love will be a distaste for a passive maintenance of the **status quo**. This will be especially in regard to our search for more and better ways to love the Lord. The problem with selfish impure thoughts, or pulling down the character of others, or losing one's temper on a regular basis will be overshadowed by positive action. One can become a member of the parish teaching force to spread the Good News of Jesus. Someone else can organize a prayer meeting. Another can look into the possibility of becoming a missionary.

When Augustine said, "Love God and do as you want," he didn't mean that we should make a pretense of loving God and then be able to do all that we wanted in the realm of sin. Rather he meant that the love of God when sought with sincerity, becomes such an all-inclusive thing that so totally takes up our time that we don't have the same attraction to evil, because of the strength of Jesus' love.

Now all this doesn't mean that we can give up on regulations. The early Church's simple concern for the four major sins of that time has had to expand as mankind has grown and discovered new behaviors that must be evaluated by the Church and the Holy Spirit.

Put another way, do we say that the Holy Spirit is wrong when now we're not terribly concerned with eating strangled animals? In Apostolic times was it "The decision of the Holy Spirit" that Christians not do this? Why the change?

That Holy Spirit is still with the Church, speaking to us through the Church just as He did in Apostolic times, giving us direction about those things which will be harmful to our growth. Still then, as now, the aim of the regulations should again and again first be a deep love for doing good rather than an overemphasis on avoiding evil. Let me avoid certain actions and then I'll be concerned with the love of Jesus. Our love should be continually maturing so that we can always be freer and freer to love.

This is what the word salvation means. I am saved,

I am free from the debilitating anxiety that comes with an over-emphasis on those things that I'm not supposed to do. With salvation I have the freedom and confidence to love Jesus to the full extent of my being.

I think that one of the most difficult hurdles to overcome for someone called by the Lord to come to Christianity is the frightening lack of freedom and joy they often see in followers of Jesus. Let's resolve to attain this freedom and joy. Let's be saved and show it to the world. People are longing to have what we have. If we become so obsessed with what we shouldn't do, we'll never have time to savor the unburdened exhilaration of doing what we're freed to do.

31

"If you find that the world hates you, know it hated me before you. If you belonged to the world, it would love you as its own; the reason it hates you is that you do not belong to the world. But I chose you out of the world . . . They will harry you as they harried me" (Jn 15:18-20).

PERSECUTION

Jesus, persecution is something I don't want. I know that it will hurt, and you know me—King Chicken of them all! If I can get out of any pain, I'll do my best to stay away. But I know that I have to take a stand sometimes. I have to confront the world that is going against your Kingdom. I have to make you present in my day just as you were two thousand years ago. Give me your courage as you went through persecution. Make sure that my love for you is so strong I will be able to go through anything to bring your Kingdom in!

Recently I had the great pleasure of having dinner with Brother Andrew. He has written a spellbinding book called **God's Smuggler.** Brother Andrew is very much in love with Jesus and wants to let others know of the wonders of His salvation. He has a special concern for those who are behind the Iron and Bamboo curtains. So what he does is smuggle Bibles into Communist Countries to let the light of Christ come to those who haven't known of His love for them. As we sat around the table after dinner listening to stories that he was telling us, I was struck by one special story. It seems that several Christians gathered one day in an abandoned Church in Russia to pray. Suddenly, the doors of the Church were flung open and a Russian soldier rushed to the front of the Church with a sub-machine gun in his hands. The moment was electrifying. In mocking tones he said that he was looking for followers of Jesus. If there were any in the Church he would like to deal with them. Everyone else could leave. The door to the back of the Church was opened, but the question of those that wanted to leave before trouble came was whether they would be gunned down in the aisles as they tried to make their escape. Several of the faint-hearted moved to the aisles and started to back away nervously. When just a handful were left, the soldier asked again, "Are there any Christians in the group?" The door was still open and no harm had befallen those who had left. The hearts of those who remained beat rapidly. Their time had come. They were now in the hands of their persecutor. Their prayers became quite fervent.

The soldier told them to close the door. Husbands held wives and children huddled close to parents. The soldier then did a strange thing. He took off his helmet and placed the machine gun on the floor. "I had to make sure that I was with only fellow Christians. I am your brother and I need your support and fellowship."

I wonder if I would have stayed or left the Church. The problem I have when speaking of persecution is that I don't have anything from experience to base it on. Still Jesus speaks to me of the inevitability of persecution, and I wonder how firmly I'm given to Jesus when I compare the troubles that a man like Solzhenitsyn went through, to my half-hearted attempts to stand up for Jesus in my world.

In today's reading, Jesus tells us that we will be hated by the world. What is that world of which he speaks? As a priest, I feel sheltered when it comes to involvement in the world that is opposed to Jesus. I tend to move in such comfortable circles. Yet I know that if I were to just stick my nose out into "the world" a little I would have to be confronted by values that run counter to the teachings of Jesus. There is the break-up of families through divorce. Do I just go along with it because so many people are getting divorces? What about abortions? When there are so many laws in the land that make it an acceptable thing, am I willing to accept persecution or do I muster up as many rationalizations as I can and go along with the stream? Then there are the values of materialism that can become so rampant in our society. Can I withstand being persecuted for finding more value in people than in things? What about standing up for the values of prayers in a family? Am I willing to go against rationalistic and world-wise people and express my strong dependence on the direction of the Lord in everything I do?

Our duty as Christians is to live the life of Jesus right now, just as His life was lived in the first century. We have to stand up for the same things He stood up for. That means that we're going to have to confront all who put more value in laws and materialism than in people. We're going to have to speak the truth when it isn't fashionable. If we're trying to do this and we don't experience persecution, then we had better take a good look at Jesus' words and examine our living them, for more than likely something is wrong.

I love the statement that's going around concerning persecution nowadays: "If you were put on trial today for being a Christian, would there be enough evidence to convict you?"

One of the most frightening aspects of persecution

is that much of our persecution as Christians comes most pointedly from fellow Christians. I think often of the persecution that Paul VI has gone through over his stand on birth control and sexual ethics.

This brings us to another sobering point regarding persecution. There are two sides to every persecution. As we are bearing the burden of hatred and disagreement from others for the stands that we take, we should develop a very open mind and not play the martyr too quickly. Perhaps the criticism that we are receiving isn't persecution at all, but justified opposition for not moving in the truth, as we live in our own little self-righteous castle of elitism. One of the greatest difficulties of persecution is the fact that we're not totally sure that the stand we've taken couldn't have been put in better words or in a context that would have been better understood. We felt that the time had come to act, and we did. Lord, help us to follow your lead and do all for your glory, to be open to the truth!

32

"Once on the Sabbath, we went outside the city gate to the bank of the river, where we thought there would be a place of prayer. We sat down and spoke to the women who were gathered there" (Ac 16:13).

THE IMPORTANCE OF QUIET IN PRAYER

Jesus, so many things are going on in my life. It's possible to get so caught up in them that I don't have time to give to you. Today I want to renew my resolve to spend more quiet time with you. Help me do that. Help me to turn off the noise both inside and outside my head. Help me to be in quiet with you so that I can get in touch with my whole self. Help me to often steal away to the mountain with you.

Today's reading strikes home. The followers of Jesus were tired and they needed to get away to have some quiet to be with Jesus whom they were preaching. Unless they had that time to be at prayer with Him their enthusiasm and fire would die out. So they think they have the spot all picked out. They were probably all filled with enthusiastic anticipation because they would finally be quiet. But what happened? When they get to the spot, their plans are turned upside down. There were a group of women there who looked hungry for the Good News, so they had to put off the retreat until another time. Oh, how familiar that sounds to me. I have some of the best plans to get away and be quiet with the Lord, and then, if it isn't the phone, it's a surprise visitor, and if it's not that, it's a call to drive into Los Angeles and there goes the day. By the time I'm back home, it's near midnight and my excitement about praying is conquered by my yawns and heavy eyes.

But I praise God that He keeps that tension alive in me to come and be with Him in quiet. I know from experience that my times alone with Jesus are the means of my getting in touch with myself. I can touch those depths of me that get stuffed under in all the hustle and bustle of my hectic schedule. I try my best to finagle a time when everyone else is out of our small chapel, and then I try to get away there for at least half an hour.

One of the biggest obstacles to overcome here is the feeling of wasting time. There could be so many other seemingly more productive activities I could be doing. But I know that I'm following in the footsteps of Jesus as He would go up into the mountain alone to spend the night in prayers or spend time in His favorite garden in Jerusalem. We need to be alone and quiet.

Sometimes when the time lies heavy on my hands and I don't know what to say and all the small talk has been spent, I do what a parishioner of the Curé of Ars did. John Vianney, the Curé, was mystified that one of his parishioners would come for long periods of time and just sit quietly in Church. St. John one day could hold back his curiosity no longer and asked the old man what he was able to talk about so long with the Lord. "Oh, I don't say anything to the Lord," was the reply. "I just sit there looking at the Lord in the tabernacle and He sits there looking at me." Sometimes we need quiet to hear all that the Lord wants to say with His magnificent love.

The first step to being quiet with the Lord is finding a special place where you can steal away to be by yourself. I know that this is especially difficult when you are dealing with a large family. Once that is taken care of there's another and perhaps bigger hurdle. This is the problem of the noises going on inside your head. It usually takes me five to ten minutes after I've settled down in my quiet place in chapel to discard all the worries about what's just happened and what's going to happen. I'm a veritable hot-bed of thoughts being thrown in my head. I find that the best way to handle these distractions is to direct the subject matter to Jesus and ask for His blessing. He is the greatest power in the world and he can handle any situation, even my distracting thought. Slowly, by calling Jesus' attention to what I'm thinking, I can settle down and be at peace with Him. I usually fix my gaze on the tabernacle. If you're a young mother, you might just worship Jesus dwelling in your infant child as he takes his mid-day nap.

Jesus' desire is to establish His kingdom in this world. That kingdom needs to first be established in our hearts, and unless we are quiet at times, we'll never be able to achieve that wholeness that has to be our continual goal.

After I've run away and scattered most of my stray thoughts and sat with Jesus, I find great strength in reading just a short piece from the Scriptures. I picture myself in the setting and think of Jesus talking directly to me. I then question how that can possibly apply to me and, sure enough, if I listen closely, Jesus tells me what I should be doing. He touches my wholeness.

Our quiet is a surrender to the Lord in a world that needs noise and activity to cover up its insecurity. In our helplessness and even our feelings of futility in His presence, we are open to special blessings.

33

"The crowd of Philippians joined in the attack on Paul
and Silas, and the magistrates stripped them and ordered
them to be flogged. After receiving many lashes they
were thrown into prison, and the jailer was given instructions to guard them well. Upon receipt of these
instructions he put them in maximum security, going so
far as to chain their feet to a stake. About midnight,
while Paul and Silas were praying and singing hymns
to God, as their fellow prisoners listened, a severe earthquake suddenly shook the place, rocking the prison to
its foundations" (Ac 16:22-26).

HOW IMPORTANT TO SING

Jesus, in you I can sing with a full voice of joy.
You are the one who has given me the wholeness
that I long for. You have given me the answers
that I seek to all the things that I can't understand. Jesus, you have given me peace in a world
of confusion. I sing to you, not with the operatic
voice I wish I had, rather with my booming but
strained voice that comes from a heart full of
gratitude. Thank you for letting me sing to you.

I'm going to let you in on a secret. Now, mind you, I'm
not about to tell you something that I've told everyone.
This is something I've been holding to myself. You know
how it is when you have something special in you and

you're afraid others will not understand you and hold
you up to ridicule. Well, I want to tell you about one
of the secret dreams that I have in my heart. Now don't
laugh. You see, I've always wanted to go to Broadway
and audition for a big production of **Man of LaMancha**
and sing the lead. Now hold on. Let me explain before
you start laughing . . . not many people have heard my
voice. I do admit that I restrict it to the shower and when
I'm zooming down the freeways with all the windows
closed. But now I'm really being honest. Not only do I
want to take the part and shake the rafters and pluck
heart strings with my rendition of "To Dream the Impossible Dream," but deep in my heart I think I have
what it takes. Granted, I might be a little rusty now.
But once I was heard by the directors and they realized
my raw talent, they would give me a voice coach and I
would soon be the envy of Robert Merrill and Howard
Keel. I say all this not too off-handedly. It was several
years ago, I remember quite clearly, I was booming forth
as my mother was trying to listen to TV. With a weak
smile she turned to me and commented, "Michael, you
have a nice strong voice." Now if that isn't unsolicited
enthusiasm, I don't know what is. I've been able to
feed my dream on that comment a good twenty years
now. Some day I'll get another compliment. Who knows,
my mom might even break out in enthusiastic praise
again and set me going for another twenty years.

There's something about singing that's magic. I mean
that real live music that you sing yourself, not the stuff
that you listen to on TV or the radio. This past summer
I was visiting relatives in Michigan. One night a good
number of the clan got together to sing. We got the
piano going and passed around the words to some of the
old songs and we must have gone for two hours. It was
fantastic! There's nothing like the joy of blasting your
lungs out with someone else to a familiar old tune. I

don't know, I think it's the way you let go. When you
sing you drop so many of the inhibitions that you have
and you are freed to be one with those you are singing
with in a way that conversation can never quite touch.
Singing is magic! I can't help thinking that with all the
problems that we're facing in the world today with
people not being able to communicate—married couples,
parents, children, races or denominations, wouldn't it
be great if we could get the people together and have
them sing one booming verse of "My Wild Irish Rose."
I'm sure that the singing would help people drop defenses and free them to love each other and feel one in
Spirit. Look what happened in today's reading. I'm not
saying that the singing was the cause of the earthquake.
Though perhaps Paul was very good on the high notes
and could even shatter things greater than glass. Paul's
singing did more than break the chains. It spoke strongly
of his faith and his joy and was a source of strength and
unity even after he had been whipped. The same idea
is expressed in the **King and I,** when "Whistling a Happy
Tune" frees us from fear. Singing can put us in close
relationship with the Lord Jesus, and open us for even
deeper love.

As a priest, I know what a difference the magic of
music can make at a liturgy. When the music is well
prepared and people are comfortable with singing loudly
and fervently, the floodgates to the Holy Spirit are broken
open. With good singing at Mass there is a dropping of
inhibitions and a great openness to the power of the
Lord moving in our lives.

But what do you do if you can't sing? I mean not
everyone has a chance like me to try out for **Man of
LaMancha** (Ah, fond dreams!). What if you can't carry a
note? This goes all the way from those who are deaf
by just one half-tone all the way up to those who make
a lot of head motions when it comes to the different

notes. The importance of singing is that it doesn't have to come from the mouth. The best kind of singing comes from the heart of your being. Jesus put a song in our hearts—a song of confidence and joy based on the fact that He loves deeply and no matter how bad things get, He'll never let us down. Just like the melody that gets caught in your head and you can't get it out, so Jesus is present to us with His power and love and makes our hearts sing. So let go! Listen to the song going on in your heart and know that it's the victory song of Jesus telling you that He loves you.

34

"As I walked around looking at your shrines, I even discovered an altar inscribed, 'To a God unknown.' Now, what you are thus worshipping in ignorance I intend to make known to you" (Ac 17:23).

CAN WE KNOW JESUS PERSONALLY?

Jesus, I want to get to know you. Knowing you isn't as simple as knowing the brother who lives in the room next to mine. There's something different. But still I know that I want to know you. Don't let me take you just as some historical person who lived a long time ago but really doesn't have to be a personal friend to me. Jesus, help me to know you.

Do you really think that you can know Jesus? No, I don't mean know Jesus on a purely historical basis. That isn't too hard, because if you can read you can go through the Bible or a life of Christ and know all the facts about Jesus that you want. But that isn't what I'm talking about. We can know all the facts about Jesus and still worship at Mass as at the shrine of the unknown God as the Greeks were doing at the time of St. Paul. We can go through our whole life doing all the right things on an external basis—going to Mass, the Sacraments, saying the Rosary, grace before and after meals and such, but never confront ourselves with the question of knowing Jesus personally in our lives.

How can you know Jesus, since you haven't seen Him? "Sure I believe that He lives right now and is in me, but all the people I know are those who have flesh and blood with whom I can sit down and have a good conversation and receive all kinds of responses from my senses. But with Jesus, it's so difficult to know if you are having a personal relationship or just projecting Him into the friends you love and live with. Knowing Jesus seems to be a very difficult thing on that level."

I have to believe that Jesus is alive today, and as such is able to be an object of my affections and knowledge on a very personal and intimate level.

Can a husband love Jesus in a manner similar to the love he has for his wife? Can we love Jesus with the same intensity with which we love a parent? At face value it would seem impossible.

But with God all things are possible. So it is in our love for Jesus. Although it seems improbable, it can be a love as personal and intimate and real as any human love we could compare it to, and even more than that! This is the wonder of dealing with a God who has created the entire universe and who can use that same power to make me feel His love for Him.

The key to experiencing this love is for us to take the frightening step of trusting in His power in our life. This means that we have to let go of the controls and the worries and the anxieties of our life and turn them over to the power of Jesus who is able to direct us. This is a very helpless and weak position we put ourselves in. But it is the position of openness that the Lord requires of us as we strive to become real and intimate with Him on a personal basis.

After we have offered to surrender ourselves to the Lord, we move into the next aspect of our love of Jesus— and that's waiting. Yes, we wait for God to give us the

gift of His personal love. The reality of loving Jesus is
not something that I can generate on my own. It's a gift.
Pure and simple. The love of Jesus is something that I
have to look for as a baby bird helplessly waiting for
its mother to come and drop food down in its mouth.
Like a baby bird I can only move into as receptive an
attitude as possible and wait. The waiting can be a real
purging, for it's only in the waiting that I experience
my weakness and helplessness and need and then can
be open to Jesus' power. We must remember again and
again the words from John, "It isn't that we have loved
God, but that God has loved us first." The waiting helps
us to take off the masks that we wear to cover up the
truth about ourself. The effort to maintain a mask is
very hard when we are tired, and there are few things
that can make us more tired than waiting for something,
helpless to make that something happen.

Our waiting is not a lethargic waste of time. No, we
don't sit back and do nothing. Our waiting must be
filled with the directives the Lord has given to us, as
to how we can be His servants. This means that we must
make Scripture a very important part of our lives.

We must hear Jesus talking to us through the Word.
We must love our neighbor as ourselves. This means
that first we must love ourselves. We must be free of the
burden of lack of self-esteem that is so prevalent in our
society and start risking the use of the talents the Lord
has given us, whether they are cooking, writing, sew-
ing, golfing, preaching or listening. We must not let the
power of God's gifts be lost. Then we must take up the
second part of Jesus' basic command and love our neighbor after we've learned to love ourselves. This means
expanding love relationships that are comfortable and
agreeable and starting to include those bothersome people who take up our time.

We are going to have to start to listen to people whose

life style seems to be a threat to our security. We're going to have to move from our domain of comfort to the weakness and vulnerability of going another mile when someone we dislike asks this of us, or turning the cheek when we've been insulted and actually loving that person, rather than just putting up with him, because that's what should be done by a Christian.

Something strange begins to happen when we wait in this manner. As we wait in growing futility, and our hunger for a real personal relationship with Jesus grows, we begin to know Him in a way that is independent of our love of others, but at the same time this love is integrally tied up with Him. It's as if Jesus were saying to us, "I want you to experience the desert as a means of purification so that you can love me really and truly, but all the while your purification will lead to a real relationship with me that will be strong and real and personal."

Yes, we can know Jesus personally, so personally that words seem futile. I do know Jesus and love Him, but that love is so much at the foundation of my being that to tell you about it would be to tell you who I am completely, and only God can handle that mystery.

35

" 'You will receive power when the Holy Spirit comes down on you; then you are to be my witness in Jerusalem, throughout Judea and Samaria, yes, even to the ends of the earth.' No sooner had he said this than he was lifted up before their eyes in a cloud which took him from their sight" (Ac 1:8).

JESUS IS GONE, BUT HERE

Jesus, the Ascension reminds me that I have a very important responsibility as your follower. You have entrusted me with the task of making you present to the world. You have left and entrusted me with all the power you had and ask that I make your life, death and resurrection a reality in the world—now. Help me do this. Help me listen to your direction so that I can help effect the revolution of your Kingdom.

The feast of the Ascension is a very meaningful celebration to me. Jesus left the world in His body but now is present in many new ways. It's good to review the presence of Jesus and know that we are integral to the meaning of His presence. Unless we take the responsibility seriously, the effectiveness of Jesus' presence will be lessened.

Although Jesus is gone, He is just as present in four different ways—different but at the same time all tied into an indivisible presence. All these ways are one driving expression of Jesus' love for us and His desire to be intimate with us.

The four presences are: in individuals, in the Church, in Scripture and the sacraments.

Jesus is present to each of us who have accepted Him into our hearts. He's taken residence in us and we participate in the divine life. This is something that can grow to greater and greater awareness on our part. Paul knew that when he grew to be able to say, "It's now no longer I that live but Christ that lives in me."

One of my favorite stories of the wonder of Jesus' presence in us is the practice of the father of the second century theologian Origen. When Origen was still an infant, his father would come into his room at night. He'd unloose his night gown and with great reverence kiss his child's chest and spend the night in worship of Jesus dwelling in his son. I need to recall this reality when I get frustrated with people. I can so want to put people off until they can fit more comfortably into my schedule. I need to remember that Jesus is dwelling in the people that annoy me. I need to remember the same Jesus is dwelling in me and I must be careful that I take care of my body by not allowing it to get caught up in sin and thus shame the presence of my saviour who's found my body to His liking.

Jesus is dwelling in the world today through the Church. When you speak of **the Church** most Catholics begin to think of the gigantic structure they're a part of—hundreds of millions strong. It's true that Jesus dwells in the Church like this but if we keep thinking so big we can easily water down the force of Jesus' presence in the Church which is our parish down the street! Our parish is a vital presence of Jesus. As we struggle to make Jesus' Good News a reality with fellow parishioners we are living the life of Jesus now. The presence of Jesus in our church is not a static thing but rather a relationship that is growing as we grow in love with the people of our parish. That means that Jesus is present as we work with our pastor who doesn't seem to have the sensitivity we would like or the obnoxious kids your children go to school with and even that family who is struggling with the prospects of a divorce despite having six children.

This is the presence of Jesus—in the group of people of your parish who seem to be spending more time struggling with the Christian ideal rather than being able to enjoy the fruits of the Kingdom. When people ask where Jesus went after the Resurrection, we can say He's right in the midst of efforts your parish is having to try to make His Gospel real, right in your home town.

More and more we Catholics are getting around to reading the Bible with greater regularity. Sad to say, the Bible was certainly something we held in great respect, but more often than not that respect meant it collected dust on a shelf. Scripture is a vital and real presence of Jesus in our life right now. The Word of God is living. This means that every time we open Sacred Scripture and read or hear it read to us, we are having a direct communication of Jesus with us. This word of God is real, as real as the presence of Jesus in our life right now. More and more we should turn to Scripture to let the Lord speak to us and express His presence to us with great love. There is a great power in the Word of the Lord in Scripture. I love to think of the words from St. Peter when he says, "The Word of God is an indestructible seed!" (1 P 1). That means that when you give the Word of Scripture to someone, even if it seems to be without effect, the Word is an indestructible seed—Jesus Christ. Jesus can not be done away with but will flourish and grow with openness and time. As Jesus calls upon us today to be His witnesses to the ends of the earth, we should remember that our key is the Word of Sacred Scripture and this should be frequently on our lips as we spread the Good News to the ends of the earth.

Jesus is also present to us in the sacraments in a real way. We meet Him and grow in a deeper and deeper relationship with Him through Baptism, reconciliation, eucharist, marriage, confirmation, ordination and anointing of the sick. These sacraments are the presence of Jesus enriching us with His wonder and intimacy. In the past there has been a great deal of stress placed on the presence of Jesus in the Eucharist which is truly a unique presence, namely, Christ is sacramentally present under the appearances of bread and wine. Not denying this in the least, we should also find Jesus present in, for example, the sacrament of reconciliation. We share with a priest the sin of our life and through the Church receive the forgiveness and reconciliation of Jesus talking to us really and truly.

Jesus is present to us. Let's not allow this power and love to go unnoticed. Let's awaken to His love and make sure that we don't take His presence for granted.

36

"You are sad for a time, but I shall see you again; then your hearts will rejoice" (Jn 16:22).

WHEN GOD IS GONE

Jesus, sometimes I'm so alone. As a matter of fact, I'm so alone that I don't even feel your consolation. I wonder where you have gone. I feel one with your disciples, who today are trying to figure out what their life is supposed to mean now that you have ascended to your Father. Lord, help me to understand aloneness. Help me to know that I can grow even when I'm afraid and confused and alone. Help me to have the underlying strength of your love to allow me to make my loss of you a time of extraordinary growth in love.

The emotions of the apostles on the first day after the Ascension must have been very confused. For three years they had been with Jesus on such an intimate basis. Now they were without His familiar physical presence. There was a definite confusion and bewilderment as to what they were waiting for in an upper room. In our lives if we are striving to know God more deeply we are going to experience times when we feel separated from Him. We are going to have times when we are convinced that God is gone.

I think of my friend who has been convinced for five

years that God is gone from her life. Five years ago her ten-year-old daughter died of leukemia, despite her begging insistence that God cure her.

The experience doesn't have to be this dramatic. We can feel forgotten by God when there's no excitement in our lives. The humdrum struggle to make a living at a job that is a total bore can gnaw at you till you're sure God is gone.

There isn't much you can do when you are alone. No amount of logic is going to solve the hurt. It takes a lot of patience with ourselves, trusting others, and acceptance of God's power over us even though we don't feel like putting up much of a fight. We aren't being hypocritical when we trust in that which we don't feel, but deep in our hearts know is present.

Today's Scripture offers a difficult direction. For a time we will be sad, but then we will rejoice. This is God's plan for our salvation. We have to suffer pain in order to rejoice. Why this difficult pattern? Wouldn't God be much more loving to have us suffer no pain but rejoice all the time? What does it mean that Christ has died on the Cross and thus paid the price for our sins? Why is it that we have to experience evil and aloneness before we can come to the rejoicing? The problem with that question is that pain and aloneness are not really bad.

In the pain of being alone I'm forced to be naked. I'm forced to admit that I'm carrying gaping holes in my life, that unless I experience a deep separation from God, I'll never be able to come to the truth of who I am as a whole person. God lets us experience His absence which isn't absence. We can't exist without His presence. But we can see where we need to have Him fill us up with His presence. When we are alone and we think that God has left, we are vulnerable and are forced to turn to the Lord to fill us up, and in this we reach wholeness. The sadness had forced us to fill ourselves up with God, but we couldn't understand our need unless we experienced the depth of being alone.

With aloneness faced and embraced we now have solid ground on which to rejoice in a way that is deeper than the pain we had felt in our desolation. In this continual process, we come to the perfection, the wholeness that God has called us to. We experience His presence and know that His love will never let us go, although we might experience His absence many times in the future.

37

"A Jew named Apollos, a native of Alexandria and a man of eloquence, arrived by ship at Ephesus. He was both an authority of Scripture and instructed in the new way of the Lord . . . He was vigorous in his public refutation of the Jewish party, as he went about establishing from the Scriptures that Jesus is the Messiah" (Ac 18: 24-28).

HUNGER FOR SCRIPTURE

Jesus, I'm so backward when it comes to knowledge of the Scriptures. Fill me up with a driving hunger to read your Word and study the insights of others so that I can be a Christian whose sole purpose in life is to grow deeper and deeper in love with you.

I'm afraid that I've developed a very bad habit as a priest administering the Sacrament of Reconciliation. After the penitent has shared his or her sins, I ask a couple of very embarrassing questions. I should stop it and perhaps start confessing my habit to my confessor rather than cause such discomfort to the people who come to me! First I ask them where they stand in their love of Jesus. "What do you mean? Of course I . . . ? Explain yourself, please Father." The second question is "Do you get much chance to read the Bible?" Sad to say, the problem with the first question tends to be closely related to the problems with the second.

In the past, the Bible hasn't played the central part in the lives of Catholics that it seems to have in the lives of our separated brethren. Now I would lay a wager that the majority of Catholic families have a Bible somewhere on a book-shelf, but when it comes to regular reading of it, we say: "It can be so confusing at times that I don't want to complicate my faith. There are so many strange sayings that leave me with more question marks than satisfaction."

So we move along, knowing that the Bible should be held in great respect but never getting the nerve to dive into it with regular reading and study.

Deep in our hearts though, there's a gnawing frustration when we come up against a Protestant who can glibly quote the Bible, even giving chapter and verse. Even worse is when they don't even bother to give the quote but are satisfied with: "And what you're saying reminds me so forcefully of Mark 23, Verse 12." Even more frustrating: at your door you find two eager Jehovah's Witnesses ready to prove to you that everything you have held sacred about Jesus has got to be re-examined and they have the Scriptures to prove it—in English, Greek, and Hebrew.

There's a revolution going on! My personal ignorance of Scripture has turned into a driving hunger. Granted I had four years of Scripture Study, but I still felt very inadequate. I've started to make up for lost ground. My first step was to get out my tape recorder and put the New Testament on cassette tapes. I went at it for half hour periods, and within a month I was finished. I then stuck my recorder at my side as I drove around Southern California. The word of God began to speak to me in a new and fresh way. But there were still so many questions. I then got real help from Bishop Sheen. He mentioned that if you ever wanted to give a priest a gift, one of the best things that you could give him was Wil-

liam Barclay's Daily Scripture Studies. I picked up one
of Barclay's books and got hooked. This Scripture scholar
has meant a great deal to me in my study. He's a man
who has a scholar's knowledge of Greek and Hebrew,
plus a great knowledge of the mentality of the Jews at
the time of Jesus. When seen from this scholar's vantage-
point, the Scripture takes on a new life and force. What
is more important than anything, Barclay is very read-
able, even for those who have ventured into the first
page of the Bible. He is very down to earth. But I haven't
stopped there. I've gone into other writers who comment
on Scripture and find that I'm being refreshed at a well
that will never run dry of surprises and insights.

One of the dangers of this hunger for understanding
Scripture is that it can develop into something that's
almost exclusively academic. The hunger for Scripture
has to be an expression of a hungering love affair. The
more that we know Jesus, the more we have to transform that knowledge into action, to love Him more.
Scripture then doesn't become a bunch of cold transla-
tions of something that happened almost 2,000 years
ago, but rather a present, intimate and real expression
of love between Jesus and me. Listening to Jesus speak
to us in Scripture at quiet moments of the morning
should set the tone for the communication that will go
on with Him during the rest of the day. The Scripture
is not only the faith-experience of the early Church,
it's a reality that is now. Let the love of the Holy Spirit
be the force beyond your reading of Scripture. It's a
wealth of love words that will enable us to touch the
ground of the meaning in our life in Jesus. Along with
commentaries, search out good Scripture study courses.
Try to encourage something on the parish level.

As we grow in our knowledge of Jesus through the
Scripture, we'll be simultaneously setting the ground

work for the entrance of the Holy Spirit in our life with an ever-renewing fire and drive.

"How do we stand regarding our relationship with Jesus?" In many ways this will go hand in hand with a growing hunger to study the Scriptures.

38

"As Paul laid his hands on them, the Holy Spirit came down on them and they began to speak in tongues and to utter prophecies" (Ac 19:6).

THE GIFTS OF THE HOLY SPIRIT

Jesus, don't let me get so caught up in rationalistic and logical categories that I can't be open to your limitless wonders. Give me the vision to help transform the world into your Kingdom of love and know I will have more than enough strength and power for this from you!

Look at all the wonders you read about in the New Testament! Can all those things have happened? So many times the wonder of Jesus seems unreal—a memory of twenty centuries ago. With all the scientific knowledge we have now, it's hard to believe in such things as walking on water or making the blind see or even the raising of the dead. Sure it could've happened back then, but now we have enough miracles to deal with, like putting man on the moon, or developing a cure for cancer, or touching the undiscovered self through psychoanalysis. Aren't these miracles more important and reasonable than making a big thing out of the wonders that Jesus was said to have performed?
I wish I could say I've never been tempted to put all my eggs into this rationalistic approach to the happenings of Scripture.

But the problem comes because I'm such a fool. I wasn't satisfied with just a rationalistic approach to everything. I felt there could be more. Being a fool, I did a foolish thing. I put faith in a greater power than a computer. I said there was greater power than what a man can develop as a cure for leukemia. There's even a greater power than all the brilliant psychoanalysis in the world.

I did the foolish thing of putting all my faith in a transcendent, but immanent God. I then asked that I might experience Him just as really as a scientist can sense the touch of a piece of moon rock or a doctor can feel a tumor or a psychiatrist can see a person cured through therapy.

I testify to you today that I've experienced God. I've touched and experienced and know as sure as I am that God has revealed Himself to me. This power of God is not something I've conjured up. It's real! I know that Jesus of Nazareth is real and is alive today and using the same power right now that He did twenty centuries ago, as recorded in Scripture. What is so exciting is that there's more power than there was in the past. Wonders that we hear about in the Good News will pale before the wonders of God that are available to us if we but reach out in trust, in foolishness as the world would have it, and be open to the power of the Holy Spirit in our lives. We have to be open to wonders such as today's reading describes.

As Pentecost nears, we're reminded that when we pray to be open and receptive to the Holy Spirit, He will come bearing gifts which will strengthen hope and awaken faith in others who have never heard of Jesus.

In the early Church, many gifts were made manifest through the Holy Spirit: speaking and praying in tongues, prophecy, teaching, preaching, healing, administration and others. All these are fine, but since we've decided to be foolish and trust in the Holy Spirit's transcendent power, why not expect even more? This is so important because we need the power of the Holy Spirit in a divided and confused world that doesn't know what it would be like to have Holy Spirit power.

When Paul laid hands on the people, they got power from God, and that's the greatest power that can ever be. That same power is ours if we can but be open to receiving it. The awareness of that power is more real than Paul's laying on of hands.

One of the greatest gifts of the Holy Spirit is peace, and this is exactly what we receive with the reception of the power of the Holy Spirit. We have a power that can overcome the fear of what others think of us or the fear of where our finances will come from or the fear of how we can ever love someone we're separated from.

The gifts of the Holy Spirit don't somehow remove us from the real world of making a living or caring for people suffering from cancer or nervous breakdowns. With the Holy Spirit we have the gift of transcendent limitless power to work wonders in our life. Let's trust in the power of Jesus rather than be fools who ignore the source.

39

"For these I pray—not for the world, but for these you have given me, for they are really yours. (Just as all that belongs to me is yours, so all that belongs to you is mine.) It is in them that I have been glorified. I am in the world no more, but these are in the world as I come to you" (Jn 17:9-11).

CHURCH UNITY AND SWITCHING RELIGIONS

> Jesus, your call is to unity in the Church. I'm confused by the number of people who are leaving the Catholic Church and going to Churches where they think they can better grow in their love for you. Help us to have a greater stick-to-itiveness to the Church and be willing to work in unproductive and discouraging situations with greater hope in your transforming power.

As a priest who has had the advantage of working with several Protestant groups on a rather intimate level, I must share with you a sorrow and question that I have concerning the great number of Catholics who are leaving their communities and starting to worship regularly at various other Churches.

A priest-friend of mine who's in a position of authority told me some sobering facts. He said that in all the Pentecostal Churches in the United States, one third of the members are former Catholics. I don't think you have to go very far, even in our own families, to find examples of people leaving the Catholic Community.

The excuses people give for leaving are many: an impossible marriage situation, resulting in a marriage "outside the Church." Since you can't participate fully in the Eucharist, why not go to a place where you can participate fully? Also there are those who disagree with the Church's teaching on birth-control or abortion.

The third type are those who leave the Catholic Church for seemingly good motives. These leave the Catholic Church because they don't think that they're getting anything out of it. It doesn't have anything to offer them. The liturgies are dull. There's no life. There's no prayer. There's no mention of Jesus in sermons. All you hear about is money and bingo games. When they look back to the days they were Catholics they can't understand how impersonal things were. No one really cared about anyone else. Mass was just a duty to be fulfilled every week.

When they go to other Churches, for the first time in their lives they find that the important thing is a personal commitment to Jesus. They start living the celebration of the Sunday service every day.

As I said before, when I hear these arguments, my blood begins to boil. Not because what they say isn't the truth. Oh, how well I know it's the truth. I know how dull believing in Jesus can be in some Catholic churches. I know that there's next to no life and enthusiasm in so many Catholic churches. I know that the leadership in so many churches seems completely void of that deep personal commitment to Jesus seen in the joy and enthusiasm of so many beautiful Protestant ministers. I know that many Protestant churches make prayer meetings the key to community. My point is that the fire of the Holy Spirit we experience needs to be channeled into the Church that has givn us our foundation in faith.

I know this is difficult to swallow. A person who's had a beautiful experience of the Lord and wants to share that life and make it grow in fellowship can be so discouraged by an over-structured and impersonal Church. "The Catholic Church is so big that there isn't the intimacy that you can find in a small congregation."

If your foundations, however feeble, are with the Catholic Church, don't you owe it to your fellow-Catholics to give them a share in the richness of the Spirit that you've received? I find the desire to leave the Catholic Church and enrich oneself with the new-found wealth of another Church the height of selfishness.

The born-again experience is not something that we sit and moon over in an ideal situation. Rather it's something that has to reach out in love to others so that they can share the fullness that we've received. We need to witness to those that are lacking our fullness, even if we're rejected and scorned by those we witness to. So if you are on fire with the Holy Spirit and find that your enthusiasm is dampened by the Catholic Church, don't go to a place where you can feel good. Rather put that fire to the dry wood of your parish and work to enrich others with your love of Jesus. Now this doesn't mean that you develop a superiority complex. Your battle plan is the same as Jesus'. With long-suffering kindness and openness and fire, you listen and serve the needs of others, but all the time with the burning desire to bring them the fullness of the love of Jesus you have aflame in your heart. A needful field of concern will go unheeded unless you do your part to make your Catholic brothers alive with the Holy Spirit on an ever-renewing basis.

"O Father most Holy, protect them with your name which you have given me, that they may be one, even as we are one" (Jn 17:11).

MARRIAGE MEANS COMMITMENT

Jesus, as I hear you pray for unity, I can't help thinking of all the heartache and disunity that is going on in Marriage. So many people have given up what was at first a firm commitment to spend the rest of their lives with another person. Now there are more and more divorces. Help me to understand what I can do to help people to have your unity in their lives. Help me to bring people the peace that you alone can give so that your revolution of love can overtake a world that's grown used to separation as if it were inevitable.

I know that I shouldn't feel this way about marriage. I mean, it's a sacrament. But for some reason there is a strong reluctance to go through the process of witnessing the marriage of a young couple. I guess that I spend so much time talking with couples who are having difficulties that I get prejudiced. I get so hesitant to involve people in something that is so sacred and wonderful to me. I want them to be so well-prepared and I don't know if I can give that preparation.

When a couple wants to get married, I want to know for sure that they are committed to Jesus and are doing this in union with Him and continually relying on His strength. So many times young couples look at marriage in the Church as something that has to be done, but they're not regular church-goers. I usually ask this question, "Why is it that you are coming to a church? Wouldn't it be much more realistic to put aside all the hassle with the gowns, tuxes, and flowers and hiring the hall, picking up the visiting relatives, and working out the ceremony? Don't go through all that! Why not just go to a quiet room all by yourself and turn the lights off. Light a candle, play your favorite love song on the record player, take each other's hands and, while looking into each other's eyes, promise that you will give yourself to each other for the rest of your lives. Now wouldn't that be more sensible? Wouldn't that be more loving and realistic? Why all the church hassle?"

To me, marriage in the Church is so much more than this. Marriage in the Church is an involvement in several deep commitments that bind and strengthen the union.

One of the first commitments in a Church wedding is the commitment to make a total abandonment to each other, not with a part-time commitment, but a total commitment. One commits oneself to the freedom of a togetherness that will end only in death! With this finality realized in your deepest heart, there is peace. This is a commitment so total that if it is broken, there's a scar left that can never be healed. There's a giving of self that can never be gotten back because of the involvement with the other.

The other commitment is that of the Catholic parish community to the couple. This is so important. Without the commitment of the Church to the couple, they'll never reach the fullness of their love. We can so easily think that love is something that only involves the husband and wife. But that just isn't so. Marriage involves the parents, and relatives, close friends and all the members of the Body of Christ in the parish, who offer all the love and direction that they can to foster this love of Jesus in the married couple. If a couple at marriage are "in love" they're going to have to go through the earth-shattering experience of not loving another person merely as a projection of his or her psyche, but rather of loving him or her for who they are, and this person might have all kinds of quirks, habits, feelings and opinions that are offensive. When love grows from being "in love" to "love" there is a strong need to have a community of understanding and support to help a couple through the transition period. The community is the presence of Jesus giving His support which is all one needs to make a marriage "work."

Commitment to Jesus is the final commitment. Prayer on a daily basis has to be a vital part of each marriage. Couples must come to Jesus each day and, if only for 15 seconds, turn to each other, and with honesty lift their union to the Lord for His help. The Lord will be there and believe me, if couples were able to do this for 15 seconds each day, with a prayer that's open and free and real, there wouldn't be a need for divorce because the commitment of Jesus to the couple would be opened and Jesus' power would transform even the most awkward marriage situation.

Prayer together for a couple who have been married for a few years can be very awkward initially. The fear of going into this type of prayer is so great that a couple would prefer to go to ten marriage counselors rather than let their masks down long enough to share their hearts with each other and Jesus for 15 seconds.

The most important part of a marriage in the Church is that it is the occasion for Jesus to say to the couple that He is willing to make a bond with them to be with them, no matter what the difficulties. He will be there to give His strength and help and will make growth a reality even in a marriage that seems to be dead!

We need to re-awaken in ourselves the reality of power—the power that comes from the Church's commitment to us in a Church wedding. Las Vegas would not be just as good. Nor would the local Justice of the Peace. What we're dealing with is the power of Jesus who is able to transform a struggling or broken relationship with His prayer for unity. All we need to do is call upon Him and ask, and He'll be there with all the power of the prayer He made to His heavenly Father to bring unity into the world. He wants unity. If we ask, He'll give us the strength. We have to listen to Him, though. We have to be willing to respond to Him even if what He asks goes against the grain.

"At this, the dispute grew worse; and the commander feared they would tear Paul to pieces. He therefore ordered his troops to go down and rescue Paul from their midst and take him back to headquarters. That night the Lord appeared at Paul's side and said: 'Keep up your courage! Just as you have given testimony to me here in Jerusalem, so must you do in Rome'" (Ac 23:9-11).

WAITING

Jesus, when I see that a job has to be done, I want to go out and do it. I am so very impatient. That's why it's hard to be a follower of yours. You move at such a different pace. It's not that you're slow, far from it. But you are so loving and all-inclusive when you answer my prayers. Help me to learn patience. Help me to be able to just wait on you and know that in the waiting I'll be able to come closer to you and show that I love you much more.

Sometimes I get so impatient with other people. When I'm trying to explain something that is very clear to me and I can't get the point across to another, I tend to get impatient. This isn't only with others. I tend to get impatient with myself. I know that I should be growing at an ever more intense pace, but my laziness and ignorance get in the way and so much of my life is just frittered away. It was at a time of great impatience that I got a great blessing from God. He reminded me how patient He is with me. If I'm honest with myself I'll have to admit that if I had responded to God's grace better in the past, I could be so much more the person that God has made me to be. But alas, I'm just myself with all my failings and reluctance to grow. But what's so great about this realization is that God is willing to wait. Sure He would like to see me farther down the road. But He is so patient with me. He doesn't bop me over the head when I don't grow up. He keeps prodding me along with such patience. I'm so glad that God can wait on me to finally come around to where I should be.

Waiting is difficult and yet it's the key to being open to the will of the Lord in my life. Without a sense and experience of waiting, we tend to be very shallow in our relationships with the Lord. Waiting in utter helplessness is an integral part of being a Christian.

St. Paul surely had to console himself with these thoughts as he spent so much of his time in prison waiting and waiting. Paul was such a fired-up man. The waiting in prison must have been a painful purification for him. Jesus too knew what it was to wait. Think of the thirty years He lived in seclusion before beginning His preaching of the coming of the Kingdom and of repentance.

But one of the most impressive examples of waiting is what the apostles went through during the time between the Ascension and Pentecost. Have you ever thought of the frustration that must have vexed the apostles as they waited for they knew not what? The day Jesus ended His stay on the earth and was ready to ascend to His Father, He gave what must have been one of the finest pep talks in history. "Go forth to the far corners of the world and proclaim what I have taught you. Baptize people in the name of the Father,

Son and Holy Spirit." Then with an exciting wonder He ascends to His Father. What would be the logical conclusion from such a commission? I would think that they would waste no time, but would immediately set out to put the world on fire with the reality of the Good News. But, what did the disciples do? They went to the upper room and waited. What an anti-climax! What a waste of time and energy! How repulsive that is to my work-a-holic mentality. What was more frightening, I'm convinced that they weren't sure exactly what they were waiting for. They knew that they needed help if they were going to be able to be the proclaimers of the Good News that Jesus wanted them to be.

What happens when you wait? Usually you get up tight. I know this is true. When I'm in the grocery store with two articles and the lady in front of me at the check-out stand has a cart-load, as I stand and wait I tend to get all knotted up inside. In my mind, I carry on the most vitriolic conversation with the lady. Or waiting in traffic! I'm on the freeway wanting to get to the other side of town for an appointment for which I'm already late. That is a disturbing experience. Another example is waiting for a person to find out what he wants to do with his life. He's twenty-four and living on welfare because he doesn't know what he wants to do. I find it hard to wait. I want to push him into something useful as soon as possible. I think too of a wife waiting for her husband or son to come back to the Church. That can hurt!

If we have the patience to look at ourselves as we're waiting, we can gain much knowledge. The only way that we can have peace in waiting is by funneling all our attention on the **now** and not get caught up in what's going to happen. As we wait we should use the present to the fullest. Listen to the sounds of now. God will be saying something to you in the birds, the hum of the

car's motor or the anguish of a confused face. Feel the
muscles in your body. Be aware of the tension in your
arm and stomach and then enjoy their relaxation as you
give the tension over to the Lord. Even try to notice
the smell of the smog or the flowers or the grocery store.
God is speaking.

As we wait, our defenses are taxed and we are able
to see things in a new way. Sure it's good to be a man
of action but when we wait we can gain the fuel for
greater and more effective action. When we wait, we
tend to be more honest with ourselves. If we can relax
in waiting and listening to God with all our senses, we
will be able to experience much the same thing that
the disciples in the Upper Room experienced for what
seemed an interminable nine days. We can be open to
the Holy Spirit who will come at us with His fire and
strength, and we too can take up the challenge of Ascension Thursday and spread Jesus' Good News to everyone we meet.

If you're waiting for the answer to prayers for yourself or others and a solution seems far off don't be afraid
to wait, and know that this can be the threshold of
a rebirth in your life.

42

"A third time, Jesus asked him, 'Simon, son of John, do you love me?' Peter was hurt because He had asked a third time, 'Do you love me?' So he said to Him; 'Lord, you know everything. You know well that I love you.' Jesus said to him, 'Feed my sheep' " (Jn 21:17).

IF YOU LOVE ME, SHOW IT

Jesus, it's easy to relate to Peter in today's reading. Three times he had said that he would stay with you, even if he had to go to his death. He failed. And now, full of forgiveness, you also want Peter to grow from his mistakes. Three times you ask him if he loves you. And now you aren't satisfied with just words. You also want action. You want Peter to feed your sheep and lambs. Lord, I've failed you so many times, despite the strong help of your grace. Help me to put my love in action by giving the food of your word to those I minister to.

How many times have I sinned when I was so resolved not to sin again. The older I grow, the greater is my fall into sin. This is because I'm more and more aware of Jesus' personal love for me and His constant efforts to keep me growing more whole and not fall into the negativism of sin. I pick myself up. I ask that the Lord forgive me and He does. How can God put up with me?

I wonder sometimes. Doesn't He know that despite my positive feelings that exist right now, I'm so often prone to falling right into the sin I'm now convinced I can avoid. He's so patient. He calls me to greater growth, but in such a gentle and loving way.

I find great comfort in Peter today. I know that Peter experienced my frustrations, wanting in his idealism to go one way, but when the chips were down and temptation was there, he even denied that he knew the Lord.

I know that Jesus will forgive me just as He was willing to forgive Peter. But in His forgiveness of Peter there's an important example for me as I accept the Lord's forgiveness. Peter is told to feed Jesus' sheep and lambs. The forgiveness of a Christian involves the concern for brothers and sisters of the Body of Christ. We have to be concerned with feeding them. We should cooperate with agencies that are involved in feeding people that don't have enough food. Working at a job that brings food to our family is integrally tied into the forgiveness we seek from Jesus. This forgiveness is in action. The one who cooks the meals should be sure that he or she does this with great love and preparation. This is a real part of being forgiven.

But there's another kind of feeding the hungry that must be our concern, as we accept Jesus' forgiveness. We must feed others with the word of God. This means we must grow in our familiarity with the words of Jesus as taught in the Bible, and then feed this food to the starving people in our life, whether they're starving because of prejudice, or sensuality, or materialism, or whatever. The Word of God must be fed to them so that they can be filled.

Another step back from this is that we can't feed others with the Word of Jesus unless we have been filled up with that Word in our lives. This means that we must take the time to read Scripture daily. We must let the

God of life and nourishment kindle us with His fire and love.

But for some reason we don't read Scripture as much as we ought. Parents don't feed their children with Scripture. Teachers can put more faith in the latest popular theories of psychology than in the Word of God. Each of us could find the answer to many of our problems by just turning to the food of Scripture.

I think one of the biggest obstacles to our use of Scripture is not that it's so difficult to understand. The problem is that the power of its splitting, two-edged reality is that it gives us more truth than we want to handle. The author of Hebrews says that the Word of God compels us to meet God's eyes. We are naked before God's Word. We would prefer to let ourselves and others go hungry rather than be exposed to such naked truth. The Greek has several meanings for the word which shows the force of Scripture's naked truth for us and others. The first definition is of an animal which is hung up and flayed. And so it is with us—we have nowhere to hide when our defenses are stripped by God's Word. The other definition presents the image of a wrestler getting such a strong strangle on his opponent that the latter can't turn away his face. And so, under the power of God's Word, we must look at ourselves and those we want to flee from rather than face the truth. The Scripture makes us look deep into the truth in Jesus' eyes, and in Him we see the sin of our life but also the love we need to be able to grow from our mistakes.

Remember Jesus' directions for Peter in His forgiveness. Show your true repentance by feeding others, both materially and spiritually.

43

"Suppose I want him to stay until I come?" (Jn 21:23).

THE SECOND COMING

Jesus, what I want in my life with you is excitement. I want to be so filled with your Holy Spirit that I want to be thrilled with your wonders day in and day out. An important aspect of this enthusiasm is being aware that your coming is imminent. Let me expect, like St. Paul, that these are the last days, and then be able to give my whole self to spreading your Gospel now and not worry about the cost, because tomorrow might be the time of your coming . . .

Have you ever watched someone running a Marathon race? The distance in the Olympics is about 26 miles. Now, I consider jogging three-quarters of a mile in the morning a monumental feat. But these guys go 26 miles. Usually it's in the heat and they are thoroughly exhausted by the time they're coming into the home-stretch. But what astonishes me is that after racing all those miles, when they come to the last 400 yards, they can put aside all the pain in their legs and lungs and start to sprint.

There's something about coming in to the home-stretch that frees us to use energy that we would have never thought possible when we were in the middle of the race. This same kind of thing happens on a long trip. Every year I make a trip from California to our college in Iowa with men who are thinking about being missionaries. The trip is over 2,000 miles one way. Although it's fun, there's still a lot of short tempers with six people living in a van for such a long time. But as we're coming closer to home, something strange happens. When we're about an hour and a half from home we start to wake up. The saddle sores don't seem so bad. We start to recognize familiar things, and that hour and a half goes by so quickly because we're almost home and we can forget all about the past. All that matters is getting home and there's real excitement and anticipation.

We should continually reawaken in ourselves our excitement about the coming of the Lord Jesus at the end of the world. We should expect Him to be coming soon. In that expectation we'll free ourselves to work all the more diligently at bringing God's Good News to our world. There is a sense of intense abandon in living in the expectation of the Second Coming. We can give that last burst of speed, even though we've been in the race for a long time. We can see new possibilities for communication and love and transformation as we come to the last few moments of the trip.

As Catholics, we are continually bombarded with reminders of the Second Coming in our liturgies. "Christ has died; Christ has risen and CHRIST WILL COME AGAIN." "I believe . . . that Jesus will come again to judge the living and the dead." "Keep us free from sin as we wait in joyful hope for the coming of our Savior, Jesus Christ."

The biggest problem with getting excited about the Second Coming is that we have visions of looking like the cartoon character who carried the sign saying when the world is going to end—day and time—and then when the time passes, the poor character is left with pie on his face. There are religions that have made much of predicting the exact day of the Second Coming, and have had to change their prediction several times. As you read through Scripture, you can find Paul all excited about the Second Coming in his early Epistles, but as he came to the end of his life his drumming on the importance of the imminence of the Second Coming doesn't seem as strong. Paul, I think, learned the lesson. Our attitude toward the Second Coming should not be one of anxiety, trying to predict the exact time or day. Jesus warned us against this extreme. But while relaxing in the power of Jesus, we need to be on fire with energy to usher in the Kingdom in our time.

It is so easy to get stuck in concern with maintaining the **status quo.** As Catholics, we belong to such a large organization with many big churches and schools and other almost corporation-size realities. We can put a great deal of time into maintaining these things and not see the importance of risking growth in the Church by reaching out to other people to become a part of the Kingdom. "But I have so much to do already."

With the awareness of the imminence of Jesus' Second Coming, we can put away much of the fear of burning ourselves out.

A key to the dynamic growth of the early Church was this urgent expectation of Jesus' imminent judgment. This expectation was made more real because of the extreme persecution that the Church was undergoing. The pain of the long race or the long trip was intense, so the longing for Jesus' final victory was more intense.

In our country, we don't experience the same kind of persecution. We won't be thrown into jail in this country for worshipping Jesus, as the early Christians might have been. Without persecution, the Second Coming doesn't seem important. Perhaps if we were in touch with the demands that Jesus is making on us through the Scriptures and the Church, we would have to stand up and be counted as persons totally dedicated to the Lord. Perhaps if we listen to Jesus and hear Him say that we have to be different from others we would experience the persecution of the early Church. During persecution, our yearning for the Second Coming would be more real.

When I was young, the idea of the Second Coming got shuffled into the idea of preparing for a holy death. Being on the lookout for my personal salvation at any time is a very important thing. But the Second Coming goes an important step further. Not only must I personally be prepared to meet Jesus, but I must have the less selfish view of wanting as many people in the world as possible to be able to share in the realities of Jesus' Kingdom of love and peace and joy and unity. My judgment is inevitable within a few years, but we need the missionary fervor of the early Church to bring as many people as possible to Jesus' love and knowledge for the Second Coming.

"When the day of Pentecost came, it found the brethren gathered in one place; suddenly from up in the sky there came a noise like a strong, driving wind which was heard all through the house where they were seated. Tongues as of fire appeared which parted and came to rest on each of them. All were filled with the Holy Spirit. They began to express themselves in foreign tongues and make bold proclamations as the Spirit prompted them" (Ac 2:1-4).

FIRE INTO BEING A CHRISTIAN

Jesus, today is the celebration of a strong wind and a fire. Come into my life with your Holy Spirit and shake up those things in me that are all firm and unwilling to move. Move in my heart with a fire that can't be quenched as I reach out to share your Good News with everyone I meet.

At half-time the game seemed all but lost. You don't go into the locker room losing a football game by 21 points and expect to turn it around. But turn it around is just what the underdogs did. The defense held, and the offense clicked, and when the gun sounded, the underdogs had won by four touchdowns. Sometimes a fire can get into a team and turn odds upside down. The same thing happened to a little girl who slipped and fell in the family swimming-pool. She was seen on the bottom of the pool by her mother who dove in and brought her out. For fifteen minutes the mother pumped air into the girl's lungs, through mouth-to-mouth resuscitation. Then there was a cough and suddenly where there was death, the red-eyed and blue-skinned girl was alive. Even where there is death, a breath of life can come and turn everything upside down. Take that parish which was coming to a resounding halt and which was suddenly being affected by a group of parishioners who decided to pray for the parish each week for an hour. Where there was death there is now a vision and a desire to preach Jesus that's starting to affect not only the parish, but the whole town.

This is the reality of Pentecost. Surprises and more surprises come barreling through. Pentecost isn't just a strange event that happened two thousand years ago and which we now read about with an unrealistic attitude. Pentecost is now, if we are open to it, if we can open our mind to possibilities that we thought never possible. Who of those 120 huddled in the Upper Room would have thought that God would work such wonders? They were simple people. Who would have ever thought they would be the ones who would bear the burden of bringing Jesus to the world ofter the Ascension? I know that if a modern-day computer-programmer was trying to work out a list of 120 people who would revolutionize the world, he wouldn't have come up with the 120 that Jesus had following Him. But the answer to the power of the Holy Spirit isn't power as the world knows power. No, the power of the Holy Spirit comes through the weakness of waiting and not knowing what's going on. The power of the Holy Spirit comes when there's frustration and real hopelessness. This makes us real in the Lord. We open ourselves in a deep way to the power of God who is willing to move through us. Look what happens to these simple men and women. They go out to

preach to the people who just a few weeks ago had killed
the man they are now preaching. In their mind, they
know that Jesus' fate can be theirs in all its ugly aspects.
But now, with the fire of the Holy Spirit, there's a new
direction and meaning. Now they are filled with so much
strength that they can confront death and be so filled
with joy and peace about it that they appear to be drunk.
Oh, how much the Holy Spirit must long to have us filled
with Him so that we can be drunk. How He must long
as He sees His priest who's lost his interest in preaching
Jesus or His child who's more concerned with sleeping
on Sunday than with celebrating with the people of God.

What is so great about Pentecost is that we can have
the same fire and strength the Apostles did on this day.
And the odds are so much better now for effecting the
Holy Spirit's revolution. Think of the effect of 120 on
the world, and now think of the number of people who
have said that they believe in Jesus. What if we all
responded to the call of the Holy Spirit moving in our
lives? What a transformation of the world!

What we should remember is that the Holy Spirit is
very much like the wind. The wind has all kinds of qual-
ities. It is unpredictable. All you have to do is listen for
a week to the news and hear the frustration of the
weather-caster. The Holy Spirit is like that. We have
to just open ourself to all kinds of excitement and know
with trust that God is going to work in ways far greater
than our finite and restricted expectations. The Spirit
also comes as a fire. When you get near fire you have to
move with great enthusiasm. This is what the Holy Spirit
does. He makes Jesus not just a law to be observed or a
person to know. With the Holy Spirit, Jesus becomes so
real that we have to tell this to others in order to live
with ourselves.

Another interesting thing about Pentecost is that the
Holy Spirit came on the 120 while they were sitting

down. Now if they knew God was coming, I'm sure that they would have at least stood, out of respect. But He got to them so unexpectedly and with such speed that they couldn't get up. Sitting down also implies that they were relaxed. They were tired of waiting to be open to the Spirit.

Pray often for the reality of Pentecost in your life. It can happen! Be strong in your faith that the Spirit will eventually come. Be open. Respond to the demand for love right now and then relax in the special care that God has for you. Never be satisfied with getting by with things as they are, because with the wonder of the Holy Spirit, we can always expect to be more!

Praise for *The End of the Free Market* and Ian Bremmer

"Many scholars have begun to analyze state capitalism. One of the clearest and most comprehensive treatments is *The End of the Free Market* by Ian Bremmer." —David Brooks, *The New York Times*

"A solid primer on the emergence of state capitalism; its operation in countries such as Algeria, Ukraine, and India; and 'how it threatens free markets and the future of the global economy.'" —*The Washington Post*

"*The End of the Free Market* is both fresh and provocative. It illuminates the subtle, yet powerful, geopolitical and economic undercurrents that must be understood by all of us." —Greg Brown, coCEO of Motorola, Inc.

"From stories of deadly rioting at a Chinese factory to the Russian prime minister's grocery shopping to the construction site of an entirely new Saudi city, this is a fascinating story with a timely and important message: American-style free market democracy might not be the wave of the future." —Fareed Zakaria, editor of *Newsweek International* and author of *The Post-American World*

"A powerful analysis of the new emerging world order by an author who is always full of insights." —George Osborne, MP, Shadow Chancellor of the Exchequer

"Ian Bremmer's understanding of international commerce and politics is peerless. *The End of the Free Market* holds essential insights for anyone conducting business on the global level." —Sallie Krawcheck, president, global wealth and investment management, Bank of America

"Ian Bremmer's book couldn't have come at a better time. An essential guide to the future of the world economy, *The End of the Free Market* describes the coming war for the soul of capitalism. It offers useful insights for investors, business leaders, and anyone interested in how to survive this coming global confrontation." —David Smick, global policy strategist and author of *The World Is Curved: Hidden Dangers to the Global Economy*

ABOUT THE AUTHOR

Ian Bremmer is president of Eurasia Group, the world's leading global political risk research and consulting firm. He has written for *The Wall Street Journal*, *The Washington Post*, *Newsweek*, *Foreign Affairs*, and other publications. His most recent books include *The J Curve: A New Way to Understand Why Nations Rise and Fall* and *The Fat Tail: The Power of Political Knowledge for Strategic Investing*. He lives in New York City and Washington, D.C.

THE END

OF THE

FREE MARKET

Who Wins the War Between
States and Corporations?

IAN BREMMER

PORTFOLIO / PENGUIN

PORTFOLIO / PENGUIN
Published by the Penguin Group
Penguin Group (USA) Inc., 375 Hudson Street,
New York, New York 10014, U.S.A.
Penguin Group (Canada), 90 Eglinton Avenue East, Suite 700,
Toronto, Ontario, Canada M4P 2Y3
(a division of Pearson Penguin Canada Inc.)
Penguin Books Ltd, 80 Strand, London WC2R 0RL, England
Penguin Ireland, 25 St. Stephen's Green, Dublin 2, Ireland
(a division of Penguin Books Ltd)
Penguin Books Australia Ltd, 250 Camberwell Road, Camberwell,
Victoria 3124, Australia
(a division of Pearson Australia Group Pty Ltd)
Penguin Books India Pvt Ltd, 11 Community Centre, Panchsheel Park,
New Delhi–110 017, India
Penguin Group (NZ), 67 Apollo Drive, Rosedale, Auckland 0632,
New Zealand (a division of Pearson New Zealand Ltd)
Penguin Books (South Africa) (Pty) Ltd, 24 Sturdee Avenue,
Rosebank, Johannesburg 2196, South Africa

Penguin Books Ltd, Registered Offices:
80 Strand, London WC2R 0RL, England

First published in the United States of America by Portfolio, a member of Penguin Group (USA) Inc. 2010
This paperback edition with a new afterword published 2011

1   3   5   7   9   10   8   6   4   2

THE LIBRARY OF CONGRESS HAS CATALOGED-THE HARDCOVER EDITION AS FOLLOWS:
Bremmer, Ian, 1969–
The end of the free market : who wins the war between states and corporations? / Ian Bremmer.
p. cm.
Includes bibliographical references and index.
ISBN 978-1-59184-301-6 (hc.)
ISBN 978-1-59184-440-2 (pbk.)
1. Communist countries—Economic policy. 2. Capitalism—Communist countries. 3. Capitalism—Developing
countries. 4. Government ownership—Communist countries. 5. Government ownership—Developing
countries. I. Title.
HC704.B72 2010
330.12'2—dc22   2009049478

Printed in the United States of America
Set in Granjon
Designed by Joy O'Meara

CONTENTS

INTRODUCTION

One Friday afternoon in May 2009, I got an e-mail inviting me to join a small group of economists and scholars "to exchange ideas and opinions on the current financial crisis" with China's Vice Foreign Minister He Yafei. Seven days later, I found myself in a conference room at the Chinese Consulate on Twelfth Avenue in Manhattan, seated directly across from a tall, friendly Chinese diplomat in a well-tailored black suit. Following formal words of welcome delivered in lightly accented English, the smiling vice minister began the meeting with a question: "Now that the free market has failed," he asked, "what do you think is the proper role for the state in the economy?"

His words hung in the air a moment. His mischievously matter-of-fact tone and the enormousness of his assumption almost drew a laugh from me. I caught myself in time, though I doubt my amusement would have offended him. His warmth was genuine, but the question was a serious one—and a quick glance at the headlines offered him plenty of corroborating evidence. For economists, signs of an impending meltdown had begun to accumulate in 2007, but the announcement on September 15, 2008, that the investment bank Lehman Brothers had filed for Chapter 11 bankruptcy protection ensured that the historic scale of the financial crisis could no longer be ignored. Within days, political officials in Washington had assumed responsibility for decisions normally made by markets in New York, a momentous shift in economic and financial power from America's capital of finance to its capital of politics. On October 3, President George W. Bush signed the Emergency Economic Stabilization Act of 2008, creating the $700 billion Troubled Asset Relief Program. Evidence appeared that global recession had taken hold. As debate intensified over a stimulus package in early 2009, a new president, Barack Obama, warned that if Washington didn't move quickly, America faced a catastrophe. Lawmakers answered the call with a $787 billion rescue plan.

He Yafei waited patiently for an answer. "Banks have clearly failed to regulate themselves, but that doesn't demand that government permanently dominate the economy," I responded. "Though I can see why political leaders might like the idea," I thought to myself. Robert Hormats of Goldman Sachs, Don Hanna of Citigroup, economist Nouriel Roubini, and others added their views to the mix. Over the next ninety minutes, my American colleagues and I made our case, and Mr. He made his. Each side scored points, and we found some common ground. But as the meeting ended, it was clear we had argued the respective merits of two fundamentally incompatible sets of political and economic principles.

In meetings of much greater consequence now taking place around the world, this inability to agree on the proper role for the state in the performance of markets will change the way we live. The most obvious example comes from the transition from an international bargaining table dominated by heads of state of the G7 group of industrialized nations—all of them champions of free-market capitalism—toward a G20 model that acknowledges the need to allow relative free-market skeptics like China, Russia, Saudi Arabia, India, and others to join the conversation. By fall 2008, the G7 had become an irrelevant institution. The financial crisis made clear that no international body that includes Canada and Italy but excludes China and India can offer credible solutions to today's most pressing transnational problems. In November, with financial panic taking hold in many parts of the world, G20 leaders met in Washington to hash out a workable emergency response.

They met again in London in April 2009 to continue to try to negotiate. Today we're living in a G20 world, and when leaders of free-market democracies diagnose what ails the global economy and prescribe their respective remedies, they now face the skeptical smile of He Yafei— and of all those across the table who believe that the free market has failed and that the state should play the leading role in national economic performance. That's an enormous problem, one that will pose important challenges for the next several decades.

How did we get here? Didn't the end of the Cold War signal the final victory of free-market capitalism? On December 25, 1991, a dazed Mikhail Gorbachev looked deeply into the lens of a single television camera and told his people that they were living in a new world. Proud that he had helped guide the Soviet people "toward the market economy," he resigned as Soviet president, shuffled the papers before him, and waited for aides to signal that he was off the air. Six days later, the Soviet Union went out of business. Within three weeks, Chinese leader Deng Xiaoping had embarked on his famous "southern tour," which created new momentum behind free-market reform in China. Within a year, even Fidel Castro had accepted the need for a little capitalist experimentation. Former Warsaw Pact states began the march toward membership in NATO and the European Union. Free-market capitalism looked to have permanently carried the day.

But as Russians discovered the hard way over the course of the 1990s, it's a long step from a command economy to free-market capitalism. The successor to a state that had once determined which products would be produced in what quantities and how much buyers would pay for them found itself managing the largest estate sale in history. Clever (and sometimes ruthless) business moguls acquired enough overnight wealth to cast doubt on the question of who really ruled Russia. Ordinary citizens, scrambling to adapt and survive, saw a level of corruption, confusion, and chaos they had never imagined. This was not the sort of "mixed capitalism" found today in the United States or in Europe. This was a brand of laissez-faire, anything-goes capitalism in which markets were regulated by those with the most to gain from exploiting them. Little wonder, then, that as Boris Yeltsin prepared for retirement in 1999, public demand grew sharply across Russia for a return to "law and order." Military and security officials led by a former KGB lieutenant colonel named Vladimir Putin stood ready to answer the call.

This is not simply Russia's story. The fall of communism did not mark the triumph of free-market capitalism because it did not put an end to authoritarian government. Chinese state officials watched the Soviet collapse and Russia's upheaval as if their survival depended on it, and they learned some important lessons. First, they recognized that if the Chinese Communist Party failed to generate prosperity for China's people, its days were numbered. Second, they accepted that the state can't simply mandate lasting economic growth. Only by releasing the entrepreneurial energies and innovation within its vast population could China thrive and the party survive. In short, China needed to embrace markets. Third, they saw that once this growth potential was unleashed, the party could only protect its monopoly hold on political power by ensuring that the state controlled as large a share as possible of the wealth that markets generate.

Nor is this simply China's story. Authoritarian governments everywhere have learned to compete internationally by embracing market-driven capitalism. But if they leave it entirely to market forces to decide winners and losers from economic growth, they risk enabling those who might use that wealth to challenge their political power. Certain that command economies are doomed to fail but fearful that truly free markets will spin beyond their control, authoritarians have invented something new: state capitalism. In this system, governments use various kinds of state-owned companies to manage the exploitation of resources that they consider the state's crown jewels and to create and maintain large numbers of jobs. They use select privately owned companies to dominate certain economic sectors. They use so-called sovereign wealth funds to invest their extra cash in ways that maximize the state's profits. In all three cases, the state is using markets to create wealth that can be directed as political officials see fit. And in all three cases, the ultimate motive is not economic (maximizing growth) but *political* (maximizing the state's power and the leadership's chances of survival). This is a form of capitalism but one in which the state acts as the dominant economic player and uses markets primarily for political gain.

To illustrate the differences between a Soviet-style command economy and these various forms of capitalism, imagine a football game or soccer match. Command economics is a game in which the state tries to predetermine the final score by ensuring that all players, referees, and spectators faithfully perform their pre-assigned roles. It's more a pageant than a sport. Post–Soviet Russian–style laissez-faire capitalism is a blood sport with few rules and referees who represent the competing interests of the spectators who wagered most on the outcome. The strongest dominate, and everyone else loses. Free-market capitalism is a game with referees who exist only to ensure proper enforcement of recognized rules and with players involved in genuine competition. Government's only role is to ensure that the rules are written effectively and fairly. It's an ideal, one to which most U.S. and European policy makers aspire. State capitalism is a match in which government controls most of the referees and enough of the players to improve its chances of determining the game's outcome. Spectators profit from some limited level of genuine competition, but the state rigs the game to ensure that favored players have what they need to score the vast majority of points on its behalf.

This book is about the emergence of this new strand of capitalism and how it threatens free markets and the future of the global economy. The main characters are the men who rule China, Russia, and the Arab monarchies of the Persian Gulf. But as we'll see in some detail, the apparent success of this new model has attracted imitators throughout much of the developing world. It's the story of how, in the first decade of this new century, *public* wealth, *public* investment, and *public* ownership have made a stunning comeback. Governments dominate key domestic economic sectors. The oil companies they own now control three quarters of the world's crude-oil reserves. They use state-owned and favored privately owned companies to intervene in global markets for aviation, shipping, power generation, arms production, telecommunications, metals, minerals, petrochemicals, and other industries. They own enormous investment funds that have quickly become vitally important sources of capital.

Chapter one tells the story of how all this happened. Chapter two offers a brief history of capitalism to uncover the roots of the current emerging conflict. Chapter three illustrates how state capitalism works. Chapter four reveals how and why governments in a dozen different countries use it, with special attention on China, Russia, Saudi Arabia, and the United Arab Emirates. Chapter five outlines why state capitalism threatens free markets and the future of the global economy. Chapter six details what those who believe in free-market capitalism can do about it.

CHAPTER ONE

The Rise of a New System

*What we may be witnessing is not just the end of the Cold War,
or the passing of a particular period of post-war history, but the end
of history as such: that is, the end point of mankind's ideological
evolution and the universalization of Western liberal democracy as
the final form of human government.*

—FRANCIS FUKUYAMA, "The End of History"[1]

In championing globalization as the defining force in international
politics and the global economy, we've spent the past several years
writing obituaries for communism, for dictatorship, and even for the
nation-state. Globalization *is* the single most important thing that governments and corporations could not afford to be wrong about over the
past two decades. But on the obituaries, we're one for three.

Communism is dead—though the Kims of North Korea and Cas-
tros of Cuba refuse to bury it. North Korea, with an economy about the
size of Warren Buffett's personal fortune, survives by blackmailing its
neighbors with apocalyptic threats. Cuba gets by with a little help from
an oil-rich friend in Venezuela. The political leaders of China and Vietnam are communist in name only. Both countries remain police states,
but neither government has remained faithful to the Marxist/Leninist/

Maoist principles from which they once drew legitimacy. Until elections in 2009, local communists had enough popular support to scuttle many promarket reforms in India. Venezuela's Hugo Chávez and Ecuador's Rafael Correa brag of their socialist "revolutions," but neither has gone much beyond nationalization of key industries. In Nicaragua, the Sandinistas' second shot at power has pushed them to make peace with the private sector. But the clearest sign of communism's demise came from the international financial crisis and the world's first truly global recession (2008–2009). Many around the world (fairly or not) blamed the meltdown on American-style free-market capitalism. If the turmoil that these crises generated couldn't breathe life into the communist corpse, it's hard to imagine what could. Communism is dead, and there will be no resurrection.

Yet no one can credibly say the same for dictatorship. In 1989, as Eastern Europe's communist states fell like dominoes and millions of Chinese students mounted a bold challenge to their government, writer Francis Fukuyama penned a provocative essay to support a surprising claim: that "history" had come to an end. He argued that though forms of government would continue to vary from place to place and that some countries had considerable catching up to do, mankind was moving toward consensus on the virtues of liberal democracy. Where authoritarian governments cling to power, the increasingly free flow of goods, services, capital, and labor would generate demand for freedoms of information, assembly, and expression—and for government that derives its powers from the consent of the governed. This was not to be simply the end of communism but eventually of all forms of dictatorship—and, by extension, of organized conflict among states. The essay quickly became the subject of intense debate.

Representative democracy *has* made considerable progress over the past two decades in the former communist states of Central and Eastern Europe, most of Latin America, in Indonesia, and post-apartheid South Africa. Though militaries still play a prominent role in the domestic politics of Turkey, Thailand, and Pakistan, all three now have popularly elected governments. India has remained the world's most populous democracy for more than six decades. Democracy has made real progress from Mali and Malawi to Mongolia, from Botswana and Benin to Bhutan. But in China in 1989, demand for democracy careened headlong into a great wall as demonstrations in Tiananmen Square ended in a surge of state-sponsored violence. Today, the country's 1.4 billion people are freer than they've ever been to determine how and where they will live, but they are still not free to directly challenge the ruling party's monopoly control of domestic political power. In Russia, after the upheaval of the Yeltsin era in the 1990s, Vladimir Putin has consolidated political power in a very few hands. Outside of Iraq and Lebanon, there is little sign that democracy is on the march within any Arab state. In Iran, the heavy-handed state response to the protests that followed the 2009 presidential election demonstrated again the limits of Tehran's tolerance for pluralism. Add North Korea, Cuba, Burma, Belarus, the five Central Asian republics, and dozens more states. In all these countries, state institutions, courts, and the media are not guardians of individual liberties but instruments of state power.

In 2008, the nonprofit organization Freedom House rated 121 of the world's 193 countries as "electoral democracies," but only 90 of them as "free" countries. In the same year, the Economist Intelligence Unit's (EIU) Democracy Index classified just 30 of 167 countries as "full democracies," 50 as "flawed democracies," and 87 (accounting for about half the world's population) as either "hybrid democracies" or "authoritarian" states. In fact, the EIU warned in its 2008 report that, "following a decades-long global trend in democratisation, the spread of democracy has come to a halt."

Freedom House and the EIU acknowledge that democracy is defined in different ways; there is plenty of gray area between Norway and North Korea. The Freedom House survey focuses on the conduct of competitive multiparty elections that are transparent, free, and held on a regular basis. EIU adds respect for civil liberties, good governance, and measures of a society's openness. Whatever the metric used, when definitions of democracy expand beyond the conduct of elections, the number of countries that have reached democracy's final destination dwindles sharply.[2] Dictatorship is alive and well.

The third obituary was for the nation-state, which a 1993 United Nations Human Development Report described as "too small for the big things and too big for the small things"[3] and author Kenichi Ohmae dismissed in 1995 as a "nostalgic fiction."[4] To understand why some believed that nation-states were headed for history's junkyard, it helps to define the word *globalization*. It's essentially a catchall term for all the various processes by which ideas, information, people, money, goods, and services cross international borders at unprecedented speed. Together, these processes have created a much more integrated global economy through trade, foreign direct investment, large-scale capital flows, the construction of global supply chains, innovation in communications technologies, and mass migration. None of these individual elements is entirely new. Global trade has existed for centuries. But the multiplier effect these forces create and the velocity with which they move make this phenomenon qualitatively different from anything that has come before. Globalization, like capitalism, is powered by the individual impulses of billions of people. It is not the result of someone's economic reform plan, and it can't be reversed by decree.

In recent years, we've been seduced by an argument that goes something like this: It isn't simply the Berlin Wall that has fallen; globalization's relentless progress is ripping down all kinds of walls. All that movement across borders will eventually strip nation-states of their power, because governments will never be able to manage the international commercial, political, social, and environmental challenges that globalization creates. Even the governments of the world's most reclusive states can't lock their citizens away forever. If cell phones from China are now flowing into North Korea, what hope does any despot have of ever again fully isolating his people from the world or from one another?[5] According to the theory, it's not just the world's most brittle regimes that won't be able to respond effectively to changes wrought by globalization. Even the governments of the world's wealthy democracies won't be up to the task. The accelerating, round-the-clock, cross-border flow of information, people, products, and cash can only really be regulated on a regional (or even a global) scale. When governments gather to agree on new rules to regulate all this activity, they will have to accept changes that compromise their sovereignty. How can China's leaders create economic growth without opening their once-isolated country to the power of the Internet? How can French legislators maintain rigid labor laws when workers from less prosperous corners of the European Union are free to enter the country and compete for jobs? Will America still be America when other countries own key U.S. assets and entire U.S. industries are outsourced to Asia and Africa? This cross-border traffic will undermine the integrity of the state in all kinds of ways. That's the theory.

But advances in communications technology have not yet proven their ability to topple dictatorships. Sometime during 2009, the number of Chinese citizens online (more than 300 million) surpassed the total population of the United States. The Chinese government has so far kept technological pace via its "Great Firewall," the system of filters and rerouters that restricts access to information on Taiwan, Tibet, Tiananmen Square, and other forbidden subjects. Foreign visitors to the Beijing Olympics in 2008 found a degree of online freedom unknown for most Chinese—though a lifting of many restrictions proved temporary. But when protests gripped Tibet in 2008 and race riots erupted between Muslim Uighurs and Han Chinese in Xinjiang province in 2009, the government quickly and efficiently restricted the flow of information into and out of the affected areas. In Iran in 2009, Facebook, Twitter, and text messaging helped shape our opinions of the Islamic Republic's politics—but they did not change the outcome of its presidential election. For the moment at least, authoritarian governments have proven up to the challenge of restricting online speech. Furthermore, new communications technologies are not inherently prodemocracy. They're simply a kind of force multiplier for messaging. If grassroots nationalism, fed by state propaganda, was a powerful force shaping public opinion in China or Russia before millions first logged on, the Internet will promote an unprecedented number of nationalist messages. Unless and until there is widespread, public demand for democracy, these new tools will simply be used for other purposes.

A wide variety of analysts, scholars, and authors warned that as a result of all this global traffic, national governments would eventually lose much of their decision-making power to organizations large and small. They would surrender sovereignty to supranational political institutions like the United Nations, European Union, International Criminal Court, International Monetary Fund, and World Bank, organizations that are not states, not sovereign, and not directly accountable to local voters. Over the past several years, we've seen the emergence of an alphabet soup of regional groups: Asia-Pacific Economic Cooperation (APEC), the Association of Southeast Asian Nations (ASEAN), the African Union (AU), the Commonwealth of Independent States (CIS), Mercosur (a South American trading bloc), the Shanghai Cooperation Organization (SCO), and many others. Most of these groups amount to little more than talk shops and "free trade blocs" in which plenty of trade barriers remain. Some include discussion of political, security, and defense cooperation. But these institutions continue to depend on the inclinations of those who govern their most powerful member states and on the political calculations that guide their actions. The G20 Group of Industrialized Nations is no different. The public officials seated at the negotiating table are concerned first with promoting the interests of their governments. Members of the North Atlantic Treaty Organization (NATO) are bound to treat an attack on one member as an attack on all, but that doesn't mean that their elected leaders will ignore popular opinion at home when deciding how many troops to commit to NATO operations abroad. As we learned again during Russia's war with Georgia in August 2008, the Organization for Security and Cooperation in Europe (OSCE) can't prevent conflict when a single powerful member state, in this case Russia, stands in the way.[6] Whenever UN officials are called on to defend institutional inaction on this or that problem, they usually remind critics that the organization is little more than an expression of the collective will of its member states. The intricate web of rules and regulations that make up the body of international law still depends on agreements among individual national governments. Only they can direct the resources needed to tackle transnational issues like climate change, nuclear non-proliferation, terrorism, and reform of the global financial system.

The twenty-seven-member European Union has become the world's most successful multinational organization, because member states have surrendered control of several key levers of national power (like monetary policy) to achieve an unprecedented level of cooperation, peace, and security—and to create a free-trade zone that takes in more than 500 million people. Via its bureaucratic center, the European Commission, the union presents a single collective face in global trade negotiations. But on many important issues, the EU can't override the veto of even a single member. Some members have opted out of core EU features like the Eurozone, where the euro is the official currency, and the Schengen agreement, which eliminates border controls between member states. And anyone who doubts that the nation-state lives on inside the European Union need only watch the crowd during a soccer match between Holland and Germany, England and France, or Portugal and Spain.

Then there was the threat from small organizations. After September 11, 2001, it appeared that militant groups and individuals empowered by globalization-assisted technological development could undermine a country's sovereignty and inflict enormous political and economic damage with relatively low-cost terrorist attacks. Some have predicted the rise of the "global citizen" as a challenge to the nation-state. The logic is simple: If you no longer depend for information on news sources broadcasting or publishing within one country, if you can quickly and easily form electronic social networks with people all over the world, if outsourcing and the advent of the global supply chain allow you to work for a company that is headquartered ten thousand miles from your home, if travel to foreign countries becomes ever easier and more affordable, and if more members of your family live and work elsewhere, won't these globalization-generated changes weaken the ties that bind you to any one country?

Maybe one day. But there is no evidence that those 300 million Chinese netizens have become any less Chinese since they first logged on. Much of what they wrote before, during, and after the 2008 Beijing Olympic Games suggests otherwise. In fact, in many ways, what they see and hear on the Internet may reinforce their sense of national identity as they decide for themselves where to travel online. Many of them have found clever ways to evade state censorship, and a few have become bolder in challenging their government to better provide for the Chinese people—though precious few are willing to openly challenge the Communist Party's political authority.[7] China's vast online community exploded with wounded national pride in early 2008 as protesters in several countries targeted the Olympic torch to protest the actions of the Chinese government. In that moment, these were not citizens of the world. They were Chinese patriots. When governments provide citizens with security and opportunity, as the Chinese Communist party has done over the past several years, large numbers of people accept a common set of values, institutions, and laws—and define themselves in opposition to those who are governed by others.

The state's most useful attribute is its ability to maintain order. In that sense, it has served the interests both of those who favor democracy and of those who don't. For those who believe that government's primary obligation is to protect the rights of each individual citizen, only the nation-state can provide a stable legal framework. For the vast majority of those who pledge loyalty to this presidential candidate or that political party, the deeper allegiance to the nation ensures that power can change hands peacefully. The nation-state also allows tyrants to project power and rally public support for their regimes. Faced with the advancing Nazi war machine and afraid that Leninist principles alone would not sustain his people's determination to fight, Joseph Stalin donned a military uniform and appealed directly to Russian national pride. Saddam Hussein, Fidel Castro, and Venezuelan President Hugo Chávez have adopted much the same strategy when times are tough. Elected officials in liberal democracies regularly advance policy goals with public appeals to patriotism. Finally, for tribal, ethnic, or sectarian groups—whether Croats, Kurds, or Northern Ireland's Catholics—achievement of an independent nation-state remains the most tangible form of universal recognition.

The Multinational Menace

No organization has been singled out as a threat to the nation-state more often or with more theatrical flair than the multinational corporation. In her 2000 book, *No Logo,* author Naomi Klein warned that "corporations have grown so big they have superseded government."[8] For a more colorful obituary of the nation-state, look back to one of the great American films of the 1970s. If you were around in 1976 to see *Network* when it was first released, you probably remember Ned Beatty as Arthur Jensen, standing in a darkened corporate boardroom and thundering at Peter Finch's disturbed and cowering network news anchor, Howard Beale:

> *You are an old man who thinks in terms of nations and peoples. There are no nations; there are no peoples. There are no Russians.*

There are no Arabs. There is no third world. There is no West. . . .
Am I getting through to you, Mr. Beale? You get up on your little
21-inch screen and howl about America and Democracy. There is
no America. There is no democracy. There is only IBM and ITT
and AT&T and DuPont, Dow, Union Carbide and Exxon. Those
are the nations of the world today.

To see the film more than thirty years later and listen again to
Paddy Chayefsky's darkly comic Oscar-winning screenplay, so much
of it seems painfully prophetic—the corporate takeover of American
television news, the public fascination with reality TV, the mass marketing of public outrage. But Chayefsky was absolutely wrong about
one thing: Multinational corporations have not made nations and governments irrelevant. Why did anyone think they might?

True, the largest of the multinational companies do have the money,
resources, and influence to play a substantive role in international politics, and their ability to operate in multiple countries limits the capacity of any one government to regulate their actions. If an international
conglomerate can operate in dozens of countries at once and headquar-
ter wherever taxes and regulatory oversight are least burdensome, what
chance do governments have to attract business and create new jobs?
How can government fill state coffers with the tax revenue needed to
provide services like security, schools, roads, ports, and other public
goods?

The establishment of subsidiaries outside their home markets has
helped companies avoid taxes, cut production costs, and target new
customers. An explosion in the number of privately owned or publicly
traded modern commercial powerhouses operating internationally
began in the 1960s with McDonald's selling burgers outside the U.S.
market for the first time in 1967. Soon after, Japanese, German, French,
and British brands began to challenge U.S. dominance. The removal
of exchange controls in Europe and the sudden OPEC-generated oil

profits after the 1973 oil crisis sharply increased the size of capital markets, tempting more banks and financial-service providers to go international. The growth of emerging markets, developing countries with newly dynamic economies, began to add hundreds of millions of new consumers to the global marketplace, creating unprecedented commercial opportunities in once-isolated states. Between the mid-1980s and mid-1990s, foreign direct investment by multinational corporations grew by about 30 percent per year.

In 2000, a report by the Institute for Policy Studies dropped a bombshell: Comparison of corporate sales of the largest multinational companies with the gross domestic products of the world's wealthiest countries revealed that 51 of the world's 100 largest economies were corporations; just 49 were countries.[9] According to the report, General Motors had become bigger than Denmark, Daimler/Chrysler bigger than Poland, Mitsubishi bigger than Indonesia, Walmart bigger than Israel, and Sony bigger than Pakistan. In January 2006, a report from a respected commentator estimated that the top 100 multinationals collectively accounted for one third of world economic output and two thirds of global trade.[10] In 2008, the UN's World Investment Report noted that the number of multinational companies had grown from 7,250 in the late 1970s to more than 60,000 three decades later.[11] These numbers set off alarm bells among critics of large corporations, who charged that they were using their enormous economic and political clout to destroy competition from small and medium-size businesses and to bribe or bully national governments into easing labor and pollution standards to help companies maximize profits at the expense of local workers and the environment.[12] Multinational corporations, they warned, had outgrown the ability of governments to regulate their actions. As a result, the state would no longer be able to meet its first responsibility: to safeguard the rights and well-being of the individual.

The list of the world's largest private companies continues to include familiar names from the United States, Europe, and Japan, but over the past decade, a wave of multinationals has begun to emerge from the developing world. Between 1990 and 2007, the percentage of global foreign direct investment originating in developing countries increased from about 5 percent to about 16 percent.[13] Some of these companies are fully public or privately held companies: Hutchison Whampoa, New World Development Co., and Jardine Matheson in Hong Kong; Formosa Plastic Group, Taiwan Semiconductors, and Quanta Computers in Taiwan; and Samsung, Hyundai, and LG Corp. in South Korea. As Antoine van Agtmael, the man credited with coining the term *emerging markets,* noted in his 2007 book, *The Emerging Markets Century: How a New Breed of World-Class Companies Is Overtaking the World,* barely a single one of these companies would have been considered world class before 2000.[14]

The Rise of State Capitalism and the Future of the Free Market

Twenty years ago, the collapse of Eastern European and Soviet Communism drove a stake through the heart of the argument that governments could generate national prosperity through direct and active management of national economies. Communist China began to generate explosive economic growth only after its leadership began to experiment with market-based capitalism in the late 1970s. When the Soviet Union collapsed in the early 1990s, millions of Russians traded the black market for the free market. Governments privatized state-owned assets in India, Brazil, Turkey, and elsewhere. In America, Reagan administration officials preached the gospel of limited government so successfully that by 1996, a Democratic president used his State of the Union address to declare, "The era of big government is over."[15] In the 1980s, Western European governments followed British Prime Minister Margaret Thatcher's lead in profitably privatizing hugely inefficient state enterprises in energy and power generation (oil, gas, coal, and nuclear), transport (national airlines, railways, and bus companies), and telecommunications. In the 1990s, they preached the virtues of free-market capitalism to their newly liberated Eastern European neighbors and began to integrate them into a single market. Global financial institutions pressed them to embrace U.S.-endorsed liberal economic theories, known collectively as the Washington Consensus.*

The results speak for themselves. Between 1980 and 2002, world trade more than tripled. The costs of doing business—especially in transportation and communications—fell sharply. Many protectionist barriers, like tariffs and import quotas, went the way of the Berlin Wall. Tariff rates (as a percentage of total import costs) were halved during this period in America, were more than halved in Europe, and fell by 80 percent in Canada. Following the 1948 inception of the General Agreement on Tariffs and Trade (GATT), eight rounds of talks helped create the World Trade Organization (WTO) in 1995. With 153 member states, the WTO promotes international trade and arbitrates commercial disputes. Both developed and developing countries have continued to protect inefficient and strategically vital economic areas, but liberalized trade policies in dozens of countries have added momentum behind the increasingly free flow of goods and services, sharpening competition, incentivizing innovation, and giving consumers all over the world better products at lower prices. By 2000, global foreign direct investment topped $1.4 trillion, a level not exceeded since. Multinational corporations and a host of smaller companies went global to both drive down production costs and target new customers: the hundreds of millions of people within emerging market states moving from poverty toward a middle-class lifestyle. Neither an economic slowdown in the early 1990s nor the damage wrought by the 9/11 attacks a decade

---

* The Washington Consensus comprises three major ideas: fiscal and budgetary discipline; a market economy, including property rights, competitive exchange rates, privatization, and deregulation; and openness to the global economy through liberalization of trade and foreign direct investment.

later could challenge the dominance of the liberal economic model. Private wealth, private investment, and private enterprise appeared to have carried the day.

But as the sun sets on the first decade of the twenty-first century, that story has already become ancient history. The power of the state is back. Over the past decade, a new class of companies has pushed its way onto the international stage: enterprises that are owned or closely aligned with their home governments. By 2008, Mexico's Cemex, now the world's third-largest cement maker, was valued on par with Coca-Cola and owned more foreign assets than Dow Chemical or Alcoa. Brazil's Companhia Vale do Rio Doce mining company (popularly known as Vale) claimed total assets worth more than traditional industry leaders like Roche, Anglo-American, and BHP Billiton.[16] Cemex and Vale enjoy close ties with their respective governments, which allow them to protect their dominant commercial positions through hostile takeovers of smaller domestic competitors. Both companies are essentially privately owned "national champions." Over the past several years, lists of the world's largest companies published by *Forbes, Fortune,* and other publications have begun to feature state-owned energy giants like China National Petroleum Corporation, Petro China, Sinopec, Brazil's Petrobras, Mexico's Pemex, and Russia's Rosneft and Gazprom. This trend toward ever larger state-owned enterprises is not just an energy phenomenon. By 2008, China Mobile claimed the largest number of mobile phone subscribers in the world (488 million). These are not traditional multinational companies, because those who run them answer first to political masters, not shareholders.

Between 2004 and the start of 2008, 117 state-owned and public companies from Brazil, Russia, India, and China (the so-called BRIC countries) appeared for the first time on the Forbes Global 2000 list of the world's largest companies, measured by sales, profits, assets, and market value. A total of 239 U.S., Japanese, British, and German companies fell off the list. The percentage market value of this latter group of companies dropped from 70 percent to 50 percent over those four years; the value of the BRIC-based companies rose from 4 percent to 16 percent. The corporate failures and government bailouts of 2008–2009 accelerated the trend. Following the meltdown and takeover of many large U.S., British, and other banks, Bloomberg News reported in early 2009 that three of the world's four largest banks by market capitalization were state-owned Chinese firms—Industrial and Commercial Bank of China (ICBC), China Construction, and Bank of China. The 2009 Forbes Global 2000 listed ICBC, China Mobile, and Petro China among the world's five largest companies by market value. In other words, privately owned Western multinationals are in no danger of replacing the nation-state as the primary actor in international politics and global markets, because the state now owns and operates some of their largest competitors.

Over the past decade, the governments of several developing countries have worked to ensure that valuable national assets remain in state hands and that governments maintain enough leverage within their domestic economies to safeguard their survival. In some cases, they've used state-owned energy companies to amass wealth or to secure access to the long-term supplies of oil and gas that their still-vulnerable economies will need to fuel further growth. They have created wealth funds from pools of excess capital and have begun to make strategic investments beyond their borders.

In 2008, this trend toward greater state power reached a tipping point. During the financial crisis and global recession, an enormous market meltdown that provided globalization with its first true stress test, political officials in both the developed and the developing worlds seized responsibility for decisions that are usually left to market forces—and on a scale not seen in decades. Governments around the world responded to the implosion of major financial institutions and key economic sectors with massive doses of state spending meant to kick-start growth and, in some cases, to bail out companies considered "too big to fail." States grabbed control of firms once considered industry flagships. They did all this because they believed it was necessary—and because no one else could do it. During the financial crisis and its aftermath, this dynamic generated a massive shift in financial decision-making power from New York to Washington. In fact, a transfer of market power from capitals of finance to capitals of political power took place all over the world—from Shanghai to Beijing, São Paulo to Brasilia, Mumbai to Delhi, Sydney to Canberra, and Dubai to Abu Dhabi. The trend was also apparent within cities where finance and politics coincide—London, Paris, Berlin, Tokyo, and Moscow.

This is an enormously important change. In emerging market countries, political factors still matter at least as much as economic fundamentals for the performance of markets. That's a useful way of understanding the intersection of politics and economics within China, Russia, India, Brazil, Turkey, Mexico, and many other increasingly influential international players. The financial crisis pushed America, Britain, and Japan in that same direction—and a global audience increasingly skeptical of free-market capitalism's ability to generate sustainable, long-term prosperity is watching closely. Their massive state-managed injections of capital were necessary to refloat a global economy unhinged by a massive failure to regulate international financial flows. Market advocates will now have to work that much harder to persuade skeptics that the world's richest states remain committed to free-market capitalism.

On both sides of the Atlantic, political officials say they've tried to rescue drowning banks and economically vital private-sector companies to breathe new life into them—before releasing them again to swim on their own. They insist they will claim victory only when all those they've saved no longer need them. But this is not how political decision makers in China, Russia, and many other emerging markets see their roles in the future of their domestic economies. Their words and actions reveal that they believe that *public* wealth, *public* investment and *public* enterprise offer the surest path toward politically sustainable economic development. These governments will continue to micromanage entire sectors of their economies to promote national interests and to protect their domestic political standing. Their market clout is growing. Governments own the oil and gas companies that now control the lion's share of global reserves. They own (or actively favor) companies in direct competition with Western multinationals in power generation, telecommunications, mining, arms production, automotives, and aviation. They own and operate investment portfolios—including sovereign wealth funds—that are fast becoming a key contributor to global capital flows.

State capitalism is not the reemergence of socialist central planning in a twenty-first-century package. It is a form of bureaucratically engineered capitalism particular to each government that practices it. It's a system in which the state dominates markets primarily for political gain. As this trend develops, it will generate friction in international politics and distortions in global economic performance. There are times when governments must protect citizens from the worst effects of underregulated markets. But over the longer term, there is no evidence that political officials regulate economic activity better than market forces can. When U.S. policy makers temporarily seize responsibility for decisions on how best to value assets and allocate resources, they inject short-term waste, inefficiency, and bureaucracy into domestic and global markets. But when officials in several of the world's most dynamic emerging markets embrace this system as a long-term means of protecting their political survival, they undermine the power of the global economic system to generate sustainable growth.

For the moment, many of the governments that practice state capitalism have profited from it—both economically and politically. This might encourage some of them to rely for future growth less on commercial ties with the United States and more on one another. If so, this trend will have important consequences for America's global political influence and the longer-term health of the U.S. economy. Does state capitalism doom the United States and China to some form of direct conflict? Will it fundamentally undermine globalization—the system that has lifted hundreds of millions out of poverty and into an emerging global middle class? Is state capitalism sustainable? If politicians fail to keep their promises to consistently generate jobs and long-term prosperity for fast-growing middle classes, will state capitalism go the way of communism? Are we on the verge of a new global struggle—one that pits free-market capitalists and state capitalists in a battle to win over countries that might still tip either way? If so, who will win?

These are the questions that will determine the future of international politics and the global economy over the next decade.

CHAPTER TWO

A Brief History of Capitalism

*A government that robs Peter to pay Paul can always depend on
the support of Paul.*

—GEORGE BERNARD SHAW

To understand why so many governments are embracing a state-dominated form of capitalism and why this trend threatens free markets and the future of the global economy, we need to take a closer look at capitalism itself. Political philosopher Kenneth Minogue once defined capitalism as "what people do if you leave them alone." It's a turn of phrase that captures the freedom and personal empowerment that many of us imagine when thinking about the only economic system proven over time to generate sustainable prosperity. But capitalism takes many forms, and freedom is a relative concept. For our purposes, capitalism is the use of wealth to create more wealth, a broad enough definition to capture both free-market and state capitalism. Generally speaking, in a capitalist economic system, most means of production—labor, land, and capital—are privately owned and traded. Money is the measurable, universally accepted means of exchange. Individuals and privately owned institutions make most of the decisions on what to buy and how much to pay, what to make and how much to charge, how much to save and where to invest. Collectively, these decisions create and sustain markets. But even this broader (simplistic) definition allows for variations, differences that are determined by the extent of government involvement in all these decisions.

Those who believe in pure or laissez-faire capitalism argue that while the buyers and sellers are buying and selling, the state should mind its own business. Beyond enforcing contracts and protecting property rights, governments enable capitalism by staying out of its way. Adam Smith, the oft-quoted father of modern capitalism, wrote in *The Wealth of Nations* (1776) of the unintended benefits that society derived from individual greed:

> *By directing that industry in such a manner as its produce may be of the greatest value, he intends only his own gain, and he is in this, as in many other cases, led by an invisible hand to promote an end which was no part of his intention.*[1]

Some students of Smith's writings might qualify this point with a reference to his earlier work, *The Theory of Moral Sentiments* (1759), in which he argues that

> *there are evidently some principles in [man's] nature which interest him in the fortunes of others, and render their happiness necessary to him, though he derives nothing from it.*[2]

Advocates of pure capitalism insist that the "invisible hand" must be allowed to work its magic—and that any effort by government to guide its actions can only burden markets and distort their natural operation. Others argue that his writings on morality and natural empathy suggest that Smith would reject much of the libertarian dogma justified in his name. In any case, pure capitalism has never existed in the real world, and only the most ideologically committed of economic anarchists believe that it should. Markets can't meet every human need, fear and greed ensure that markets will never work perfectly, and no market participant enjoys perfect information.

Market failure didn't begin with the global recession of 2009, the bank failures of 2008, the credit crunch of 2007, the savings-and-loan crisis of the 1980s,[3] or even the stock market crash of 1929. Those investing heavily in the South Sea Company in 1720, the victims of irrational exuberance over the firm's monopoly on trade in the South Seas, might have saved themselves some heartache had they learned the lessons of the Dutch tulip mania of 1637.[4] Each successive market meltdown creates a temporary surge of momentum behind government efforts to ensure that it never happens again. That's why the state's role in enabling modern capitalism extends well beyond the provision of a social safety net. Even in America, home to many a free-market champion, government is expected to referee the game to ensure that players observe the rules, to serve as lender and guarantor of last resort, and to provide public goods like national defense, a criminal-justice system, public education, environmental protection, health insurance for the elderly and poor, air-traffic control, and disaster relief. These services are too important to social well-being to entrust them to private enterprise.

This combination of free-market competition and limited government intervention creates a "mixed" capitalist economy. The dominant model among developed countries since the end of World War II, its influence has spread around the world since the collapse of the Communist bloc two decades ago. There are variations within even this single category of capitalism, because some states involve themselves in their domestic economies much more often and more directly than others. Yet all mixed capitalist systems share faith in the principle that only free markets can generate long-term prosperity and that government should never become the dominant player in an economy. State capitalism represents a direct challenge to that belief.

Capitalism and Political Free Markets

It's not mere coincidence that Adam Smith published *The Wealth of Nations* in the same year that America's founders signed their Declaration of Independence from Britain. The movement that eighteenth-century philosopher Immanuel Kant called the Enlightenment inspired all sorts of people to demand all sorts of freedoms—both economic and political—from priests, lords, and kings. Modern capitalism began to take shape as the Industrial Revolution transformed economies from dependence on manual labor to more dynamic models based on mechanized farming and manufacturing. The Industrial Revolution's inventions and practices (mass employment in single factories, for example) spread quickly throughout Europe, its colonies, and the United States, empowering economic creativity and output on an unprecedented scale. More people than ever built a genuine stake in their domestic economies. A share of wealth (however modest) provided a broad range of citizens with a compelling incentive to demand better government, and emerging elites on both sides of the Atlantic insisted that taxation entitled them to political representation. Autocrats reluctantly accepted new political entitlements, giving birth to a more mature social contract between leaders and those they led. The right to vote spread gradually. In the nineteenth century, economic development created opportunities for the growth of ideologically delineated political parties and movements for social reform that fought to abolish slavery, mandate standards for working conditions, establish child-labor laws, and create universal primary education and mass sanitation. In the twentieth century, economic opportunities spurred demand for political rights for women, labor representation and collective bargaining, and an end to various forms of discrimination.

Over time, political scientists, economists, and sociologists discovered a trend in the European and American heartlands of modern capitalism. Free markets, they argued, produced greater prosperity;

prosperity created middle classes; middle classes demanded better government. "Better government" implied more open government, the right of citizens to know much more about what their elected representatives were up to and to hold them accountable—at the ballot box and even in court. Transparency and accountability were essential for the proper functioning of free markets. The basic economic freedoms that underpin capitalism became conceptually inseparable from core political liberties. At the heart of both lay the conviction that no person or institution can exercise these rights on someone else's behalf. They're not on loan from government, and the state has no right to revoke them. A marketplace for goods and services needs a marketplace for ideas. In other words, economic free markets function best within the supportive embrace of a political free market, because the full exercise of economic freedom depends on public access to information, a court system and a press that are independent of government, freedoms of speech and assembly, broad access to higher education, and the freedoms to travel and trade.

Practitioners of state capitalism don't agree.

What's in a Name?

The term *state capitalism* hasn't yet caught on, but it isn't new. It probably had its debut during a speech by Wilhelm Liebknecht, a founder of German social democracy, in August 1896. Before Marxism took on undeniable geopolitical significance following the Bolshevik Revolution in October 1917, it was the object of a seemingly endless series of heated internal debates. Some, like Liebknecht, railed against the half measures of those who failed to denounce capitalism forcefully enough. Liebknecht assured a socialist congress in Paris that, "Nobody has shown more distinctively than I that State Socialism is really State Capitalism."[5] He was arguing that it's not enough for the state to seize the means of production. It must surrender political power to the proletariat. Once Marxism gained a real-world foothold following the creation of the Soviet Union in 1922, this debate began to get ugly.

Liebknecht was long dead by the 1920s, but the argument gained new force among some within the Bolshevik elite. "We waged revolution on behalf of the working class," they argued. "If the state is now to run the new economy, hasn't the working class simply inherited new masters?" Thus was born the first common use of the phrase state capitalism, a term of abuse favored by those who worried that leading Bolsheviks weren't communist enough. As early as 1922, Austrian economist Ludwig von Mises, a later hero of the libertarian movement, identified and attacked this usage:

> *The Socialist movement takes great pains to circulate frequently new labels for its ideally constructed state. Each worn-out label is replaced by another which raises hopes of an ultimate solution to the insoluble basic problem of Socialism—until it becomes obvious that nothing has changed but the name. The most recent slogan is "state capitalism."*[6]

Describing the Soviet experiment as a "revolution betrayed" in 1934, Leon Trotsky warned that state capitalism "has the advantage that nobody knows exactly what it means," arguing that it "conceals the enigma of the Soviet regime."[7] This debate continued through Joseph Stalin's purges and World War II, but it attracted virtually no attention outside the communist movement. The term then reappeared in headline form when Soviet leader Nikita Khrushchev denounced Stalin during a speech in February 1956. A divide began to develop between Khrushchev and Chinese leader Mao Zedong, who increasingly asserted China's leadership for the communist world. From 1956 until the late 1970s, China's Communist Party often used state capitalism much as Liebknecht and Trotsky had—to spit at those who practiced

an impure form of socialism. Ironically, a few among the world's dwindling band of hard-line Maoists now use the term to condemn China's
economic reforms of the past thirty years.

Some committed capitalists used the phrase to attack socialism from
the other side. Murray Rothbard, a disciple of von Mises, attached it to
Nazi economic management in Germany, fascist rule in Italy during the
1930s, and the postwar economies of the Soviet bloc. For Rothbard, state
capitalism was the economic equivalent of political tyranny—and an
invention that could only survive within a totalitarian political system.
He argued that free-market capitalism is to state capitalism as "voluntary
mutual exchange" is to a "hold-up at gunpoint." He considered laissez-
faire capitalism an efficient and self-replenishing network of small exchanges of goods or services based on free will, including a buyer's right
to refuse new exchanges if the first one left him unsatisfied. All taxation was "purely and pristinely robbery." He forecast the inevitable self-
destruction of central economic planning and insisted that free-market
capitalism was "the only moral and by far the most productive system
[and] the only viable system for mankind in the industrial era."[8]

Beyond Rothbard, there are three ways in which the term *state capitalism* has been used over the years within the free-market world. First, the
term is sometimes used to describe a system in which government allows
privately owned companies to monopolize entire industrial sectors. In late
nineteenth-century America, the men who built enormous private-sector
monopolies (and near monopolies) in oil, shipping, railroads, banking, and
the telegraph cultivated close relations with senior officials in Washington.
That's in part how the Carnegies, Rockefellers, Vanderbilts, J. P. Morgan,
and others amassed considerable fortunes. The backlash against state-sanc-
tioned monopolies culminated in antitrust laws—most of which, in one
form or another, remain in place today.

Second, the term is sometimes used to describe the ways in which
governments commandeer free-market economies during wartime.
Many leading German, French, and British companies remained in pri-

vate hands at the outbreak of World War I, but as a conflict many expected would end quickly settled into a costly stalemate, governments were forced to adopt a high degree of central economic planning. The mobilization of national resources during World War II benefited what outgoing President Dwight Eisenhower christened the military-industrial complex in 1961.[9] All governments, including those presiding over a relatively free market, provide for the defense of the country's territorial integrity.* In the process, they create space for a state-guaranteed market in which privately owned defense companies can develop a privileged position, distorting the competitive playing field. Security provisions which make many defense-related technologies secret and require time-consuming security clearances for some private-sector employees make it all but impossible for smaller firms to enter the market.

Third, state capitalism sometimes involves the choice of political officials in a free-market democracy to keep particular industries in public hands. Before Margaret Thatcher privatized a long list of large companies, British Airways, British Gas, British Steel, British Telecom, and British Petroleum, as well as large shipbuilders, regional water and electricity companies, airport operators, parts of the nuclear and coal industries, and even Rolls-Royce were all publicly owned. Even Thatcher would not privatize Britain's National Health Service, however, which remains Europe's largest employer with more than 1.5 million names on the payroll.

Mercantilism

Had the fall of the Berlin Wall truly marked the final triumph of free-market democracy, the term *state capitalism* might have quietly passed

---

* Even in Costa Rica, which has no armed forces, the government operates a Ministry of Public Security that oversees a Civil Force, a kind of special police force devoted to combating drug trafficking and other crimes. The ministry is responsible for protecting the country's sovereignty.

from the scene. But these words have now taken on a distinctly new meaning, one that will become enormously important for international politics and the global economy over the next ten years. This book defines twenty-first-century state capitalism as "a system in which the state plays the role of leading economic actor and uses markets primarily for political gain." But to really understand the roots of this phenomenon, it's useful to look briefly at an earlier version of it—one that revolutionized economic life and defined the prevailing order for nearly three hundred years.

Mercantilism is economic nationalism for the purpose of building a wealthy and powerful state.[10] The preeminent global economic model from the early sixteenth until the late eighteenth century, it's an economic system in which governments use state regulation to amass national wealth and power at the expense of all other governments. In postfeudal Europe, mercantilism was based on two false assumptions. First, mercantilists believed that a nation's wealth was exactly equal to the money and other treasure it controlled. Precious metals, especially gold, were the period's most widely accepted measure of wealth. As Adam Smith, the system's most famous critic, put it, mercantilism was based on "a popular folly of confusing wealth with money," leading to the conclusion that any increase in the money supply, namely bullion, made everyone richer. Second, mercantilists assumed that the total volume of global wealth—and therefore of international trade—was fixed. They believed that the pie could not grow larger and that success meant securing the largest possible slice. Trade was practiced as a zero-sum game, and because one country could only gain at another's expense, commercial relations were bound to spark conflict.

These two assumptions led to a single dominant national objective: to accumulate precious metals through a positive balance of trade. The importance of maximizing exports while minimizing imports became an article of faith. The aim was to control trade via a few large monopolies that could be managed and monitored by state officials; via captive overseas markets, called crown colonies, which were barred from trading directly with others; and via a host of other protectionist measures, like punitive tariffs on imports, particularly of finished goods. At home, government promoted national self-reliance as a defense against dependence on potentially hostile foreigners. In particular, governments championed domestic industries that produced essential goods like clothing, candles, and food.

Mercantilism was much more capitalist than Marxist, because it drew inspiration from the basic human drive for security through the accumulation of wealth. This sword and shield of gold were expected to make the nation richer, less vulnerable, and more powerful. But over time, those who profited from the growing bureaucracies that were needed to administer this system developed an interest in growing their personal power and privileges. The corporate state became more expensive, producing higher taxes, greater unrest and insecurity, and deeper state dependence on the bureaucracy. The wealthiest and most powerful among the merchant class fought to preserve their state-guaranteed competitive advantages by forming alliances with well-placed bureaucrats, whose role expanded into mutually profitable enforcement of an ever-expanding web of state regulations.

Why the preoccupation with gold? There was no obvious alternative. The world had no internationally accepted global reserve currency. National currencies were barely exchangeable. But wherever they traveled, even among the most primitive societies, mercantilists encountered the universal human fascination with precious metals. Generally speaking, Europe's mercantilists had two methods of increasing their stockpiles: by building a positive trade balance (more gold coming in than going out) and by conquering the lands where new reserves were discovered. The latter was a powerful incentive for financing an age of exploration. Privately funded ventures like the merchant Marco Polo's gave way to state-subsidized projects led by explorers like Columbus, Vasco da Gama, John Cabot, and Magellan, men charged with opening new trade routes and helping their benefactors amass new wealth—and in some cases, new territory. The acquisition of new land brought fresh supplies of raw materials with which to produce goods for export in return for more gold. Conflicts over trade routes and colonies became inevitable.[11] So did transatlantic slavery. Growing bureaucracies, colonialism, and trade competition stoked conflicts. To thwart the efforts of competitors to build a positive trade balance, mercantilist governments imposed tariffs, taxes, and quotas on imports, particularly of manufactured goods, while promoting the interests of their export merchants through subsidies, tax rebates, and monopoly licenses. Monarchs commissioned the construction of ever-larger cargo ships to carry more goods at lower cost. The ships charged with protecting them became larger too. Budgets swelled, sometimes forcing the imposition of still higher taxes. Navies became as important as armies as symbols of political power.

In the commercial realm, monopolies ruled. Kings and queens provided a few companies with *letters patent,* exclusive rights to act in the monarch's name. The British and Dutch East India companies were set up within two years of each other at the very start of the seventeenth century. These were privately owned companies, issuing stock, with a board of directors chosen from among shareholders. But they were also royally commissioned and enjoyed exclusive privileges, partnerships of political and commercial elites that were essentially the earliest examples of government-backed "national champions." Denmark, Sweden, and France followed the leaders, creating similar companies as trading monopolies, but the British and Dutch versions were by far the most successful. For most of the seventeenth century, the Dutch company paid its shareholders annual dividends of between 10 percent and 60 percent. It was a central player in a series of Dutch-Spanish wars over six decades that eventually forced the Portuguese (then united with Spain) from much of present-day Indonesia and Indian coastal regions and established a global monopoly of the spice trade. In 1652, the Dutch

East India Company established the first European settlement in South Africa. This is the company that discovered and settled New York, then known as New Amsterdam, before ceding it to the British.[12]

The British East India Company was even more successful. Oliver Cromwell's government granted it monopoly rights[13] to trade with India in 1657, and the company then effectively became the unchallenged sovereign power in much of India for more than a century. The company maintained its own administrative bureaucracy, militia, and navy, which at times were larger than Britain's. When the British government formally took political control of India in 1784, it made East India Company director Warren Hastings its first governor-general and allowed the company some governmental and military functions for another fifty years. The British East India Company also enjoyed a monopoly on trade with China and purchased Singapore in 1819. When commercial rivals appeared, it either crushed them or bought them out.

Political policy makers bolstered these companies. The British Acts of Trade of the second half of the seventeenth century (also known as the Navigation Acts) decreed that only English ships with mostly English crews could transport foreign goods to and from England and its colonies. All colonial trade with countries outside the empire had to pass first through English ports, where taxes were to be paid on particular commodities like sugar, indigo, rice, and tobacco. These laws contributed directly to more than a century of Anglo-Dutch wars, which started one year after the first act effectively excluded the Dutch from the transportation of all products traded with England and its emerging empire. The laws also planted the seed of rebellion in the American colonies by forcing colonists to buy relatively expensive sugar from the British West Indies and, more famously, by giving the East India Company a monopoly on the duty-free import of tea. But the laws did have some positive effects for England: Even Adam Smith praised their role in creating a military and economic superpower by promoting the need for a huge merchant fleet with a large enough navy to protect it.[14]

What of the merchants themselves? By their own accounts, they were hard-nosed realists. At times, they considered themselves warriors on the front lines of a great national effort to secure a larger share of the world's wealth. Some claimed that they were bringing God, civilization, and modernity to primitive peoples. Many of them flaunted their good fortune, building opulent homes filled with the sorts of prizes found only at the edge of the world. The most successful of them used their political influence and personal connections to rig the game to their advantage.

These were the first state capitalists.

The End of Mercantilism

There are several reasons why, by the end of the eighteenth century, mercantilism had begun to die. As transportation over land and sea became easier and more common, governments discovered that banning the import of certain products could not prevent large-scale smuggling. As a broader range of citizens began to gain political influence, it also became more difficult to defend lucrative monopolies against those, including some political officials, who demanded a piece of the action. Finally, the Industrial Revolution mechanized manufacturing on an unprecedented scale, sharply expanding society's productive potential. For all these reasons, it became increasingly obvious that, over time, governments would have much less control over the flow of commerce.

In the late eighteenth century, mercantilism came under attack from Adam Smith, David Hume, and others.[15] Taken to its logical extreme, a growing chorus of critics argued, mercantilism could not be sustained. There could never be a world in which everyone exports and no one imports. Smith insisted that producers could not rely indefinitely on a system that cheated consumers by depriving them of choices. He argued that when every individual and every nation produces within the area of its comparative advantage, allowing specialization and competition to produce better products at less expense, trade can benefit all who participate in it. Smith, Hume, and others also ridiculed the assumption that an increase in the money supply enriched all of society. They demonstrated that a country that hoards gold would eventually have so much of it that its value relative to other goods would fall—and that countries that lacked gold couldn't afford to buy the products that gold-rich nations wanted to export.

The system didn't die everywhere at once. In the nineteenth century, Britain shed mercantilism to become the world's leading proponent of free markets and free trade. Others, including Bismarck's Germany and the United States, lagged behind. Basing his views on Alexander Hamilton's philosophical support for mercantilism,[16] Abraham Lincoln often championed protectionism.[17] The post–Civil War period was marked by trade barriers and internal monopolies. In the late nineteenth and early twentieth centuries, the United States caught the free market wave, overtook all others, and built what is still the world's leading economy. Over the past century, America has remained closer than any other major economy to the laissez-faire end of the market spectrum, but state intervention has helped successive U.S. governments survive free-market excesses, from the Great Depression of the 1930s to the financial crisis of 2008.

Even in the greatest economic boom times, no populous country has ever embraced pure free-market capitalism. All have adopted some form of regulated free-market capitalist system. The debate now revolves around the relative merits of the Keynesian view that increased government spending and reduced interest rates can stimulate demand, minimize unemployment, and return a damaged economy toward its natural equilibrium. In fact, John Maynard Keynes approved of some aspects of mercantilism, arguing that a trade surplus could spur demand growth and increase the national wealth.[18] Few Western economists argue that mercantilism is the wave of the future, but elements of the system remain with us, and state capitalism has given them new life.

Mercantilism and State Capitalism

State capitalism is not simply twenty-first-century mercantilism. To believe that the size of the global economy is fixed and that one nation's gain must be another's loss is to have missed two centuries of growth. As the World Trade Organization (WTO) puts it, "The data show a definite statistical link between freer trade and economic growth. . . . Liberal trade policies—those that allow the unrestricted flow of goods and services—sharpen competition, motivate innovation and breed success."[19] Today, no one in charge in any of the world's leading industrial nations doubts the power of trade and investment to fuel prosperity in several countries at once. Just as a Western financial crisis was generating a global recession, leaders of the G20 nations gathered in London in April 2009 to discuss how they might cooperate to turn things around. Following their summit meeting, even Hu Jintao and Dmitry Medvedev, presidents of China and Russia, the world's leading practitioners of state capitalism, signed on to a communiqué that read: "World trade growth has underpinned rising prosperity for half a century. We will not repeat the historic mistakes of protectionism of previous eras."

Pledges aside, the numbers tell the story. According to the WTO, the volume of merchandise exports increased from $59 billion in 1948 to $13.62 trillion in 2007. More than half of that growth has come since 2000, and trade in services has more than doubled in value over the same period. Economic growth will always be cyclical and uneven, but these statistics reflect changes in global politics. After the collapse of large-scale command economics in the late 1980s, former communist and other emerging markets began to integrate more fully into the global economy. The volume of world trade grew at just under 20 percent in 1995 alone and just over 20 percent in 2004. China's share of global trade has increased about tenfold since its free-market reforms began in the late 1970s, from about 0.7 percent to 7.7 percent. The growth of emerging-market countries and their export markets has cut America's total share of the global merchandise export market in half over the past sixty years, from 28 percent to about 14 percent.[20] In other words, many more countries have embraced capitalism in recent years, and most of the world's international financial institutions reflect the change.[21]

Mercantilism is dead, but its influence continues. Governments are again intervening in their economies to promote declared national interests, and they have found subtler and more effective ways to practice protectionism. Even states considered among the world's foremost advocates of trade liberalization and free-market capitalism refuse to yield ground on especially sensitive trade issues. The European Union, the world's largest trading bloc, continues to use import tariffs to protect its farmers against products that European consumers could buy for less from the developing world.[22] The EU's agricultural policies are in some ways a legacy of extreme wartime food shortages. But decades later, local farmers and food remain powerful symbols of a nation's heritage. Today, the financing of agricultural subsidies and tariffs still amounts to more than 40 percent of EU spending—on a sector that employs less than 5 percent of its population. When Europeans argue that developing states should liberalize their trade practices, the governments of those countries often counter that their own "food security" is under greater threat than in any rich-world country and that protectionism is therefore to be expected. State-capitalist governments—and those most likely to adopt state capitalism in the future—use these arguments to justify their own interventions and to argue for the merits of their economic model. This is where the history of mercantilism provides insight for today's global economy and where it might be headed. Those who favor free-market capitalism argue that competition and trade generate prosperity at home but also serve the general good. As with mercantilism, state capitalists use markets to build state power. Forced to choose between protection of the rights of the individual, economic productivity, and the principle of consumer choice, on the one hand, and the achievement of political goals, on the other, state capitalists will choose the latter every time. They reason that if political survival doesn't depend on this choice today, it might tomorrow.

The Western financial crisis and global recession created serious threats for China's political stability. How did its central government respond? First, aware that the downturn in America, Europe, and Japan had deprived Chinese manufacturers of some of their biggest customers, Chinese officials spent a significant portion of a $586 billion stimulus package to subsidize the export sector's survival. The global recession had already forced large numbers of Chinese manufacturers to halt operations and put workers on the street. Subsidies were designed to prevent more closings—and to minimize the risk that millions more unemployed migrant workers might generate civil unrest that threatened political stability. Second, just as mercantilists worked to maintain a positive trade balance, the Chinese government has invented new ways to limit imports through sometimes hidden forms of protectionism that shelter favored companies and manage the flow of capital. Third, just as mercantilists hoarded gold, the leadership manages the value of China's currency to spur exports and increase its holdings in foreign reserves—cash that can then be used to advance China's interests around the world. Mercantilists relied on colonialism to provide the raw materials needed to fuel further growth. Likewise, China's twenty-first-century foreign policy is designed to lock down the long-term supplies of oil, gas, metals, minerals, and other commodities needed to fuel China's continued economic expansion, to generate prosperity at home, and to safeguard the Chinese Communist Party's political capital.

Among the world's leading state capitalists—China, Russia, and

Saudi Arabia—politically connected modern mercantilists profit from close ties with institutions (like the Chinese Communist Party or the Saudi royal family) or with individuals (like Vladimir Putin and his political entourage). These business leaders operate comfortably within states where laws are designed and enforced to protect lords at the expense of vassals. Their willingness to act as instruments of state power wins them official protection from commercial rivals, foreign and domestic. In the case of state-owned companies, governments are no ordinary shareholders. The threat alone that they will change the regulatory rules of the game discourages competitors from challenging them. The world's largest state-owned companies and privately owned national champions may never have the clout of the East India companies, but they enjoy many of the same advantages.

In short, state capitalism has become big business—with serious implications for international politics and the global economy. The next chapter details how it actually works.

CHAPTER THREE

State Capitalism: What It Is and How It Happened

The main feature of this crisis is the return of the state, the end of the ideology of public powerlessness.

—FRENCH PRESIDENT NICOLAS SARKOZY, January 8, 2009[1]

State capitalism is a system in which the state dominates markets, primarily for political gain. But the division between state-capitalist and free-market countries isn't always clear. There is no iron curtain separating the two sides neatly into opposing camps. Every country on Earth features both direct government involvement in regulating economic activity and some market exchange that exists beyond the state's reach. No country's economy is either purely state capitalist or purely free-market driven, and the degree of government intervention within each country fluctuates over time. That said, there are crucial differences among countries in how their governments regulate commercial activity and in their power to extend their influence.

The following illustration will help put state capitalism in context. It represents what we might call the market spectrum. At each end are the ideological extremes of a state's role in an economy. On the far left is utopian communism, with absolutely no free-market activity. It's a game in which the referees have absolute control of every player's every move. This extreme has never existed, because even in the most tightly controlled state, black markets generate supply to meet demand. On the far right is utopian libertarianism, which some call anarcho-capitalism. At this extreme, there is no government—and no other authority that can manage, regulate, or interfere in any way with the operation of markets. It's a game with no referee at all.

Market Spectrum

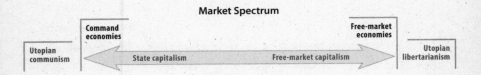

Between these extremes are real-world forms of capitalism, which include command economies with sharply limited free-market activities (like today's Cuba) on the far left and free-market economies with minimal government involvement (like late-nineteenth-century America) on the far right. Within this narrower spectrum, we have systems that vary mainly in how involved each government is in the workings of its economy. All of them, even the most tightly controlled, have some free-market activity going on. The economies of every country in the world lie somewhere along this spectrum.

How do we know where any given country would fall along the line? A few caveats. First, this is a profoundly simplistic model. It's offered only to illustrate the broad contours of the idea behind this book. Second, any particular country's place on this line is a snapshot of one particular moment in its history. Every country is in constant motion back and forth along this line—though some move much further and much more often than others. In 2008, a financial crisis, a recession, and presidential and congressional elections brought greater direct government involvement in the U.S. economy—a move from right to left. The political tug-of-war over this issue in America often plays out as a debate over taxes. Republicans tend to argue for lower taxes and less government interference, because consumers tend to spend their money much more efficiently than government can. Democrats counter that, left to its own devices, the private sector will never provide safe, high-quality public goods and services at affordable prices—like education for the poor or health care for the elderly.

But the U.S. move to the left was a relatively modest one, as the Obama administration spent much of 2009 wrestling with the political and economic forces that limit any American president's ability to bring about change within a system with strong checks and balances. For a much larger move along the spectrum, think of Russia's transition from communism in the 1980s to capitalist chaos in the 1990s or of China's creation of "special economic zones" in the late 1970s and 1980s, small experiments with capitalism, which produced big results that were eventually extended throughout much of the country. With far fewer limits on its power than an American president must accept, the Chinese Communist Party has made a significant shift from left to right over the past thirty years—though as we'll see, there's a limit to how far China's leadership has been willing to travel.

In fact, over the past three decades, there has been more movement to the right than to the left. Most of the former communist states of Eastern Europe have moved far enough right to meet the free-market demands of membership in the European Union. In the 1990s, countries like India, Brazil, Turkey, South Korea, and South Africa emerged by privatizing previously state-owned sectors of the economy and reducing regulation, subsidies, and monopoly practices to empower free enterprise. In exchange for access to cash and credit, many developing countries moved to the right by accepting demands from the World Bank and International Monetary Fund (IMF) for cuts in government budgets, for deregulation, and for other free-market reforms. Supposedly leftist politicians like Bill Clinton and Tony Blair administered last rites to the era of big government and supported the sort of economic liberalization that they opposed as younger men.

There is no precise tipping point that separates state capitalists from free marketers. But generally speaking, the left half of the market spectrum is populated by states in which governments play the role of lead economic actor, and the right features countries with established legal limits on the state's ability to regulate the actions of private companies and investors. Most countries have elements of both models. The U.S., German, Chinese, and Saudi governments all regulate some economic sectors much more tightly than others. In any country, a company that sells shoes will face fewer government-mandated rules than one that sells medicine. But the spectrum can help us understand how likely a particular country is to undergo a fundamental reordering of the role of government in its economy and how large a share of the global economy state capitalists might eventually own.

The Free-Market Camp

The governments of China, Russia, Saudi Arabia, and other countries had begun building their own versions of state capitalism long before the Western financial crisis sparked a global recession. But the market meltdown of 2008 proved a turning point, because it reversed a move toward less government intervention in the United States and Europe—and discredited free-market capitalism for many in the developing world.

After all, the recession originated in the United States, where poorly regulated credit markets, limited restraints on speculative leveraging of borrowed capital, and the nonregulation of the so-called shadow banking system (mainly hedge funds and private-equity firms) inflicted heavy damage on markets around the world. These shadow banks traded heavily in underregulated "derivative" financial products like packages of mortgages or other debt (known as collateralized debt options) and insurance against the failure of these options (known as credit-default swaps). By 2007, the United States had moved far to the right along the market spectrum—especially in the financial-services sector. This shift over the past three decades produced successive pieces of deregulation—like the repeal in 1999 of the barriers between commercial banks and more speculative investment institutions, which had been in place since the Glass-Steagall Act of 1933. As lawmakers removed regulatory hurdles, decision makers within many of these banks decided that prosperity (or perhaps survival) depended on willingness to embrace ever-higher levels of risk. This logic produced a kind of hypercapitalism that led some to offer credit to consumers who should not have accepted it, creating an enormous bubble in which many of the assets, particularly real estate, were considerably overvalued. This was a massive failure of government oversight and regulation in which hunger for short-term profit and a post–Cold War capitalist triumphalism allowed too many people to believe that markets can regulate themselves.[*]

Since 2008, the global recession has pushed dozens of governments back toward the left side of the spectrum. Policy makers and legislators in Europe and America have embarked on the largest state economic intervention since the 1930s. Less than one month after taking office, President Barack Obama signed into law a $787 billion stimulus plan, a package of government spending and tax cuts meant to kick-start U.S. growth and create millions of jobs. Intervention on this scale is meant to prevent a huge market failure—to move left along the spectrum so that the economy can recover its balance following a thirty-year-long lurch to the right. But America's massive government intervention in markets was not simply a victory of Democrats over Republicans. Before leav-

---

[*] The 2007 asset bubble, like many before it, grew from a huge overestimate of the true value of underlying assets. The term *hypercapitalism* refers to a situation in which an unregulated market overheats in a wave of unchecked but irrational exuberance. In these cases, it is mistakenly believed that money, rather than wealth, creates more wealth; that financial practices should be given free rein to create monetary value with as little government involvement as possible; and that additional monetary value does not need to be backed by proportionate increases in real economic productivity.

ing office, President George W. Bush fought to create a program that allowed the U.S. Treasury Department to spend up to $700 billion to purchase or insure so-called troubled assets, a move supported by both Barack Obama and his Republican presidential rival, John McCain.

Has America become a state-capitalist country? Hardly. All free-market countries have elements of state intervention, particularly during an economic downturn. But free marketers and state capitalists have very different core beliefs about the relationship between the individual and the state—and the role of government in an economy. In the United States, Europe, Japan, Canada, Australia, and many other like-minded countries, large-scale state intervention during the financial crisis was designed (intelligently or not) to save the free market, not to bury it. Even if Barack Obama were a socialist, as some of his less credible political rivals insist, no president of the United States has the power to fundamentally change his country's economic system. Obama's record suggests he is a believer in free trade and free enterprise—though he ran for president at a moment when neither would win him many votes among core Democratic voters in the labor and trade-union movements. There is clear political consensus among U.S. lawmakers of both political parties that once the banking, automotive, and other troubled sectors and companies can safely be removed from the endangered species list, government should restore their independence and allow them to compete.

The United States is not the only free-market country in which government has moved to bolster the free market through state intervention. After World War II destroyed most of its industry and capital stock, Japan experienced one of the longest sustained periods of rapid economic growth in history, recovering within three decades to become the world's second-largest economy. For much of that period, the Japanese government effectively ran the country's industrial policy via the Ministry of International Trade and Industry (MITI), created in 1949 to help revive a shattered economy and build a new industrial base.[2]

The ministry functioned as both a regulator and an interventionist policy maker. It orchestrated strategic industrial cartels, research and development, and mergers and investment decisions. It established and enforced environmental, health, and safety standards. It settled disputes between companies and unhappy customers. Its administrators guided the development of new technologies. It shielded vulnerable Japanese companies from foreign competition. Until the 1980s, this economic and political powerhouse produced most of Japan's prime ministers.[3]

But MITI was never intended to give the Japanese government total control of Japan's economy. It had relatively little influence, for example, in industrial sectors that produced motorcycles, cameras, robotics, and electronic consumer goods. Honda resisted attempts by MITI officials to force it to merge with a larger automotive cartel. Despite MITI's advice, Sony forged ahead with the production of transistor radios in the 1950s. Beginning in the 1970s, MITI's influence gradually declined as the yen was allowed to float freely against the dollar, trade policy was liberalized, and global trade agreements demanded new antitrust measures. By the 1990s, MITI was helping foreign companies sell products in Japan.

In short, Japan's was never a command economy. None of its internationally competitive corporate powerhouses were state owned, and even when MITI's clout was strongest, it was never Japan's leading economic actor. Though an extreme real-estate and equity bubble created a decade of economic stagnation in the 1990s and the global recession of 2008 to 2009 pushed the Nikkei stock market toward lows not seen in more than twenty-five years, Japan remains a free-market country.

No wealthy Western countries appear more skeptical of free markets than those of Scandinavia—Sweden, Norway, Finland, Denmark, and Iceland. Among larger countries, they have both high standards of living and narrow gaps between rich and poor. Few countries have come closer to eliminating poverty and illiteracy.[4] According to the 2008 Human Development Index from the United Nations, which ranks 179 countries according to a composite score that includes life expectancy, educational achievement, and wealth, all five of these countries appeared among the top 13 in the world.[5] How have they done it? Remember the firestorm during the 2008 U.S. presidential campaign over Barack Obama's comment that it's good for all when government "spreads the wealth around"? Since World War II, Scandinavian officials have imposed some of the highest levels of tax and income redistribution and created some of the most extensive social-welfare systems in the industrial world. They have embraced elements of centralized wage bargaining and wage equalization to ensure that employees in different firms within the same sector earn similar salaries. But there has never been widespread nationalization in the Nordic countries, and several of the relatively few state-owned companies have been privatized. State involvement in Nordic economies has not prevented several local public companies from making it big on the global stage. Denmark's Maersk, Finland's Nokia, and Sweden's Volvo, Ericsson, Electrolux, and IKEA are globally competitive because they make world-class products. On the whole, the governments of these countries have favored free trade and opposed protectionism. For all the state spending on social-welfare and poverty-eradication programs, the free market is the primary driver of economic growth in these countries.

What about France, symbol of everything that American free-market conservatives despise? Before 1940, France had a relatively fragmented laissez-faire economy powered by small and medium-size family-owned businesses and few large industrial heavyweights. But World War II wiped out entire French industries. After 1945, policy makers sought to spur economic development by appealing to French national pride. For years, the country moved left along the market spectrum, defining its economic model in opposition to the "Anglo-Saxon model." Successive French governments adhered to an economic policy of *dirigisme*,[6] a system that allowed the state to exert strong direct influence over (though not control of) postwar redevelopment. The state created a central economic plan designed by a central government body (the Commissariat au Plan). It directed mergers or provided incentives for private companies to merge into favored national enterprises. It mandated direct state ownership of the railways, airlines, and the aerospace, defense, telecommunications, gas, and electricity industries. It used huge subsidies to create prestigious national projects, including a large network of nuclear power stations, the TGV high-speed train network, and the Concorde supersonic aircraft.

But even in the early 1980s, as President François Mitterrand presided over a wave of nationalizations in banking and other industries, the French government never owned more than relatively few French companies. Since then, *dirigisme* has ceded substantial ground to economic realities, and many formerly state-owned enterprises have been privatized.[7] The French government continues to subsidize local farmers (as American lawmakers do) and to enforce relatively restrictive wage and labor laws. It has resisted fully extending the EU's single market beyond goods into services, and it maintains comparatively high levels of government spending as a percentage of GDP. The 2008 financial crisis reawakened some of the French *dirigiste* impulses by, for example, encouraging the government to protect the nation's auto industry by closing French-owned production lines in other EU countries if necessary to protect jobs at home. But the vast majority of French companies, whether publicly or privately owned, do business without direct government involvement in their operations.

The State-Capitalist Camp

There are two fundamental differences between free-market and state capitalism. First, policy makers don't embrace state capitalism as a temporary series of steps meant to rebuild a shattered economy or to jump-start an economy out of recession. It's a strategic long-term policy choice. Second, state capitalists see markets primarily as a tool that serves national interests, or at least those of ruling elites, rather than as an engine of opportunity for the individual. State capitalists use markets to extend their own political and economic leverage—both within society and on the international stage.

State capitalism is not an ideology. It's not simply communism by another name or an updated form of central planning. It embraces capitalism, but for its own purposes. Many of its practitioners came of age within authoritarian political and economic systems, where governance is the art of risk management. In such a system, power is an all-or-nothing proposition, and the outcomes of all the various political and economic games they play can determine their very survival. Faced with such a game, it's best to control both the referee and the strongest players.

There is no single model of state capitalism, though its leading practitioners share a well-developed sense of risk aversion. It's no accident that the two most internationally influential of them are China and Russia, countries that have only recently shed communism and embraced markets. Fear of chaos long predates communism in China, and a tradition of secrecy and centralized control has shaped Russian political life for centuries. It's little wonder, then, that when governments in Beijing and Moscow finally decided to welcome the increasingly free flow of ideas, information, people, money, goods, and services from beyond their borders, they would try their best to control these processes—and to carefully micromanage the risks they create. As we'll see in detail in the next chapter, this organic relationship between state capitalism and autocracy is also visible within the Arab monarchies of the Persian Gulf, where personal, political, and commercial interests are tightly interwoven within royal families. It's also visible in energy-rich authoritarian states like Iran, Venezuela, and others.

But state capitalism is not socialism, and it does not represent a retreat from participation in markets toward command economics.

Vladimir Putin, a committed state capitalist, once said that "any Russian who doesn't regret the disintegration of the Soviet Union has no heart, but one who wants to revive it has no head." Those who practice state capitalism know, often from bitter personal experience, that command economies are bound to fail eventually, because governments can never direct supplies of scarce resources and attach values to goods and services as efficiently and intelligently as markets can. Instead of eliminating markets, they try to harness them for their own purposes. Socialism often represents a long-term commitment to progressively greater state control, a sort of "slow boat to communism"—eventual state ownership of all means of production. This boat may never reach port, but its captain is ideologically committed never to change course, no matter how heavy the storms that stand in his way.[8] The current governments of China and Russia, on the other hand, have no intention of pushing their countries back toward communism. They want as much control as possible over economies that remain dynamic and innovative enough to produce explosive and sustainable growth.

To some extent, the left-to-right positioning of countries along the market spectrum is similar to their arrangement along the conventional political spectrum we use to tag various politicians, political parties, governments, and ideologies as "left" or "right." When Americans think of Democrats on the left and Republicans on the right, they're thinking of political differences between the two parties over the proper role of government in American life. Generally speaking, we think of leftists as those who argue that governments have a moral responsibility to correct injustice, promote fairness, and create opportunity. Those on the right counter that state interests often run counter to the rights of the individual, and that governments cannot be trusted to impose standards of justice or fairness. They argue that markets, not bureaucrats, fuel prosperity.

But the market and political spectrums are not the same, because some countries that have not embraced genuine political pluralism encourage free enterprise. That's true, for example, in Singapore, where the ruling People's Action Party, which has exercised nearly total control of parliament for more than fifty years, works to promote entrepreneurialism and economic competition. The regulatory and tax hurdles the government creates for businesses are famously low. In both 2008 and 2009, the World Bank Group's Doing Business index ranked Singapore first of 181 countries for the ease with which private commercial enterprises can create and conduct business. Yet, Prime Minister Lee Hsien Loong has reportedly warned that *political* competition can "cripple decision-making."[9]

The Tools

To manage state capitalism, political leaders use a variety of intermediary institutions. The state doesn't always exert day-to-day control, but it has considerable direct influence over these tools. The most important of these are national oil (and gas) corporations (NOCs), other state-owned enterprises (SOEs), privately owned national champions, and sovereign wealth funds (SWFs). The presence of some of these institutions does not automatically make a country state capitalist. The government of Norway manages a sovereign wealth fund and owns more than 60 percent of StatoilHydro, the world's largest offshore oil and gas company. It's not the tools that count; it's how they're used. But countries that have all four of these institutions tend to be state capitalist.

National Oil (and Gas) Corporations—NOCs

Governments of countries all over the world, particularly those that import oil and gas, have begun to invest substantial sums in the development of hydrocarbon energy alternatives. Some hope mainly to limit the financial and political risks generated by rising oil and gas prices.[10] Others want to reduce their dependence on hostile or potentially unstable energy-producing countries. Still others want to reduce carbon emissions to slow the process of climate change. Many are motivated by a combination of these factors. But for a variety of reasons, oil and gas will be fueling the global economy for many years to come.

Oil was first used for commercial development in the United States in 1859. At the dawn of the twentieth century, it supplied just 4 percent of the world's energy, but by the outbreak of World War II in 1939, it had become the world's most important fuel source. Today oil accounts for about 36 percent of the world's total energy consumption. Add natural gas and the total climbs to about 59 percent. Few credible forecasts suggest this figure will fall below 50 percent by 2030, largely because rising demand for oil and gas in emerging powerhouses like China and India will (at least partially) offset technological breakthroughs in fuel efficiency and the development of hydrocarbon alternatives.[11]

Many industry experts expect global oil production to peak before 2030, and some believe we'll reach the downhill slope much sooner. U.S. crude-oil production peaked in 1970, and confirmed discoveries of new oil reserves around the world have been trending lower for decades. But the world isn't about to run out of oil next year. Industry experts estimate that the human race has so far consumed about 900 billion barrels of oil. Most forecasts suggest that between 1.2 and 1.3 trillion barrels of proven and likely reserves remain to be recovered—two thirds of them in the Middle East. In early 2008, the world used nearly 86 million barrels per day. If current consumption rates continue and there are no further discoveries of exploitable reserves, the world will have enough oil for another forty years and enough natural gas for another sixty.[12]

Though the oil will last a little while yet, there is plenty of evidence that it will become more precious. Short of a catastrophe that punches a hole the size of China in the global economy or a miraculous technological breakthrough in alternative energy,[13] there is no way global consumption will remain at today's levels for the next forty years. There are plenty of statistics that help tell the story of emerging markets and rising energy consumption. For the sake of simplicity, let's focus only on automobiles. In 2009, about a thousand brand-new cars hit the streets of Beijing every twenty-four hours, and only about 4 percent of Chinese consumers already own automobiles. In other words, China offers a vast—and still largely untapped—market for cars. Worldwide, there were about 700 million cars on the road in 2009. By 2025, that number will probably top 1.25 billion.

Who will profit from all that new consumption? The phrase "big oil" conjures up images of Western multinationals like ExxonMobil, Royal Dutch Shell, and British Petroleum. But three quarters of global crude-oil reserves are now owned by national oil companies like Saudi Aramco, Gazprom (Russia), CNPC (China), NIOC (Iran), PDVSA (Venezuela), Petrobras (Brazil), Abu Dhabi National Oil Company, Kuwait Petroleum Corporation, and Petronas (Malaysia). These state-owned giants are the world's largest energy companies measured by reserves. The biggest multinationals collectively produce just 10 percent of the world's oil and gas and hold about 3 percent of its reserves. The largest of them, ExxonMobil, ranks just fifteenth in the world. In fact, the fourteen largest state-owned energy companies control twenty times as much oil and gas as the eight largest multinationals.[14] Faced with fewer opportunities to acquire new reserves, decision makers within some multinationals have begun to shift their business models toward the sale of services and technology to the national oil companies. One day soon, that may be the only comparative advantage they have left.

This tectonic shift is a relatively recent one. It's largely a result of the sharp spike in oil prices between 2003 and 2008 and the enormous profit opportunities it created for the governments of energy-producing countries like Russia, Venezuela, Nigeria, Libya, Angola, and Algeria, which scrapped foreign-investment-friendly policies in favor of higher taxes on foreign firms operating in the energy sector and legal mandates for a larger state role in the development of new fields. Especially in Russia and Latin America, political officials often justified these moves as long-overdue safeguards against resource exploitation by outsiders. This development has fundamentally changed the relationship between governments and private oil companies. Some of the multinationals once expected to take over the world are energy companies, firms that must now negotiate contract terms with foreign governments that own sizeable stakes in some of their commercial rivals.

There are important differences among these national oil companies. Some of them are the nationalized remnants of oil industries that multinationals developed many decades ago, while others are postcolonial inventions. Not all of them are wholly state owned. Some have much greater technical capacity than others. Operational independence varies considerably, but none are entirely immune to political interference. As a group, they undermine the growth of global oil production, adding constant upward pressure on prices, and they can threaten the political stability of the governments that own them.

History offers plenty of examples. The Mexican constitution mandates that only the state can own domestic energy resources. Since 1938, state-owned Pemex, now the largest company in Mexico, has controlled every aspect of the country's oil production. Over the years, the company has accounted for as much as 40 percent of total government revenues, but its production is now in decline because the taxes it pays sometimes exceed its profits. Pemex's debt has compromised its ability to borrow in international capital markets, further reducing its ability to spend on exploration and production. Its reserves have been falling for a quarter century.

Further complicating its operations, Pemex's operating budget must be approved each year by congress. That ensures that its effective shareholders are lawmakers with interests to serve and votes to win, making long-term investment decisions all but impossible. In 2007, lawmakers approved reforms that reduced taxes on the company and gave it greater freedom to decide how to spend its profits. Yet Pemex continues to produce less oil and less revenue every year.

Iran has the world's third-largest reserves of oil and second-largest reserves of natural gas. Its energy exports account for as much as 70 percent of government revenue.[15] But investment in the sector has yet to recover from the Iran-Iraq war of the 1980s. Its oil and gas fields, overseen by the National Iranian Oil Corporation (NIOC), aren't aging well, and U.S. and UN sanctions, imposed to force Iran to renounce its nuclear ambitions, have weighed heavily on foreign investment in the energy sector. The problem is exacerbated by government use of energy resources to protect its popularity. To appease a population increasingly frustrated by economic mismanagement, high inflation, and rising unemployment, Iran's government spends more than $20 billion per year, money that could be invested in energy infrastructure, on subsidies to help consumers afford gasoline and heat their homes. The government has diverted billions more into state spending on projects that have nothing to do with long-term energy development and everything to do with short-term efforts to appease angry citizens. A 2007 U.S. National Academy of Sciences study warned that without substantial investment to upgrade its infrastructure, equipment, and operations, NIOC might not be exporting any oil at all by 2015.[16]

Venezuela's Petróleos de Venezuela S.A. (PDVSA) has even bigger problems. Nationalized in 1976, PDVSA has become Venezuela's largest employer, accounting at times for one third of the country's GDP, half of government revenue, and 80 percent of its export earnings. In 2002, nearly half of PDVSA's employees went on strike to protest President Hugo Chávez's bid to impose a board of directors on the company that would give him greater control of its operations. Chávez responded to the strike by firing about eighteen thousand workers, including some of the company's most talented and experienced engineers. The resulting turmoil brought operations to a virtual standstill. Eight years later, PDVSA has yet to fully recover.

In 2006 and 2007, the Chávez government grabbed majority control of previously foreign-owned joint ventures in the country's oil-rich Orinoco Belt and seized assets from several international oil companies. PDVSA's average stake throughout the Venezuelan oil industry jumped to 80 percent. Eager to use an ever-increasing percentage of PDVSA's profits to finance politically inspired spending sprees, Chávez forced the company to pay the government higher royalties and taxes. In 2006–2007, PDVSA's bill increased by 16 percent, even as its revenues fell by 3 percent. The government also required that PDVSA make direct "social payments" to various domestic programs, including power-infrastructure upgrades and urban-development projects, and to buy and distribute food to help the government cope with shortages. By early 2009, PDVSA's production had fallen by 15 percent in less than four years, and the downward trend continues.[17]

But some national oil companies have more going for them than access to large amounts of oil. They have managers with the skills, experience, and operational autonomy to compete successfully with the best of the multinationals. Though it manages the largest exploration and production budget outside the Persian Gulf, Brazil's Petrobras enjoys a relative freedom from government interference that Pemex, NIOC, and PDVSA can only envy. The government of Malaysia created Petronas (Petroliam Nasional) in 1974 and allows its management to make most of its own strategic decisions and to reinvest a healthy percentage of profits back into the company. Formed in 1963 from the nationalized assets of mostly French oil companies, Algeria's Sonatrach began life as the domestic partner for foreign firms active in the country's oil-and-gas sector. Since 2006, Algerian law has mandated that Sonatrach must own at least a 51 percent stake in domestic upstream, pipeline, and refinery projects, but the government tends to let the company's managers guide the company's commercial development, raising money instead via increased taxes and royalties from foreign operators.

The presence of a national oil company alone does not suggest that a country's government has embraced state capitalism. No NOC is run more like a privately owned multinational than Norway's StatoilHydro, which is hardly surprising, given Norway's political and economic cultures.[18] Despite its relatively generous state spending on public health, child care, and social-welfare programs, Norway's government has never signaled a desire to become the country's leading economic actor. StatoilHydro is now the world's third-largest net supplier of crude oil and controls about 60 percent of Norway's oil production. Direct state involvement in its management is minimal. One of the world's wealthiest countries, with a population (4.6 million) half the size of North Carolina's, Norway's government has little need to divert StatoilHydro funds toward politically inspired spending projects.

Going Abroad

Over the next decade and a half, China's population will likely grow by more than 300 million people, a number equal to the total population of the United States. To continue to power the country's economy and create jobs, the Chinese leadership has sent its three national oil companies out into the world to win access to the long-term supplies of oil and natural gas that China will need. From Algeria to Angola, in Nigeria, Niger, and Ghana, state-owned Chinese companies are competing with Western multinationals for energy supply contracts.[19] China's trade with Africa topped $100 billion in 2009, a figure ten times higher than in 2001. This trend is not limited to China, nor is Africa the only playing field.

National oil companies have considerable competitive advantages. They have direct (often aggressive) support from officials back home, who can offer foreign governments attractive political and financial incentives. They can work with other national oil companies, particularly within countries where local laws limit the involvement of multinationals in the oil and gas sectors or where there are political motivations for partnership. That's why, for example, there is considerable cooperation between the governments of Iran and Venezuela. Beyond membership in the Organization of the Petroleum Exporting Countries (OPEC), the two also share deep hostility for the government of the United States. Their energy partnership is more about political stagecraft than commercial cooperation, but that's little consolation for the Western multinationals that are shut out of potentially lucrative business with both governments.

The national companies have still more advantages. They can invest in large-scale partnerships with repressive regimes that multinationals can't approach. A private-sector company must protect its reputation with customers, investors, and shareholders. State-owned companies, protected from public scrutiny by state restrictions on freedom of the press, don't have that problem. In addition, political officials in states like Iran, Sudan, and Burma are far more likely to violate an agreement with private shareholders than one made with a powerful foreign government.

Some national oil companies exist to achieve political goals, acting on behalf of the governments that own them to, for example, lock up long-term access to badly needed energy supplies. Turning a profit is secondary. That's why the best-funded of the NOCs can afford to pay above-market prices for resources, taking losses that multinationals can't easily afford and driving prices higher for consumers everywhere. Many of them have relatively low labor costs, because they hire non-union workers that multinationals can no longer use. In the process, state capitalism distorts the performance of energy markets and limits available energy supplies for consumers around the world by putting reserves in the hands of companies that are ill equipped to quickly, efficiently, and fully develop them.

The impact of national oil companies is not simply economic. Gazprom, Russia's state-owned natural gas monopoly, made headlines in January 2006 and again in January 2009 by cutting gas supplies to neighboring Ukraine. Company officials claim the action was taken in retaliation for Ukraine's unwillingness to resolve a dispute over debt and pricing, but cutting off heating supplies in the dead of winter amounts to a none-too-subtle reminder that Russia's government has the power to create turmoil inside its neighbor. By turning off the taps on Ukraine, Gazprom also briefly suspended supplies ultimately bound for Europe, which now depends on Russia for one quarter of its natural gas.

In theory, the government of a country blessed with rich deposits of oil and gas would benefit most by selling access to them to the company that can find them, extract them, and move them to market as quickly and cost-effectively as possible. After all, governments can earn enormous sums by taxing the company's profits. The largest of the multinationals have the talent, experience, and technology to get the job done, and there is evidence that efficiency gaps between privately owned companies and their state-owned rivals are wider in the energy sector than in any other area of an economy.[20] Multinationals offer higher wages, attracting better workers. They're more likely than state-owned companies to benefit from economies of scale. They're more innovative. Their managers and engineers are more experienced, and they use better equipment. These advantages will continue to matter in places like the Gulf of Mexico, Venezuela's Orinoco Basin, Brazil's Tupi field, and Russia's Far East and Arctic regions, where the technical demands of bringing oil to the surface are extraordinarily high.

Available evidence suggests that when governments pass oil assets from privately owned companies to state-owned firms, oil output and the revenue it produces fall. So why do they do it? They want to use the natural wealth for political purposes. Some want to steal the profits for themselves. Others, like Hugo Chávez, want to use a state-owned company as a cash cow. Still others, like some within the Russian political elite, want to use oil and gas as weapons with which to reestablish dominance throughout the territory of the former Soviet Union. But in each case, the primary motive is *political*. This is what separates a government like Norway's from one like China's. StatoilHydro exists to generate revenue. China National Petroleum Company exists, at least in part, to help the Chinese Communist Party maintain monopoly control of China's domestic politics.

Resource Nationalism

The use of oil, gas, and other commodities as political tools and strategic assets, a practice known as resource nationalism, can be an essential part of state capitalism. For a country blessed with oil wealth, the temptation to use it for political gain can be enormous. All governments that export significant amounts of oil use the revenue it generates and the promise of access to it to accomplish political goals. Few do it as nakedly or with as much gusto as Venezuelan President Hugo Chávez. As global oil prices rose sharply between 2003 and 2008, Chávez used the extra cash to bankroll social-spending projects at home and to sell oil at bargain-basement prices to friends in need, like Cuba's Fidel Castro. The government sometimes requires that job applicants at state-owned PDVSA pledge political loyalty and attend progovernment rallies. Chávez warns periodically that unless Washington does what he wants, Venezuela, America's fourth-largest oil supplier, will halt exports to the United States.

But nowhere is resource nationalism played on a grander scale than in Russia. In October 2006, after a decade of negotiation, the Russian government abruptly rejected bids by five major multinationals (Conoco-Phillips, Chevron, Statoil, Norsk Hydro, and Total) for a share of the enormous Shtokman gas field beneath the Barents Sea. A year later, state-owned Gazprom secured a 51 percent stake in the project, with Total and Statoil as junior partners. In December 2006, the Russian government informed Shell, Mitsubishi, and Mitsui that it had revoked their environmental permits as project managers for the $22 billion Sakhalin 2 project, forcing them to halve their respective holdings and give Gazprom a majority stake. This act of political hardball instantly wiped out 2.5 percent of Shell's global reserves. In June 2007, the private Russian-British consortium TNK-BP agreed under pressure to sell Gazprom its 63 percent stake in Rusia Petroleum, the company that held the license to develop the huge Kovykta gas field in eastern Siberia, and its 50 percent share in the East Siberian Gas Company. This is how Gazprom became the world's largest producer of natural gas with rights to about one quarter of the world's known reserves. The company has also become an important tool of Russian foreign policy and a source of considerable revenue for its government and ruling elite.

Russia holds no monopoly on the recent wave of resource nationalism. In 2006, Ecuador accused U.S.-based Occidental Petroleum of espionage and environmental damage and ordered troops to seize its oil facilities. In 2007, the Bolivian government nationalized the country's oil and gas fields. Kazakhstan suspended development of the Kashagan oil field in the Caspian Sea, then the world's largest new crude-oil discovery in many years. By 2009, state oil company KazMunaiGas, had doubled its stake from 8 percent to more than 16 percent by drawing shares from six privately owned members of the consortium. There are plenty more such examples from around the world.

In most of these cases, governments seemed to have learned an important lesson from earlier nationalizations: They can deprive the multinationals of majority stakes, but they'd better not run them off entirely. They know that their state-owned companies will need access to foreign expertise and technology if they are to succeed. As Bolivia's Vice President Álvaro García Linera said in 2007, "We offer our humble contribution to what we see as 21st-century-style nationalization, which means that foreign companies with capital and know-how are present in the country with their machinery, and they can earn profits, but never again can they be owners of the gas and petroleum."[21]

State capitalism pushes oil prices higher, and higher oil prices enrich the resource-rich governments that practice state capitalism. Their added wealth—and their increased geopolitical importance for countries that need their energy supplies—allows countries to behave more aggressively on the international stage.[22] This problem was never more obvious than in the summer of 2008, when crude-oil prices climbed past $147 per barrel. During this time, Russia defied the international community by launching a brief but destructive war on neighboring Georgia. Iran test-fired nine medium- and long-range missiles. Chávez threatened to cut all oil supplies to the European Union and traveled to Russia for discussions on possible formation of an OPEC-like natural gas cartel. When prices fall, the risk rises that these same countries will face market-moving political instability—and they will divert still larger shares of "their" oil revenue toward spending projects meant to restore order.

Beyond Petroleum

State-owned enterprises extend well beyond the energy sector. These companies are not simply a relic of communism—or even of postwar European social democracy. Every large economy in the world has at least a few. In the United States, the Postal Service, Amtrak, and the Corporation for Public Broadcasting are all essentially state-run enterprises. But in sectors as diverse as petrochemicals, power generation, banking, the mining of metals and minerals, iron and steel production, ports and shipping, weapons manufacture, automotives, heavy machinery, telecoms, and aviation, state-capitalist governments look to dominate entire industries and to use them to enhance their political power.

China is home to many of the world's largest non-oil state-owned companies. Electric utilities like State Grid Corporation of China and China Southern Power Grid, financial institutions like China Development ment Bank and Agricultural Bank of China, automotive-sector giants like China FAW Group Corporation, Dongfeng Motor Corporation, and Shanghai Automotive Industry Corporation are among the largest and best politically connected. There are state-owned enterprises on every continent and in dozens of economic sectors. Endiama, Angola's national diamond company, is the exclusive concession holder for the only sector outside oil that generates substantial export revenue in one of Africa's fastest-growing (but still poorest) countries. Like Sonangol, Angola's national oil company, Endiama still partners with private-sector companies to develop new reserves. Yet there is no guarantee that this openness will continue if the Angolan government decides it no longer needs the expertise, technology, and financial resources that privately owned foreign companies have to offer. Kazakhstan holds about one fifth of the world's known reserves of uranium ore, a core ingredient in the production of civilian nuclear power.[23] The fully state-owned Kazatomprom aims to become the world's largest single producer of uranium by 2010. Morocco's Office Chérifien des Phosphates is the world's largest supplier of phosphates. It controls nearly half of known global reserves, a large enough share to play a major role in setting its price. Phosphates are an essential ingredient in fertilizer—and therefore in global food production.

Privately Owned National Champions

Afraid that the financial crisis and global economic slowdown would damage Brazil's economy with an election year on the horizon, President Luiz Inácio Lula da Silva pushed mining giant Vale in 2009 to invest larger amounts of money within the country's borders. The Lula administration insists that Vale, a formerly state-owned company that operates mines and infrastructure under government concessions, has a responsibility to invest its profits in ways that create jobs for Brazilian workers. Instead, Vale responded to the slowdown as many other profit-driven companies did: It protected its bottom line by laying off hundreds of workers and cutting spending for the year by more than 35 percent. Lula wants Vale to help stimulate Brazil's economy. Vale wants to maximize profits. To get what he wants, Lula can threaten to push a tax increase or to rewrite regulations that would force Vale to surrender some of its concessions to the state. To protect its profits, Vale can appeal to opposition politicians to argue the company's case in congress. As economic conditions improved in 2009, Lula backed off a bit, and Vale has promised to spend more in 2010 and to invest in steel projects that will create jobs. But Brazil's government and its mining champion will continue to negotiate their way through these tensions in years to come.

National champions are companies that remain in private hands (though governments sometimes hold a large minority stake) but rely on aggressive material support from the state to develop a commanding position in a domestic economy and its export markets. Bidding on state contracts is often rigged in their favor. They have access to cheap financing from state-owned banks, tax breaks from central and local governments, and near-monopoly control of entire economic sectors. There are plenty of large U.S.- and Europe-based companies that become global players at least in part with support from their governments. U.S. and European firms competing abroad for state contracts often rely on their governments' diplomatic influence. But state capitalists create these national champions to build a reliable competitive advantage both at home and abroad, primarily for political reasons.

This is not a new phenomenon. Japan achieved a postwar economic miracle partly through the creation, with support from MITI, of large integrated business groups called *keiretsu*. Companies like Mitsubishi, Mitsui, Toyota, and Sumitomo were created to integrate all stages of the manufacture of single products or many different types of products through subsidiary companies operating under one umbrella. The South Korean version of this government-backed conglomerate, the *chaebol*, includes names like Samsung and Hyundai. Both the *keiretsu* and the *chaebol* helped their governments build an industrial base. In return, they won government contracts, credits, and loan guarantees that helped them maintain their domestic dominance. But today neither the *keiretsu* nor the *chaebol* are as formidable as they used to be.

How do state-capitalist national champions differ from other privately owned companies? The governments that create and promote them face far fewer legal and political limits in how they go about it. The companies themselves are much more secretive about how they operate and can more easily force smaller domestic rivals to merge with them. In Russia, no large business can succeed without good relations with the state, and a small group of oligarchs with strong ties to the country's political elite control most of them. This includes companies like Norilsk Nickel (mining), NLMK (Novolipetsk Steel) and MMK (Magnitogorsk Metallurgical Combine), Evraz (mining, steel, and other metals), Severstal ("Northsteel"), and Metalloinvest (steel). In China, Lenovo (computing), Huawei (telecoms), and the AVIC (Aviation Industries of China) empire have all become state-favored giants.

Then there are the hybrid countries. In 1969, the Malaysian government responded to an explosion of ethnic violence between Malays and the country's Chinese and Indian minorities with the so-called New Economic Policy, which favored companies owned by Bumiputeras, ethnic Malays, and other indigenous groups. As the United Malays National Organization broadened and deepened its control of government, the policy began to produce results. In 1980, Bumiputeras made up 60 percent of the population, but there were still no Bumiputera-owned companies among the top one hundred firms listed on the Kuala Lumpur stock exchange. By 2003, there were sixteen such companies, and the rest were legally required to ensure that 30 percent of equity was owned by ethnic Malays. The Malaysia Mining Corporation now has a leading position in ports, energy production and distribution, and construction sectors.

Some emerging market-based national champions have expanded their international clout by buying up companies based in developed countries. Vale, privatized in 1997, used government support to acquire Brazil's second-largest iron-ore producer (MBR) and, in 2007, the Canadian company Inco for nearly $17 billion. Vale has now become the world's second-largest mining company. India's Tata Group has become the country's largest corporation, partly through acquisition of iconic Western brands like Britain's Tetley Tea, Jaguar, Land Rover, and Corus (formerly British Steel). Tata now operates across multiple industrial sectors in more than eighty countries.

Sovereign Wealth Funds—SWFs

To finance all these state-owned and state-supported companies, governments could simply print the money they need, but they would lower the value of their currencies, stoke inflation, and undermine the value of their assets in the process. To pull the money directly from state budgets, they would have to either raise taxes or spend less money on other projects. Neither choice will do much for the government's popularity. This is where sovereign wealth funds (SWFs) come in. These are state-managed pools of excess cash that can be invested strategically. Governments can use the profits they generate for political purposes. They can also use the funds themselves to buy stakes in strategically valuable companies and institutions, primarily abroad.* Some of these funds are created by governments that don't practice state capitalism. Here again, it's not the tool that matters but the way it's used.

Sovereign wealth funds draw their capital from three main sources. First, there is foreign currency earned from the export of natural resources, mostly oil and natural gas, a major source of income for Russia, Arab states of the Persian Gulf, and several North African countries. Second, there is the extra cash left over from a positive balance of trade. For example, China finances sovereign wealth funds with the foreign currency it earns by exporting huge volumes of manufactured goods to the United States, Europe, and Japan. The money can also come from the profits produced by state-owned enterprises, the proceeds from privatizations, taxes collected by governments that spend less than they save, or via transfers from government-run pension plans. Third, sovereign wealth funds are occasionally bankrolled via direct one-off transfers from a federal budget or foreign-exchange reserves.

These funds generally include a range of financial assets in their portfolios with varying degrees of risk: foreign currency, stocks, government and corporate bonds, precious metals, real estate, and other assets. They buy stakes in (and sometimes majority ownership of) domestic and foreign companies, including hedge funds and leveraged-buyout firms. What makes them different—and poses challenges for free markets—is that those who manage their investments don't answer to shareholders. A sovereign wealth fund has one stakeholder: its parent government.

These funds are not bank savings accounts that earn a modest interest rate and help governments save for a rainy day. They're investment

---

* The IMF defines SWFs as "special purpose investment funds or arrangements, owned by the general government. Created by the general government for macroeconomic purposes, SWFs hold, manage, or administer assets to achieve financial objectives, and employ a set of investment strategies that include investing in foreign financial assets. The SWFs are commonly established out of balance of payments surpluses, official foreign currency operations, the proceeds of privatizations, fiscal surpluses, and/or receipts resulting from commodity exports."

vehicles that take on significant risks to maximize returns. They're distinct from risk-averse central banks that hold foreign-exchange reserves in cash and make short-term investments in low-yield assets like government bonds and money-market instruments. The IMF recommends that central banks maintain enough cash to cover three to four months of imports. Sovereign wealth funds often have a much longer-term outlook and can amass a net worth that far exceeds any short-term government need for added liquidity or management of foreign-exchange balances.

These funds aren't new. They've been around for more than half a century. In 1953, eight years before Kuwait gained its independence, its British administrators created the Kuwait Investment Authority, now the world's fourth-largest SWF. Though market players barely noticed, Abu Dhabi Investment Authority, Singapore's Government Investment Corporation, and other significant funds were created in the 1970s and 1980s. Only in 2005 did anyone publicly use the term *sovereign wealth fund,* as SWFs' growing importance for the global economy began to become obvious.[24] Several more countries have followed the leaders: Qatar in 2003, Australia in 2004, and South Korea in 2005, Vietnam, Libya, and Dubai in 2006, and Russia in 2008.[25] Against a backdrop of global recession, Brazil announced plans in 2009 for its first SWF. Officials in India, Angola, Bolivia, and Thailand may soon join the club. Depending on precise definitions, there are now about fifty sovereign wealth funds, at least half of which have been created since 2000—a natural by-product, in many cases, of the enormous pools of foreign currency collected by emerging-market exporters. The IMF estimates that these reserves tripled to more than $6 trillion between 2001 and 2007. China alone controls about one third of that total.

Unlike most state-owned companies and national champions, sovereign wealth funds of every description took an enormous hit during the Western financial crisis. A few have gone under, and others are struggling to reorganize their assets. Some took their heaviest losses from investments in Western financial institutions. Crisis-inspired risk aversion has already persuaded several of the governments that own these funds to fire some of the Western investment professionals they had hired to manage them, tightening operational control under state officials.

There are several reasons why governments create and use sovereign wealth funds. First, in countries that export large amounts of oil, gas, metals, minerals, and other valuable commodities, these funds can help transform finite, nonrenewable assets buried deep in the ground into financial assets that, if managed intelligently, can generate wealth indefinitely. They can also help governments survive the natural volatility in commodity prices. Some Persian Gulf Arab states learned the importance of this strategy the hard way. They sharply increased state spending when oil prices surged in the mid-1970s. But as oil prices tested new lows in the 1980s, their budget problems multiplied.

Second, the sudden infusion of large sums of cash from export earnings or fiscal surpluses can fuel inflation, weaken the local currency through an oversupply of foreign exchange, and create consumption bubbles. Diverting excess capital into a sovereign wealth fund can help keep an economy from overheating. These funds can provide governments with cash when they need it to limit the damage of sudden capital flight from the country or attacks by speculators on their currencies. SWF reserves can help provide a fiscal stimulus to boost economic demand, save jobs, and bail out failing financial institutions. In extreme circumstances, sovereign wealth funds can help a government avoid having to ask the IMF for help, encouraging skittish foreign investors not to flee and alleviating the need to cut a deal that might come with strings attached. After U.S. forces drove Iraqi troops from Kuwait in 1991, the Kuwaiti government relied heavily on the Kuwait Investment Authority to help rebuild a war-ravaged economy.

Sovereign wealth funds tend to be as transparent—or as secretive—as their governments.[26] Norway's Government Pension Fund (NGPF) oversees that country's huge oil wealth and provides the best example of a transparent large sovereign wealth fund. In fact, it's arguably more transparent, more accountable, and has clearer governance structures than many private institutional investors. The fund employs 120 investment professionals and publishes regular reports, which provide details on the assets it manages, in what currencies and in which companies. It reports its investment returns and lists Western companies it will not invest in for ethical reasons (including Walmart!) based on a company's environmental record and its operations in countries with poor human-rights records. Norwegian state officials play little or no role in the fund's day-to-day operations.

Other countries with relatively transparent SWFs include Chile and South Korea, both of which hire external fund managers to oversee a large majority of their assets. Singapore's Temasek and funds in Australia and New Zealand are rated as transparent as Norway's. Temasek, though state-owned, is formally a private corporation governed by the same company law that applies to the private sector.* The United States has no federal sovereign wealth fund, but the states of Alaska, Alabama, New Mexico, and Wyoming started down this track more than a generation ago.

Other funds operate with a little more secrecy. Most analysts consider the Abu Dhabi Investment Authority (ADIA) to be the world's largest sovereign wealth fund.[27] It is wholly owned by the ruling al-Nahyan family of Abu Dhabi, the largest and wealthiest of the United Arab Emirates. His Highness Sheikh Khalifa bin Zayed al-Nahyan worked for ADIA for several years as a European equities analyst. He now chairs the fund and appoints its directors. Many company officials have also worked in UAE government ministries—though nearly 800 of its 1,100 investment professionals are foreign nationals. Its cash comes almost entirely from oil exports. ADIA has never publicly re-

---

* Some argue that Temasek is not a sovereign wealth fund. But its money belongs to the government, which appoints its senior management. Temasek does invest more of its money at home than any other large fund.

leased documents that reveal exactly how big it is, what countries and economic sectors it invests in, or how well it has performed, but it is beginning to become marginally more transparent. Its management granted its first public interviews (with *BusinessWeek*) in 2008, revealing that it had averaged 10 percent annual returns for more than twenty years and invested more than half its funds in stocks in developed markets.[28] ADIA has begun to publish more data, revealing among other things that Abu Dhabi used ADIA to bail out neighboring emirate Dubai after the financial crisis wreaked havoc there. Its more recent foreign investments included stakes in two U.S. private-equity firms in 2007[29] and a huge loss from a $7.5 billion stake in Citigroup in mid-2008. Funds from Bahrain, Kuwait, Malaysia, and Singapore fall into this category of midlevel transparency.

At the more secretive end of the spectrum, China created its latest SWF—the China Investment Corporation (CIC)—in September 2007 with $200 billion from the Chinese central bank's huge foreign-exchange reserves. Closely linked to China's Finance Ministry and overseen by administrators who answer directly to Premier Wen Jiabao, CIC publishes almost no information on its investment processes, returns, or decision-making strategy. The fund appears to invest at least some of its money at home, but it generated headlines around the world by venturing into the U.S. financial sector with a $3 billion stake in the Blackstone Group private-equity firm (May 2007), $5 billion in Morgan Stanley (December 2007), and an 80 percent share in its own private-equity fund run by J. C. Flowers (set up in early 2008). A second large Chinese sovereign wealth fund—the State Administration of Foreign Exchange (SAFE)—has managed most of China's reserves since 1997, but it has also invested in global equities with the purchase of a $2.8 billion stake in French oil company Total in April 2008. It appears to have taken heavy losses by buying a piece of U.S. bank Washington Mutual via an American intermediary, but the details are unclear, because SAFE's management practices are even murkier than CIC's.

China has no monopoly on opaque sovereign wealth funds. Libya's Investment Authority, Algeria's Revenue Regulation Fund, Nigeria's Excess Crude Account, and Kazakhstan's National Fund are among the most secretive. In 2008, following pressure from the United States and other G7 governments, the IMF persuaded twenty-six countries to endorse "generally accepted principles and practices" for sovereign wealth funds on timely disclosure and sound risk management and governance structures.[30] But even if these principles were established in international law, there is no way to enforce them. And SWFs are hardly the only financial institutions that keep billion-dollar secrets. Hedge funds and private-equity funds zealously guard sensitive information about their operations, sometimes by domiciling in offshore tax havens. Yet hedge funds and private-equity firms aren't owned and operated by governments, and they're far less likely to put political considerations ahead of profits in making investment decisions.

Unfortunately for advocates of openness, the largest sovereign wealth funds are found in authoritarian state-capitalist countries. Abu Dhabi, Saudi Arabia, and China top the charts, with Russia playing catch-up. This lack of transparency, including secrecy about the extent of losses during the financial crisis and global recession of 2008 to 2009, complicates efforts to gauge their relative sizes. But several independent sources have constructed estimates based on available evidence, and we do know that some funds took heavy losses by providing international banks with tens of billions of dollars in capital before the extent of the banking crisis became clear.[31] The table on page 76 provides a snapshot of the relative size of the largest sovereign wealth funds in March 2009. The numbers are based mainly on figures gathered by the Sovereign Wealth Fund Institute, *Sovereign Wealth Funds News* (sovereignwealthfundsnews.com), and International Financial Services London Research. For SWFs valued at more than $100 billion, the lower range reflects relatively skeptical estimates from Deutsche Bank, Morgan Stanley, the Council on Foreign Relations, the Peter G. Peterson Institute for International Economics, and others. The size of some of these funds is literally a state secret. But despite the considerable guesswork behind these estimates, they do provide some insight.

Country	Fund Name	Estimated Rounded Net Value Range ($billion in March 2009)
1. UAE	Abu Dhabi Investment Authority	300–650[32]
2. Saudi Arabia	Monetary Agency (SAMA)	430–500
3. Norway	Government Pension Fund	396.6
4. China	SAFE Investment Company	300–350
5. China	Investment Corporation	288.8
6. Kuwait	Investment Authority	200–260
7. Singapore	Government Investment Corporation	200–250
8. Hong Kong	Monetary Authority Investment Portfolio	193.4
9. Russia	Reserve Fund and National Welfare Fund	178.5[33]
10. Singapore	Temasek	85
11. China	National Social Security Fund	82.4[34]
12. UAE	Dubai Investment Corporation	82
13. Libya	Investment Authority	50–70
14. Qatar	Investment Authority	65
15. Algeria	Revenue Regulation Fund	47
16. Australia	Future Fund	40.4
17. Kazakhstan	National Fund	38
18. Brunei	Investment Agency	30
19. South Korea	Investment Corporation	27
20. U.S.	Alaska Permanent Fund	26.7

China/Hong Kong and the United Arab Emirates (with five funds each) probably control more than 40 percent of all SWF assets worldwide. Saudi Arabia, Norway, Kuwait, and Russia control another 40 percent. Most of those countries land on the state-capitalist side of the market spectrum.

Sovereign wealth funds are likely to play a steadily increasing role in the global economy over the coming decade. In early 2008, before the effects of the global slowdown had become apparent, SWFs are believed to have reached $4 trillion in total value. In January 2009, with the depth of the recession still unclear, estimates fell to between $2.5 and $3.5 trillion, an amount still greater than the value of all global assets of private-equity and hedge funds combined. The IMF has estimated that collectively all sovereign wealth funds might be worth $10 trillion by 2013,[35] based on conservative assumptions about the recovery of the global economy, commodity prices, and return on investment. That's why many more countries are likely to jump on the bandwagon—and governments that already have one sovereign wealth fund are likely to create more. That's an enormous (and fast-growing) amount of capital in state hands.

What happened to all those post–Cold War assumptions that public wealth had become a thing of the past and that private wealth was the wave of the future? In fact, state capitalism began to take root long before the 1990s. It has developed in four waves.

The First Wave—Oil as a Weapon

State capitalism first began to pay dividends for a few resource-rich countries with the formation of OPEC in 1960.[36] National oil companies have been around since the 1940s, but only in late 1973 did the world's most important commodity become one of its most potent foreign-policy weapons. That's when OPEC cut production to several countries and imposed embargoes on the United States and the Netherlands in retaliation for their support for Israel during the Yom Kippur War. The price of crude oil, which had barely increased in real terms since the end of World War II, quadrupled from $3 to $12 per barrel in a matter of weeks. For OPEC member states, the crisis put an end to decades of perceived political and economic impotence, and the price shock forced the United States into a deep recession, triggered inflation, generated various forms of oil and gasoline rationing in America and Europe, and boosted the foreign-exchange reserves of the Soviet Union—buttressing its economy at a crucial historical moment.

Modern resource nationalism was born, as oil producers found that by acting together, they could control international production levels and grab a much larger share of the revenues generated by Western multinationals. At a stroke, the balance of market power shifted from consumers to producers. Newly valuable national oil companies came under tighter government control. The Saudi government fully nationalized Saudi Aramco, and other countries followed suit, allowing OPEC to become a virtual cartel. In other words, the conflict had enormous and lasting consequences for international politics and the global economy.

The Second Wave—Fast-Emerging Markets

The second wave of state capitalism made landfall during the 1980s and early 1990s with the liberalization and economic expansion of the so-called emerging markets—China, Russia, India, Brazil, South Korea, Mexico, Turkey, and others. Trade liberalization produced a surge in consumer demand in dozens of countries, the global economy has since gained hundreds of millions of new participants, and most of the emerging markets have a history of relatively direct state involvement in economic decision making. China and Russia depended for decades on command economies. In some of the others, large enterprises—often run by wealthy, well-established families—enjoyed virtual monopolies in certain economic sectors. India under Jawaharlal Nehru and Indira

Gandhi, postwar Turkey, Mexico under seven decades of single-party rule by the Institutional Revolutionary Party, and Brazil under alternating military and nationalist governments never fully embraced the view that only free markets can produce durable prosperity. Their political cultures predisposed them to the conviction that key economic sectors should remain under effective government management—in part to avoid exploitation by U.S. and European capitalists.

Though governments of many of the emerging markets enacted reforms that freed businesses to compete, to keep more of their profits, to invest as they saw fit, to export to new markets, and to welcome foreign investment, their commitment to free-market principles has remained tentative. The officials who introduced these reforms may be willing to experiment, but many of them gained their formative educational and professional experiences inside state-run institutions that were created to continually replenish the ranks of authoritarian and secretive governments. These are places where demonstrations of loyalty (not creativity or entrepreneurialism) were essential for advancement. Some of these officials have genuinely embraced free-market capitalism. But political cultures change slowly, and history provides enough examples of exploitation by outsiders to continually renew faith in state control of national wealth.

Economic liberalization has created robust growth in China, Russia, and several other emerging markets without independent courts to protect the rights of the individual, an independent press to check the power of those who profited most, or a culture of openness to bring predictability to development. In an emerging-market country, political factors matter at least as much as economic fundamentals like supply and demand for a country's development and the performance of its markets. Western governments scrambling to adapt to this shift in the global balance of power—and companies willing to ignore all sorts of risks in the gold rush for hundreds of millions of new customers and workers—may well pay a heavy price for their complacency.

These risks will grow over time. Since a team of Goldman Sachs economists first coined the term BRIC (Brazil, Russia, India, and China) in 2001, these countries have captured the collective imaginations of multinational companies, the international investment community, and the Western media. In a Global Economics paper titled "Dreaming with BRICs: The Path to 2050," published in 2003, the firm's economists argued that, given sound political decision making and good luck, "in less than 40 years, the BRICs economies together could be larger than the original G6 [the United States, United Kingdom, Germany, France, Italy, and Japan] in dollar terms."[37] With sustained long-term economic growth comes new political clout. Once Brazil, Russia, India, and China wield greater influence over the rules governing global financial flows, intellectual-property rights, and trade issues, the United States, Europe, and Japan will face a very different set of political challenges than they do today.

But the Goldman Sachs analysts argued that the BRICs would hit their long-term targets only if their political leaders committed themselves to "maintain policies and develop institutions that are supportive of growth." India and Brazil are more likely than China or Russia to maintain that commitment, because the state capitalists in charge in Beijing and Moscow back progrowth policies mainly as a means of ensuring domestic stability. If either government one day believes it must choose between economic growth and social order, they will restore order—and the state's considerable resources will help them do it. That kind of conflict is more likely in China and Russia, authoritarian countries where political dissent has fewer acceptable outlets. For the moment, major political players in India and Brazil appear to accept a more modest role for government in their countries' economic development. But there is no guarantee that significant levels of social turmoil—or, in Brazil's case, the temptations that come with a major oil discovery—won't one day change their minds.

The Third Wave—What to Do with the Wealth?

The third wave came ashore with the flood of cash produced by the growth of emerging markets and the rise of commodity prices of recent years. These forces haven't "lifted all boats," but they have drawn large numbers of consumers, from South Asia to Eastern Europe to Latin America, into an emerging global middle class. Brazil's growth rate, which averaged around 1 percent for the quarter century before 2001, reached nearly 7 percent in 2008. India's averaged 6 percent between 1988 and 2003 and peaked at 9.6 percent in 2007. Russia's averaged nearly 7 percent a year from 1998 to 2008, thanks in large part to surging prices for oil, natural gas, and other commodities. China's economy has grown by an astonishing 9.5 percent per year for three decades. Its exports of manufactured goods to the United States and European Union brought windfall after windfall of foreign-currency reserves. Together, these trends generated huge amounts of excess global capital and created the need for sovereign wealth funds.

When those who direct these funds make an investment decision, are they looking for profits, political leverage, or some combination of the two? It's impossible to know for sure, because many of these funds operate in the shadows. But if Western sovereign wealth funds like Norway's or pension funds like California's factor politics into investment decisions—in divesting from Iran or Sudan, for example—it's reasonable to assume that secretive, authoritarian states will do the same.

The Fourth Wave—Crisis and Opportunity

In the fall of 2008, Western governments began intervening in their economies on a massive scale. In Europe, a tradition of statism* and social democracy make nationalization and bailouts a little more politically palatable, but Western Europe has not known such large-scale state economic intervention since the World War II era. Japan, Australia, and other free-market heavyweights have followed suit. U.S. lawmakers have rolled up their sleeves and reached deeper into American financial institutions and key industries than at any time since the 1930s.

Many of the state-capitalist countries took a hit from the slowdown too. Following the fall in oil prices from $147 per barrel in July 2008 to less than $40 in February 2009, Russia faced its first budget deficit in a decade. The Russian government has had to bail out several state-owned enterprises and private national champions, manage a careful devaluation of the ruble that might have panicked millions of consumers, and prop up plenty of banks. During an interview with a Russian daily newspaper in October 2008, President Dmitry Medvedev sought to reassure depositors: "I have kept all of my bank accounts. I have not withdrawn any funds, nor have I converted my rubles to dollars. . . . I am convinced there is no threat to my savings, just like there is no threat to the funds of all Russian savers."[38] It's never a good sign when the president comments publicly on the safety of his bank account.

China had much less exposure to the toxic assets that spread like a virus through the global banking system, but large numbers of manufacturers were forced to close their doors in 2008, because U.S. and European customers stopped importing the products they sold. The rise in unemployment created serious risks for even-higher-than-usual levels of social unrest. But the Chinese economy has proven remarkably

---

* For our purposes, *statism* refers to a concentration of economic controls and planning in the hands of an often highly centralized government. It can be a defining element of both communist and fascist regimes.

resilient—and countries like India and Egypt, which are less exposed to global trade flows and toxic bank assets than many other emerging-market countries, sustained less damage from the global slowdown and have recovered from it relatively quickly.

That's why, for the next several years, a global economic meltdown widely blamed on free-market capitalism will undermine the arguments of those who believe that intelligently regulated private-sector competition is essential for long-term growth. With that problem in mind, it's essential to understand how state capitalism actually works in China, Russia, and many other countries—to recognize its strengths, spot its weaknesses, and figure out how it's likely to change our lives in years to come.

CHAPTER FOUR

State Capitalism Around the World

Tyranny is always better organized than freedom.

—CHARLES PÉGUY

On August 29, 2005, Venezuelan President Hugo Chávez announced a plan to provide low-cost heating oil and gasoline to hospitals, nursing homes, schools, and local organizations representing poor communities. "If you want to eliminate poverty, you have to empower the poor, not treat them as beggars," said Chávez as he announced plans to expand the program three weeks later. This is the kind of story that would normally generate headlines only in Venezuela's state-run media. In this case, it drove media attention all over the world, because the recipients of Chávez's state-sponsored largesse were victims of Hurricane Katrina in the United States. The plan was for Citgo Petroleum Corporation, a wholly owned subsidiary of state-owned oil firm Petróleos de Venezuela S.A. (PDVSA), to set aside 10 percent of the oil it refined for Americans in need. In this case, Chávez used his country's state-owned natural resources to provide direct support for people who needed help—and to score propaganda points by sticking a finger in the eye of President George W. Bush.

State capitalism is not a single coherent political ideology. It's a set of principles that a government can adapt to meets its particular needs. As we'll see, Saudi royals, Russia's elite factions, and China's senior party leadership design policies intended to extend their domestic power within very different political environments. Even in democracies, especially those in which one party has historically dominated the country's politics, governments use some elements of state capitalism to promote their interests. India's Congress Party uses state-owned enterprises to protect jobs and generous subsidies in some areas to control prices. South Africa's ruling African National Congress and Malaysia's United Malays National Organization use these and other state-capitalist tools to protect their political capital by serving the interests of historically disadvantaged majorities. Within democracies where power often changes hands, governing institutions can enshrine state-capitalist principles. Mexico's constitution has blocked efforts to liberalize the country's energy sector for decades. A huge offshore oil find may push Brazil's government in the same direction.

That said, democratically elected governments will never have as much freedom to develop state capitalism as authoritarian governments do, because they answer to voters, journalists, legislatures, and courts—all of whom have an interest in ensuring that no government can ever amass too much political and economic power. For example, China's party leadership can never be sure that a regional government will properly carry out its orders. But it faces nothing like the problems that India's central government must tackle in overcoming resistance from provincial governments controlled by rival political parties or local leaders who use courts to their advantage. Where elected leaders have access to state-capitalist tools, it's usually a remnant of a less democratic past (as in South Africa and Ukraine), some form of anticolonialist resource nationalism (as in Mexico and Malaysia), and limited to a few economic sectors.

As we'll see in some detail, state capitalism distorts the politics and domestic economies of countries throughout the Middle East, in South and Southeast Asia, and in Africa and Latin America. But if the Chinese, Russians, and Saudis didn't practice state capitalism, we wouldn't be talking about it. These countries each play a large enough role in international politics and the global economy to make this system a fundamental challenge to the future of free markets.

Saudi Arabia

As you enter King Abdullah Economic City, a multibillion-dollar building project due for completion in 2020, you pass through an enormous gate ornamented with the king's image and the words, "The vision of our leader has embodied our dreams."[1] According to the city's official Web site, its purpose is "To become the single greatest enabler of social and economical growth for the Kingdom of Saudi Arabia."[2] Two million Saudis are expected to live, learn, and work within this desert fortress of state-of-the-art skyscrapers, schools, and shopping malls that will one day cover 150 square miles. This is just one of six megacities the Saudi government intends to invent over the next decade, projects imagined by state contractors and built largely by the Saudi construction and service companies that win lucrative government contracts.

In Saudi Arabia, grand-scale state capitalism is a natural fit. Most authoritarian governments now recognize that change is inevitable. The more a regime fears for its long-term survival, the more likely it will try to micromanage the processes of adaptation and reform. Saudi Arabia's ruling royals survive and thrive by using the kingdom's massive oil revenues ($288 billion in 2008) to buy the political allegiance of its citizens. Given the need to spend billions on projects designed to bolster their popularity and on added security where necessary, they will continue to ensure that as much wealth as possible remains in state hands—and that economic changes don't enrich and empower potential rivals or militants devoted to their destruction.

The al Saud family has been a central political and economic player on the Arabian Peninsula for centuries, but its leaders know the kingdom must evolve to remain in (relative) harmony with an outside world determined to develop oil alternatives and powered by an ever-accelerating cross-border flow of information. Over the past several years, Saudi vulnerabilities have become more obvious. Though it holds nearly one quarter of the world's oil reserves, the kingdom's large population (about 28.7 million) ensures that the average Saudi enjoys a much smaller share of the wealth than his neighbors in Qatar, Kuwait, Bahrain, or the United Arab Emirates. Even with the sharp drop in prices in the second half of 2008, oil still accounts for about one third of total GDP. Saudi leaders have acknowledged for years that the kingdom can't afford to rely so heavily on oil for future income. Economic diversification has been a constant refrain, but progress remains slow.

In addition, the age gap has widened between senior royals and their subjects. In 2009, King Abdullah turned eighty-five, ailing Crown Prince Sultan reached eighty-three, and Interior Minister and political heavyweight Prince Naif hit seventy-six—but more than 60 percent of those they rule have not yet turned thirty. State officials say that 10 percent of Saudis are unemployed, but the real number (particularly among young people) is much higher. As growing numbers of students try to enter a job market that can't provide for them, some may turn their anger on their government. A few will embrace the kind of militancy that inspired the kingdom's most infamous native son (Osama bin Laden), most of the 9/11 hijackers, and domestic al Qaeda–affiliated groups.

Yet state capitalism serves the interests of both the royals and those they rule. Capitalism and free trade are hardly foreign concepts within the kingdom, but its political system and its oil-dominated economy have historically generated hands-on state management. Saudis don't pay taxes, because the government can draw wealth directly from the ground, and citizens see their royal family as a provider of wealth, jobs, and opportunity—not as public servants they can hold accountable.

The Saudi private sector, which accounts for 45 percent of domestic economic output, relies heavily on the state to provide commercial opportunities. When Abdullah became king in August 2005, he launched a series of market-friendly reforms meant to modernize the country by shifting the Saudi economy toward greater reliance on an expanding private sector for new growth and new jobs. The king pushed for diversification away from dependence on the oil sector and promoted his country's bid to join the World Trade Organization. In December 2005, the kingdom became the WTO's 149th member. Membership was motivated in part by a Saudi plan to secure greater global market share in the production of petrochemicals, but it was also designed to professionalize private-sector Saudi companies by forcing them to compete with international corporations, which WTO rules now allow onto Saudi territory in larger numbers. This strategy turned out to be the economic equivalent of teaching a child to swim by throwing it in the ocean, and when large numbers of Saudi companies began to slip beneath the waves, their government rescued them, renewing its commitment to state economic dominance. Why compete, many in the Saudi private sector might wonder, when we know the state will provide?

The global recession heightened Saudi risk aversion still further. As the price of oil plummeted from $147 per barrel in July 2008 to about $35 per barrel just a few months later, the Saudi government recognized that lagging economic performance might provoke social unrest. Any delay in completion of the massive and expensive state-funded social, industrial, and educational projects already under way could undermine the state's ability to ensure job creation—along with non-oil-related growth and foreign investment. At a moment when public fear of a stock market collapse and huge financial losses for local investors raised anxiety levels throughout the country, the Saudi leadership decided it could not afford to move quickly from state dominance of the economy toward a liberalized (and potentially volatile) economic model. After injecting $5 billion into struggling local banks, the government budgeted for still more economic development programs.

Whatever the near-term future of Saudi Arabia's private sector, its economy will depend on oil for the bulk of its revenue and international political leverage for many years to come. Reliance on oil means reliance on state-owned Saudi Aramco, the world's largest oil company. Aramco illustrates both the power of state capitalism in Saudi Arabia and its limits. The Saudi royals are unlikely ever to allow private ownership of "upstream" assets—those that are closest to the point at which oil is discovered and brought to the surface. But state-owned Aramco operates with much less direct interference from political officials than national oil companies in countries like Russia and Venezuela. Aramco's budget and operations are overseen by the Ministry of Petroleum and Mineral Resources and a "supreme council" chaired by the king himself. For the most part, Saudi kings have allowed Aramco officials, highly trained professionals recruited from outside the vast royal family, to draw up the company's commercial strategy and control its operations.

Aramco is not the only tool with which Saudi royals dominate the domestic economy. The Saudi Basic Industries Corporation (SABIC), another enormous state-owned company, plays a similar role in the petrochemical sector, drawing on state backing to invest in major downstream projects around the world. Outside the company, little is known about its day-to-day operations. In February 2009, SABIC abruptly announced that the global economic downturn—and the steep drop in oil prices—had forced the firm's management to freeze bonuses and promotions for about seventeen thousand employees. The move generated plenty of discussion and anxiety inside the kingdom, where the company has long been considered one of the most stable state-run enterprises. Fears that such a company might have cash problems prompted many Saudis to wonder about the government's plans for it—though the move was probably no more than a measure of global-recession-inspired caution.

Saudi Arabia also has its privately owned national champions. Beyond companies like the Olayan Group (trading and industrial infrastructure) and the Dallah Albaraka Group (media, banking, and construction), there is another family-owned, state-supported heavyweight with a familiar name. The construction and equity-management conglomerate Bin Laden Group has dominated its local competitors for decades. The families that run these companies have deep and durable ties with the Saudi royals. Other companies are owned directly by members of the family. The most successful of these is probably the Kingdom Holding Company, operated by Prince Alwaleed Bin Talal Alsaud, nephew of King Abdullah, and the man *Time* magazine has called the "Saudi Warren Buffett." Some Americans remember him as the man who presented then–New York City Mayor Rudolph Giuliani with a check for $10 million to help finance 9/11 relief efforts. Giuliani famously refused the money when Alwaleed publicly expressed hope that the United States would "reexamine its policies in the Middle East" in light of the attacks. He made news again in January 2008 when he partnered with the Singapore Government Investment Corporation (GIC) and others to provide embattled Citigroup with $12.5 billion in much-needed capital.[3]

The Saudi state directly manages the kingdom's oil revenues and sets its long-term global investment strategy. The country's assets are essentially managed by the Saudi Arabian Monetary Agency (SAMA), which acts as both the country's central bank (for regulatory purposes) and a sovereign wealth fund (for investment). It answers directly to the king. SAMA has long had a reputation as a place where less scrupulous members of the royal family plundered state assets to amass personal fortunes. Abdullah's February 2009 appointment of respected technocrat Muhammad al-Jasser as SAMA's governor may mark a significant change in management of the kingdom's financial assets, but that remains to be seen. In May 2009, the state launched the Saudi Arabia Investment Authority, Sanabil Al Saudia, a sovereign wealth fund that could become a global leader over time.

Outside the hydrocarbon sector, there is less protectionism than there used to be. Enactment of an investment law in 2000 has allowed full foreign ownership in many sectors, and foreign companies have been allowed to apply for loans and bid for government contracts. Both foreign and privately owned Saudi firms are entering multiple economic sectors in larger numbers. The king's decision to create a legal system in which commercial courts, not religious tribunals, resolve business disputes bodes well for the future of foreign investment. It wasn't always so. In 2001, the kingdom's mufti, Saudi Arabia's highest religious authority, issued a religious edict (fatwa) banning the popular children's game Pokémon on the grounds that some of its symbols promoted Judaism and Israeli interests, Christianity, and gambling. The ban hit Japanese firm Nintendo hard, depriving the company of an increasingly large youth market without any possibility of appeal. Problems with enforcement of contracts will continue without much greater transparency in Saudi Arabia, limiting foreign investment.

International investors also await the chance to invest freely in the Saudi stock market, but the 2008 financial crisis may have convinced Saudi leaders that the more connected they are to international markets, the greater their risks of economic (and political) instability. The famously low risk tolerance of senior royals and the strength of their grip on power ensure that Saudi state capitalism won't be going away any time soon.

United Arab Emirates

No Middle Eastern country has profited more handsomely as a fashionable international business destination than the United Arab Emirates (UAE), thanks mainly to the determination of powerful political officials among the various ruling families to drive and control the local and federal economies. But in at least one respect, the UAE differs sharply from other state-capitalist powerhouses: It's not a highly centralized state. Since the seven emirates established independence as a federation in 1971, each of them has maintained its right to pursue its own political and economic policies. Only the two largest—Abu Dhabi and Dubai—have the political and financial clout to dominate the UAE's governing institutions. Political and financial rivalries among the emirates and their ruling families are a constant fact of life.

Before the financial crisis, no emirate shone brighter than Dubai, where dwindling oil reserves had already forced some creative strategic thinking on the city-state's economic future. In the mid-1990s, oil accounted for about one third of Dubai's GDP. By 2009, it was believed to account for just 5 percent.[4] That shift reflects a deliberate state-directed move away from reliance on oil toward development of the emirate as a major regional business hub—with financing from wealthier Abu Dhabi. The early success of this project stoked the ruling al-Maktoum family's ambitions to promote Dubai as a global capital of international finance. Within a decade of implementing this strategy, the city-state had become a futuristic luxury tourism destination and a trendy regional base for heavyweight international companies and financial institutions. The UAE's other five emirates, which also lack Abu Dhabi's oil wealth, have followed Dubai's lead in relying on financial backing from the Abu Dhabi–dominated federal government to diversify their economies, though on a smaller scale than Dubai and with varying degrees of success. Abu Dhabi's ruling al-Nahyan family has moved much more slowly and carefully toward diversification to ensure that it doesn't undermine the regime's hold on power.

Beyond their idiosyncrasies, the seven emirates have something basic in common: To one degree or another, they're all state capitalists. Dubai has experimented on a grand scale with foreign investment and open markets without approval from Abu Dhabi, but its development has still been state driven and directed. The federation's largest corporate groups and financial institutions, whether owned by shareholders or directly by the state, are dominated by either the UAE's federal government or a member of one of the seven ruling families. Despite a heavily hyped embrace of foreign investment and free-market capitalism, the UAE remains a typical Persian Gulf monarchy. Emirati nationals, who represent just 20 percent of a population of about 5 million people made up largely of low-skilled workers from developing countries in South and Southeast Asia, accept heavily subsidized goods and services in return for political loyalty.

Dubai's colorful ruler, Sheikh Mohammed bin Rashid al-Maktoum, has taken a corporatist approach to managing his emirate. He's the hands-on proprietor of most Dubai-based large corporations and investment institutions and manages its internal affairs with no federal supervision. To promote the commercial real-estate sector, Sheikh Mohammed created companies whose only purpose was to buy homes from the real-estate-developing companies he owns. His developers reportedly sold soccer star David Beckham a lavish home at an unusually low price to attract international attention and a more high-profile clientele. (Beckham has since given the home to his in-laws.) Then there's the al-Nahyan family, led by UAE President and Emir of Abu Dhabi Sheikh Khalifa bin Zayed al-Nahyan and his half-brother Crown Prince Mohammed bin Zayed al-Nahyan. Together they dominate Abu Dhabi's business community, in part via an organization known as the UAE Offsets Group, a collection of thirty to forty men with ties to both the al-Nahyans and the UAE's largest companies and development projects. For many years, relations between the al-Maktoums of Dubai and al-Nahyans of Abu Dhabi have generated friction, competition, and rivalry.

The financial crisis and credit crunch of 2008 hit Dubai especially hard, fundamentally shifting the balance of power within the UAE toward Abu Dhabi and the al-Nahyans. As money stopped flowing into Dubai from abroad, large-scale infrastructure projects ground to a halt, shrinking the local labor force. Thousands of foreigners lost work permits in the construction sector. Thousands more, saddled with loans they could no longer repay, simply abandoned their property and left the country. By January 2009, local police complained that about three thousand cars had been abandoned at the airport. Dubai found itself buried beneath a mountain of IOUs, and for a few days in February 2009, the financial world lost faith. The emirate's credit score tanked, and foreign investors began to plan for the once unimaginable risk that Dubai would default on its sovereign debt. Dubai then announced a $20 billion bond program to raise the needed cash. In February 2009, Abu Dhabi moved in with a $10 billion bailout, underwritten by the UAE's central bank. By December 2009, Dubai was still $5 billion short, and a credit crisis involving state-owned Dubai World had markets again on edge. The al-Nahyans can't and won't provide Dubai with a blank check, but the bursting of Dubai's real-estate bubble and the sudden collapse of its economy will likely allow them to buy a larger share of the al-Maktoums' assets.

What lessons have Emirati officials taken from all this? Like a frugal parent chiding a spendthrift child, the al-Nahyans charge that Dubai's Sheikh Mohammed al-Maktoum has paid the price for betting too heavily on free-market capitalism. Abu Dhabi dominates the federal Emirati government, and state officials with ties to the al-Nahyans claim that the financial crisis, Dubai's reliance on foreign capital, and the bursting of its real-estate bubble justify the need for tighter, more prudent, and more centralized supervision of local investment decisions. They warn that the other emirates should now accept as an economic model Abu Dhabi's reliance on a huge sovereign wealth fund and its more conservative approach to development. Not surprisingly, Abu Dhabi's bailout of Dubai has generated tensions between the two ruling families, mainly over how and when the debt should be repaid.

Some of the al-Nahyans have demanded stakes in Dubai-based companies that the al-Maktoums consider the family's crown jewels. After unveiling the world's tallest skyscraper in January 2010, officials in Dubai renamed the tower for Sheikh Khalifa bin Zayed al Nahyan, Abu Dhabi's president. It's clear that the UAE as a whole will only rely more heavily on state-managed growth strategies in the years to come.

Oil will remain the federal government's best insurance against political instability and economic volatility. It creates the wealth with which the government can buy the public's loyalty and ensures that smaller emirates remain dependent on the central government in Abu Dhabi. Each of the seven emirates has its own state oil company, but the most important (by far) is the Abu Dhabi National Oil Company (ADNOC), which sits atop the world's fifth-largest oil reserves and manages the 2.7 million barrels that the emirate produces each day. ADNOC has closer links to Abu Dhabi's ruling family than Saudi Aramco has to the House of Saud. It is chaired by Abu Dhabi's Sheikh Khalifa. Unlike its Saudi counterpart, ADNOC allows foreign ownership in upstream energy projects, though it reserves the right to own up to 60 percent of any given venture. This openness to foreign investment comes not from faith in free markets but from the al-Nahyans' recognition that the company still needs access to state-of-the-art technology and technical expertise. Once they believe that ADNOC has raised its game, the state will have far fewer incentives to share profits with outsiders.

Unlike the situation in Saudi Arabia, where the Saudi Arabian Monetary Agency controls the bulk of Saudi assets, the Emirati central bank holds just $40 billion in foreign-exchange reserves. The Emirati government controls much more within opaque sovereign wealth funds like the Abu Dhabi Investment Council, the Abu Dhabi Investment Authority, and the International Petroleum Investment Company. To diversify their holdings, UAE-based funds have bought large stakes in recent years in institutions like Citigroup, HSBC (formerly Hongkong and Shanghai Banking Corporation), and Sony.

Most of these investments took a significant hit during the recent collapse in global equities during 2008 and 2009, and the political firestorm that erupted in Washington when state-owned Dubai Ports World tried to win the right to manage several U.S. ports in 2006 still stings. But the ruling families have placed a long-term bet on global economic recovery, and their sovereign wealth funds will likely remain powerful players in international equity markets for the foreseeable future.

The UAE's private sector is dominated so heavily by companies owned directly by various members of the seven families that the concept of national champions doesn't really apply. These firms exist to further family business interests, not the UAE's international political leverage. Abu Dhabi's crown prince controls Mubadala Development Company and Aldar—firms that with their subsidiaries own a combined $40 billion in assets. Dubai's emir owns names like Nakheel, Emaar, and Dubai World, which generated an estimated $50 billion in combined annual revenue before the onset of the global recession. When foreign investors bid for big government procurement contracts, they can expect that these local heavyweights will have every advantage the ruling families can afford to give them.

It's not all bad news for foreign investors. The UAE has set up a number of free-trade zones where profits are plentiful—though outside these enclaves at least 51 percent of any business must be owned by an Emirati citizen, group, or institution. The in-country distribution of imported goods must be conducted through an Emirati partner, but there are no controls on access to foreign currency or the transfer of profits across borders. To attract more foreign investment, there has even been talk of legal reforms that would allow foreigners a fair hearing on commercial disputes. Dubai's International Arbitration Center has already become one of the leading institutions of its kind in the region.

The global financial meltdown has made it more politically palatable within the UAE for members of the al-Nahyan family to expand their authority over the other emirates and to ensure a more centralized political and financial decision-making process. The risk is obvious that the UAE will become more authoritarian, more secretive, and more willing to rely on state capitalism for future growth. In early 2009, the UAE's Federal National Council, an advisory board, approved a proposal to slap fines of up to $272,250 on journalists and media outlets that criticize the head of state, the seven royal families, or their deputies.[5] As initially drafted, the new law would force media organizations to post a security deposit from which fines for future infractions could be taken. And if you live within the UAE and want your own copy of Christopher Davidson's *Dubai: The Vulnerability of Success,* or *Abu Dhabi: Oil and Beyond,* you'll have to leave the country to find it.[6]

Egypt

State capitalism extends well beyond the Gulf monarchies into other parts of the Arab world, though some of them have taken concrete steps toward genuine market reform. Government dominance of the domestic economy has deep roots in Egypt, where political officials have been managing (often mismanaging) development since the revolution that deposed King Farouk I in 1952 and elevated Gamal Abdel Nasser. Formally elected president in 1956, Nasser and his supporters committed themselves to socialist principles and built an enormous state bureaucracy to implement their plans. How enormous? Nasser promised government jobs for every Egyptian who graduated from college—a law that's still on the books. Since President Hosni Mubarak inherited power from the assassinated Anwar Sadat in 1981, economic liberalization has advanced in fits and starts, sometimes under direct pressure from the International Monetary Fund.

But in the summer of 2004, things began to change. Mubarak appointed Egypt's first technocratic government, led by Prime Minister Ahmed Nazif. With Finance Minister Youssef Boutros-Ghali and the head of the newly created investment ministry, Mahmoud Mohieldin, allies of Mubarak's market-friendly son Gamal began reshaping Egypt's economic policies. Gamal Mubarak, a senior member of the ruling National Democratic Party who is considered likely to succeed his father, gained insight into market operations as an investment banker with Bank of America. In short, for the first time since 1952, those in charge of crafting economic policy in Egypt are ideologically committed to market liberalization. Hosni Mubarak is still the country's ultimate decision maker, but reform advocates have real space in which to craft policy.

Under their direction, the Egyptian government has begun to sell off major state assets. In 2002, foreign direct investment in the country remained at about $500 million. By 2008, that figure pushed past $13 billion. In 2006, an Italian bank[*] was allowed to buy 80 percent of the Bank of Alexandria, making it the first state-owned financial institution to be privatized. The regime has since adopted a more market-friendly approach to regulation, cut corporate taxes, and streamlined investment policies.

Crucially, since the onset of the financial crisis, Egyptian authorities have reaffirmed their commitment to free-market policies. As global recession took hold in 2009, Mubarak chose not to fire anyone within the economic team, a decision interpreted by investors inside and outside the country as a vote of confidence in reform. The state did pass a nearly $3 billion stimulus package in early 2009 and a budget that sharply raised the deficit. But senior officials claim the country will weather the crisis, saying that when the global economy bounces back, Egypt will again see high growth and investment. The country has a number of national oil and gas companies, but they aren't becoming more dominant within the domestic energy sector, and the government hasn't interfered in bids to attract energy investment from abroad. State

---

[*] Sanpaolo IMI, later Banca Intesa.

officials have announced that they mean to reform the huge and un-wieldy Egyptian General Petroleum Company.

Orascom Group leads the way among Egypt's national champions. Orascom Telecom, the most successful within the group, has become a highly profitable multinational company with interests around the world. Though the Sawiris family, which owns the largest stake in the group, enjoys close ties with the government, authorities have not un-dermined the company's major domestic competitors. Mobinil, Oras-com's mobile network, was the first in Egypt, but the government has awarded licenses to two of the company's commercial rivals in recent years. There are certainly direct links between business and politics in the country. Ahmed Ezz, a member of parliament, key player within the ruling NDP, and close friend of Gamal Mubarak, is also the biggest shareholder in Ezz Steel, the largest steel producer in the Middle East and North Africa.

The Egyptian economy navigated the global recession relatively well, largely because its trade ties with the outside world remain rela-tively weak, giving it little exposure to the slowdown in Europe and America. But if future market volatility generates large-scale social un-rest, as it did briefly during a bout of global food inflation in 2008, Hosni Mubarak has both the power and the personal inclination to tighten the state's grip on Egypt's economic development. When it comes to reform, the president lacks his son's risk tolerance, and market-friendly government ministers have no popular support base of their own. For the moment, Egypt is moving cautiously from state dominance of the economy toward a tentative embrace of free markets.

Algeria

Not so in Algeria, where the state's grip on economic policy is tighter than ever. Since winning independence from France in 1962, Algeria's government has dominated its economy, directing economic policy via Soviet-style five-year plans. The country's political leadership trumpets its refusal to embrace globalization as a mark of discipline, a symbol of integrity, and a badge of honor—seizing on the global recession as vindication of its wisdom. This statist tradition is driven by two publicly popular commitments. First, the regime claims its embrace of socialism reflects its determination to promote social justice. Second, the state pledges never to leave the people of Algeria at the mercy of predatory foreign investors. President Abdelaziz Bouteflika loosened state control of the oil and gas, telecom, and real-estate sectors between 2002 and 2005, because he saw opportunities to grow the economy beyond hydrocarbons. But as he embarked on the politically risky path of abolishing constitutional term limits to give himself an opportunity to serve a third presidential term, he reverted to a state-dominated approach. With ample revenue from oil and gas exports to support weak state industries that employ lots of Algerians, Bouteflika did not want to risk introducing private-sector competition.

Algeria features more than one thousand state-owned companies, firms that produce everything from ceramics to mattresses. The largest and best known is energy giant Sonatrach, Africa's largest company and Europe's second-largest supplier of natural gas. Sonatrach is officially run by a technocratic CEO, but real authority over its operations remains with political officials loyal to Bouteflika. Even a partial privatization of Sonatrach has become unthinkable, because without this state-owned corporate giant, none of the hundreds of unprofitable state-run enterprises could continue to pay their workers. In 2002, it appeared Sonatrach might share more of the domestic energy sector with foreign companies to boost oil and gas production, which was starting to reach a plateau. But since 2006, it has become more difficult than ever for foreign companies to operate in Algeria. The state has increased taxes on oil production and now requires foreign firms to partner with local companies. When awarding contracts, it favors foreigners willing to do business with Sonatrach on Sonatrach's terms, without much regard for the commercial merits of a particular bid. Strengthening the state giant is vitally important, because it employs 120,000 people, and its labor union carries considerable clout.

Algeria has just one private-sector national champion, the agro-industrial firm Cevital, which profits from the full range of food manufacturing and distribution from farms to store shelves. Cevital has no formal ties to the state. Its CEO, Issad Rebrab, owns an influential French-language newspaper that retains a reputation for independence without falling afoul of the government. The company has built its dominant market position by buying land from the state for agricultural production. Following Algeria's declaration of independence in 1962, all land owned by French colonists reverted to the state, providing the new government with enormous domestic economic leverage. Confusion over land rights has stunted the growth of Algeria's private sector, because the process of securing land for factory construction, agricultural production, and other commercial uses is often held hostage to the vagaries of an absurdly bloated bureaucracy and political infighting fueled by corruption. Making matters still more complicated, nearly half a century after large numbers of French citizens fled the country after independence, it's often unclear who owns the land they abandoned. French retailer Carrefour has canceled plans to open supermarkets in Algeria, because it hasn't been able to secure land rights that it believes would stand a legal challenge or political test. Cevital, in particular, would use its considerable influence within government to oust the foreign company.

Foreign investment in Algeria slowed to a trickle in 2009 following measures introduced by Prime Minister Ahmed Ouyahia that limit the independence of foreign companies and make it difficult for them to take profits out of the country. Some of these companies fled Algeria altogether when the government abruptly approved legislation that forced them to give a larger share of profits to local partners. Here as in other state-capitalist countries, the Algerian government is allowing a few state-owned and state-dependent companies to flourish to continually strengthen its hold on domestic political power.

For some of the countries emerging from the shadow of communism, state capitalism may prove a step along the path toward free markets. But for those that have yet to enjoy the European Union's welcoming embrace, the journey could be a long one. Then again, state dominance of their domestic economies may prove less a passing phase than a modern reconfiguration of an authoritarian past.

Ukraine

Nearly two decades after escaping the Soviet Union, Ukraine's political leadership pledges to promote free markets in the country, and its ambition to one day win Ukraine a place in the European Union reflects a commitment to economic liberalization. There are two large caveats. First, that's a long-term project. The state still maintains a heavy presence in sectors it considers crucial to national security and economic development—like oil and gas, agriculture, and transport. State-owned companies are usually managed by industry professionals, not political appointees, but government officials don't always resist the temptation to interfere in their commercial decisions. Progress has been slow on the privatization of some of the larger remaining state-owned assets. Second, Ukraine's politics are so dysfunctional that it's hard to predict what attitude political officials might take to these questions five years from now, particularly if elections oust the current government—and if neighboring Russia, which already casts a long shadow over Ukraine's politics, increases its influence.

As in any country still struggling to build a dynamic economy from the ashes of communism, it's much easier to promise reform than to deliver it. The privatization of large state-owned enterprises can put large numbers of people out of work, leaving elected officials vulnerable to populist attacks from political rivals. The drafting of laws and regulations intended to promote economic growth and protect the fairness of market operations is subject to all kinds of pressures from powerful vested interests. Enforcement of regulations can be arbitrary. The judicial system remains vulnerable to coercion from both the political and business elites, and corruption is a constant problem. Ukraine faces all these challenges.

The current government assumed power in 2005 following the so-called Orange Revolution, which upended a bid by outgoing president Leonid Kuchma and Russian-backed candidate Viktor Yanukovych to rig a presidential election and elevated Viktor Yushchenko, who pledged to bring Ukraine closer to Europe and Western institutions. Yushchenko became president and Yulia Tymoshenko was chosen prime minister. Both have encouraged foreign investment and pursued ambitious privatization plans, most notably when multinational giant ArcelorMittal was allowed to buy the country's largest steel works in 2005.

But to protect the country's independence from the powerful and predatory energy producer next door, Ukraine's political leadership relies on state control of the domestic energy sector. No company better illustrates the willingness of supposedly promarket Ukrainian politicians to use a market player for power politics than Naftohaz Ukrainy, the fully state-owned oil and gas firm. It's a weak company, especially since a fight with Russia in 2006 stripped it of some of its best customers. Yet Ukraine's government sees Naftohaz as "too useful to fail." It has a clear interest in maintaining control of the company and in returning it to profitability by helping it repay foreign debts and providing it a lead role in oil and gas exploration in Ukraine's portion of the Black Sea. Though Tymoshenko claims to welcome foreign investment, even in the energy sector, her government canceled offshore exploration and production licenses in 2008 that had been awarded to American and British companies. To justify the move, she claimed the original deal had been negotiated on unfair terms and criticized the involvement of Russian companies. Some suspect she also wanted to destroy a deal that benefitted Rinat Akhmetov, a political rival.

The state owns all agricultural land, though lots can be leased for farming. The state holds majority ownership stakes in railroads, telecommunications, electricity, chemicals, heavy machinery, and civil aviation (via Ukraine International Airlines). The government, which badly needs the cash, promises to fully privatize all of them, but political infighting has repeatedly delayed the process, in part because the businessmen profiting from the current system lean heavily on their political contacts to oppose any market liberalization that might create more domestic and foreign competition.

These businessmen exert a powerful influence on state economic policy. Akhmetov's name appears often in discussions of Ukraine's domestic politics, because he's arguably the most influential among a group of conspicuously wealthy businessmen who control major assets in important sectors of the economy, thanks to close personal and commercial ties with some of the country's most powerful political leaders. Akhmetov controls steel, power generation, and coal-mining assets. He is a powerful and popular figure in the country's mainly Russian-speaking eastern provinces and a major supporter of the opposition, antireformist Regions of Ukraine party. He's also one of several Ukrainian oligarchs who have used their financial clout to win seats in parliament. Tymoshenko, who was successful in the gas-trading business before entering politics, became prime minister in part by pledging to sever the close ties between the political and business elites. That hasn't happened, and some of her critics charge that she relies on key oligarchs for support. Their privileged positions come without the obligations to serve state interests that Vladimir Putin has imposed on Russia's oligarchs, mainly because no Ukrainian politician has the muscle to exercise Putin-scale market intervention.

But Russia's gravitational pull is still there and provides a strong countermodel for Ukraine's economic management. There are still influential communists and other left-leaning politicians within the country who push for greater state involvement in the economy, including the outright nationalization of assets. Russia's recent experience reveals how the rise of a strong leader within a weak political system can shift the country's policies from a loosely free-market-based system to one of heavy state intervention. Until Ukraine develops new strength and self-confidence, it will remain vulnerable to Russia's state-capitalist influence.

Russia

Imagine you're a senior executive at X5 group, Russia's largest retail food chain. Hard at work in your office, you're informed that, for reasons unknown, Prime Minister Vladimir Putin wants to talk to you. With television cameras recording your every gesture, you find yourself walking alongside Russia's most powerful man for a surprise inspection of the meat counter at one of your neighborhood supermarkets, where he informs you that you charge too much for pork. You assure him that prices will soon be slashed. Unimpressed, Putin heads for the dairy aisle. This was the fate that awaited Yuri Kobaladze as he arrived for work on June 24, 2009. The next day, X5 announced a "grand sale," with steep discounts on all sorts of things. Four days later, Russia's Federal Anti-Monopoly Agency announced an investigation into price collusion between retail chains and distributors in a number of product categories.

No story better illustrates Russian-style state capitalism, which combines a drive to manage the performance of markets with a habit of deflecting blame onto available scapegoats when things go badly. The Kremlin relies on both direct government intervention in key sectors of the Russian economy and control of politically connected businessmen to further the political and commercial interests of the Russian state and those who run it. That said, Russia's political leaders have no interest in a return to Soviet-style central economic planning. As president from 2000 to 2008, Putin was the chief architect of his country's current political and economic structure. Now prime minister, he has repeatedly affirmed his conviction that only capitalism—in this case, state capitalism—can generate prosperity in Russia and restore the country to great-power status.

State capitalism in Russia has come a long way in a short time. During its chaotic first post-Soviet decade, the weakness of Boris Yeltsin's government left it at the mercy of grasping oligarchs, who offered him financial and other forms of support in exchange for the chance to buy valuable national resources and other assets at bargain-basement prices. In its second decade, the balance of power shifted back to the state as surging economic growth, fueled (largely but not exclusively) by a sharp spike in oil prices, allowed Vladimir Putin to corner the oligarchs, to expand state control over many of their assets, and to use them to advance his domestic political agenda and Russia's international interests. Nowhere is the expansion of state power more obvious than in the energy sector.

Russia's political elite now practices a concentrated form of resource nationalism, treating the country's vast oil and gas reserves as tools that can help protect its financial and political independence and project Russian power abroad. Gazprom accounts for nearly 90 percent of Russia's gas production. Though the state still controlled the company's management and cash flows when Putin was first elected president in 2000, the government's direct stake in Gazprom had fallen below 50 percent. By the time Putin passed the presidency to chosen successor Dmitry Medvedev eight years later and assumed the role of prime minister, Gazprom was again in state hands and held an official monopoly on gas exports. During the Putin presidency, the state expanded its control of Russia's enormous oil output from less than 10 percent to nearly 50 percent.

Since 2003, the Russian government has applied legal and regulatory pressure on both foreign and domestic energy companies to push Gazprom and state oil champion Rosneft into dominant positions in the country's energy sector. In the process, Putin's government used regulatory harassment to force foreign companies to surrender control of valuable projects. It also dismantled an emerging domestic giant, the Yukos Oil Company, when its president, Mikhail Khodorkovsky, made plans to build an independent pipeline to China, moved to merge with a foreign oil company, and began to chart an independent political course. But the state-capitalist trend was hardly limited to oil and gas. In aerospace, shipbuilding, arms exports, civilian nuclear power, and other advanced technology sectors, the Kremlin has created new state-controlled holding companies and a special category of quasi-sovereign state corporations to tighten the government's grip on them and to produce revenue for the officials who control them.

There is plenty of overlap between political and economic elites in many countries, but Russia is an extreme case. Before becoming Russia's president, Dmitry Medvedev served simultaneously as first deputy prime minister and Gazprom's chairman. When he left to succeed Putin as president, he was replaced at Gazprom by then–Prime Minister Viktor Zubkov. Current Prime Minister Putin is now chairman of state development bank Vnesheconombank (VEB), one of the state's most important tools in managing the fallout from the financial crisis. Deputy Prime Minister Igor Sechin, a key Putin aide and reputed architect of the attack on Yukos, is chairman of state oil company Rosneft. Deputy Prime Minister Sergei Ivanov chairs the board of state-controlled Unified Aircraft Company, and Finance Minister Alexei Kudrin doubles as chairman of Alrosa, the world's second-largest diamond producer. Sergei Chemezov, who heads the rapidly expanding state corporation Russian Technologies, and Vladimir Yakunin, who chairs the Russian Railways monopoly, are friends and former KGB colleagues of Putin's. Alexander Voloshin has moved from Kremlin chief of staff to chairman of former state electricity monopoly RAO UES to chairman of Norilsk Nickel, a company that controls one fifth of the world's nickel (vital for steel and auto production) and half its palladium. Before serving as Norilsk's CEO, Vladimir Strzhalkovsky, a former state security agent, headed the state tourism agency.

Beyond the informal ties, the state's expanded control of Russia's economy was codified in a 2008 law that identified forty-two "strategic" economic sectors in which restrictions applied for foreign investment. To buy sizable stakes in Russian companies in these sectors, foreign investors must have approval from a prime-ministerial commission. The rules are especially stringent for nearly any valuable resource that must be pulled from the ground. Without special approval, no foreign investor can hold more than a 10 percent stake in any Russian company that controls a field containing more than 70 million tons of oil, 50 billion cubic meters of gas, 1.6 million ounces of gold, or 500,000 tons of copper. Fields containing other rare or military-use minerals are also restricted.

Aware that the state can't micromanage the development of every economic sector and that consumer demand is best fueled by free markets, Russia's political elite allows many large segments of the domestic economy to remain relatively open for private (including foreign) investment. Consumer-driven sectors like retail, construction, real estate, automotive, and wireless telecoms are mostly free of direct political interference. In many cases, political officials have found, it's better to control those who run a company than to accept direct and public responsibility for its performance.

Political officials and the oligarchs clearly serve one another's interests, though in the Putin era, the state's needs will always come first.

During the first months of his presidency, Putin gathered most of the oligarchs and outlined Russia's new rules of the road. The state would allow those who played by these rules to keep the wealth they had amassed (under often murky circumstances) and support their business activities at home and abroad. In return, the oligarchs were to steer clear of any independent role in Russian politics and, whenever necessary, to subordinate their interests to those of the state. Oligarchs who refused to accept this new arrangement fled into exile or came under direct attack from Russia's security services, tax police, and other instruments of state power. But most of them have abided by the informal agreement, because the rewards of accepting state dominance are considerable. Not only have Russian government officials allowed these men and women to remain wealthy, they have used the state's political leverage to help them win telecom, energy, and manufacturing contracts in the Middle East, Europe, Asia, and the Americas.

To prove their loyalty, some of the oligarchs have put their financial muscle behind community development projects in regions hit hard by Russia's economic slowdown and have pledged to invest in state-supported ventures they know will lose money—like construction for the 2014 Winter Olympics in the Russian resort town of Sochi. Russian companies, especially those owned directly or indirectly by the oligarchs, are expected to do all they can to protect jobs to avoid the sorts of public protests that can damage a government's popularity. As the economic crisis swept through the country's metals, mining, and manufacturing towns in 2008 and 2009, companies cut work schedules, slashed salaries, and pushed older workers into early retirement or younger ones into make-work jobs as part of "social responsibility" projects meant to prevent social unrest before it started.

Oligarchs who missed the message came in for rough treatment. In June 2009, just days before he went grocery shopping with Yuri Kobaladze, Prime Minister Putin helicoptered to the beleaguered town of Pikalyovo, about 150 miles southeast of St. Petersburg, to persuade oligarch Oleg Deripaska to reopen a cement plant he had temporarily closed to cut costs. Laid-off workers had captured the Kremlin's attention by barricading a federal highway in protest, and Putin arrived to berate Deripaska and other local business leaders for their failure to protect local jobs. With TV cameras rolling, Putin tossed a pen at Deripaska and ordered him to sign an agreement that would reopen the factory and pay his employees the same day. Deripaska signed, Putin took back his pen, and workers were immediately paid with cash that the government had already transferred into the company's state bank account to ensure that Putin's exit produced the desired theatrical effect.

This is a dangerously expensive show, because there's a risk that the state is creating a precedent. Allowing oligarchs to manage large companies helps the Russian government practice state capitalism without accepting direct blame when workers lose their jobs. On the other hand, a government struggling to stop the bleeding when a poorly diversified economy takes a large hit—as Russia did in 2009—must hoard as much cash as it can. The surge in oil prices between 2003 and 2008 helped Russia build a stockpile of foreign reserves estimated at $600 billion, an enormous war chest, but the urgent need to defend the value of the ruble and to help Russian companies pay their foreign debts reduced that amount by one third in the final four months of 2008 alone. By playing the role of superhero and bailing out the workers of Pikalyovo, Putin has invited the employees of other floundering companies to stir up enough trouble to again bring his helicopter to the rescue.

That's not the only example of the dysfunction that can plague a state-capitalist government when things go wrong. As the Russian economy failed to quickly respond to state attempts at artificial resuscitation, the government responded with political arm-twisting to force banks to extend more loans. Putin has dictated "acceptable" lending rates to banks and warned bank executives not to take vacations until they loaned out all the state funds they had been given. At the same time, the Russian government was warning banks to guard against the growth of bad loans. In 2009, Russian banks took legal action against large numbers of borrowers who had defaulted on loans, but they did it knowing that forcing a business that employs large numbers of people into bankruptcy might spur public protests and draw an unfriendly visit from the prime minister.

Russian-style state capitalism can also create confusion among private shareholders. In July 2008, Putin accused Igor Zyuzin, head of the publicly traded Mechel steel company, of tax evasion. Assuming that Putin was preparing the ground for more drastic action against the company, investors quickly began unloading Mechel shares. The company lost half its value in a matter of days. But the state never intended to take Mechel apart. In advance of an expected surge in government spending on infrastructure projects, Putin intimidated coal and steel producers to lower the price of construction materials. He generated turmoil in equity markets, but he accomplished his political goal.

Then there's the risk for foreign companies. With a drop in global demand for steel in 2009, international giant ArcelorMittal was considering scaling back production and laying off workers from some of the coal mines it operates in the area around Kemerovo province in central Russia. On July 9, Kemerovo Governor Aman Tuleyev sent the company a telegram to inform its leadership that the company would keep the mines open, at a financial loss if necessary, or "hand them over without compensation."[7]

Here again, political leaders needed a scapegoat. Sometimes, it's a bewildered grocery-store executive. At other times, it might be a regional governor like Tuleyev. But if that local official is fast on his feet, blame might fall instead on the faceless foreign company that's about to lay off workers. Given the financial stakes involved—ArcelorMittal is the world's largest steel maker—Tuleyev might well have had prior approval from Moscow. After all, Russia's regional governors are hand-selected by Russia's president, not elected by local voters.

Kremlin officials know they must protect what's left of the country's badly damaged reputation as an investment destination. Threatening a multinational heavyweight with expropriation of valuable assets unless it's willing to operate at a loss is a poor way of doing that. But the Russian political leadership had a more immediate problem: Hundreds of workers were about to lose their jobs. Russia's federal government can't afford to bail out every struggling local company, as Putin did in Pikalyovo. Allowing Tuleyev to play the heavy, Moscow could withhold comment, and Tuleyev could score points with workers in his district. This is the injection of politics into what would otherwise be a market decision, and foreign investors in any industry that employs large numbers of Russian workers will have to think twice before putting money on the table.

The state also works to ensure social stability by managing price fluctuations. In June 2009, the Russian government enacted a plan to establish price controls for "socially important" food products, but only in an "emergency." This program illustrates that difference between Soviet-style command economics and Russian-style state capitalism. In announcing the plan, senior Russian officials were adamant that it would not include strict price controls. Yet it's the government, not the market, that determines which products are socially important and what exactly constitutes an emergency.

There are also times when the state has to crack down on citizens themselves. In December 2008, the government decided to protect Russia's struggling domestic automakers—and the more than 1.5 million workers they employ—by sharply increasing tariffs on imported used cars. The move triggered surprisingly large demonstrations in Russia's Far East, where thousands of local businessmen and workers make their living via the import of used Japanese cars and parts. Rattled by the size and intensity of the protests fed by local communists, the Kremlin increased subsidies to encourage consumers to "buy Russian"—and flew specially trained riot police nine hours from Moscow to Vladivostok to quell the unrest. The confrontation turned violent, sparking protests elsewhere in Russia. Though demonstrations continued for several weeks, the government did not back down.

President Medvedev has signaled on several occasions that state dominance of Russia's economy is simply a stage in its economic development. But its political leaders are unlikely to empower the independent governing institutions needed for substantial free-market reform anytime soon. Under Putin, Russia had a strong president, but it was the man, not the office, that commanded respect—and not much has changed since he traded his old job for a new one. That's not a strong foundation on which to build the corporate culture, rule of law, and freedom of speech that enable markets to grow and mature. The global economic crisis made things worse by playing on Russian fear of chaos and heightening the state's risk aversion. After the creation of so many enormously powerful political and economic stakeholders, dismantling the current order would produce the kind of internal conflict that the Kremlin desperately wants to avoid. As long as oil prices are high enough to finance Russian state capitalism, the country will remain stable, but a lasting economic slowdown could force a day of political reckoning.

Almost all the countries profiled so far have some form of authoritarian government. But some democratic governments also use state-capitalist tools to achieve political goals.

India

It has become conventional wisdom that from independence in 1947 until at least the late 1980s, India's economic policy reflected the statist personal views of prime ministers Jawaharlal Nehru and his daughter, Indira Gandhi. During that time, successive governments enforced state dominance of many economic sectors, rigid market regulation, and laws that protected local companies from foreign competition. But in 1991, an Indian government facing financial crisis embraced free-market reform as a matter of political survival. It began breaking up state monopolies and unshackling India's private sector, welcoming unprecedented levels of trade and foreign investment. In recent years, market reformers have begun freeing the country's entrepreneurs to drive India toward a future as an economic powerhouse.

There's a lot of truth in this historical simplification, but India remains poised between the state-dominated economic model of an earlier era and one driven by private enterprise. There are three main reasons why India's government continues to resist a full embrace of free-market capitalism. First, few Indian politicians will say publicly that free markets produce faster growth. Second, India's poorest citizens vote in unusually large numbers, and state officials fear the price these voters will exact if government imposes long-term reforms that inflict near-term pain. Third, true state dominance is a tough habit to break—particularly when it's the state that must break it. Indian governments have liberalized the country's industrial and trade policies over the past twenty years to make life easier for large Indian companies, but officials explain these plans in different ways to different audiences. There is now more confidence within the leadership that markets sometimes deliver where the state cannot, and that has triggered a genuine debate within society over how best to fight poverty and spur development. With the 2009 elections, India's Communist Party, a major obstacle to reform in recent years, won its smallest vote percentage since 1952. But that debate is not yet won, and it will always be politically safer to avoid serious discussion of cuts in state subsidies or the reform of dysfunctional social-welfare programs. The strength of the Congress Party–led government's commitment to any particular plan is tested each week with the release of new economic statistics and political opinion polls.

India's government still organizes economic policy according to five-year plans that are created, implemented, and monitored by a state planning commission chaired by the prime minister. State involvement in some sectors remains high, particularly when it comes to politically sensitive products like food, fuel, fertilizer, electricity, and water. Subsidies are useful, because they allow the government to manipulate prices for political reasons. But they also cost state-owned enterprises in these sectors large amounts of money, and state budgets take a considerable hit. That's why the Indian government has forced state-owned companies to compete with privately owned rivals in sectors like oil and gas, airlines, power, metals, and defense. Privatizing state-owned firms offers trade unions and rival parties a chance to score political points at the government's expense. It's safer to simply remove their advantages and force them to adapt.

This may be the long road to reform, but it has begun to pay dividends. Privately owned companies now play a much larger role than they used to in generating wealth. In the mid-1980s, the public sector accounted for more than half of investment. By 2008, this figure had fallen to less than 25 percent. In addition, state-owned Indian companies now tend to be run by former state officials chosen for their managerial ability, not political cronies handpicked for their loyalty.

The state still owns more than half of India's forty largest companies and more than two hundred firms in total. Local governments throughout the country own a thousand more. Some of these companies dominate their respective sectors, and their total contribution to national GDP has fallen only slightly in recent years, from 17.5 percent in 1994 to 13 percent in 2007.[8] The largest of them is Indian Railways, with 1.4 million employees. But India's entrepreneurial energies have changed things, even inside this state-owned giant. A 2009 report from the Organisation for Economic Co-operation and Development (OECD) lauded its success: "From a loss making and heavily subsidized enterprise, it has become one of the relatively few state-owned railway systems in the world generating sufficient earnings not only to meet operational and capital costs, but also to undertake a large modernization program while contributing to the public purse."[9] Eighteen state-owned companies (with operations in power, steel, oil and gas, and telecoms) have been awarded the title *navratna*, literally "nine precious jewels,"* giving them a degree of financial and managerial autonomy that other state-owned firms don't have. These companies are free, for example, to partner with privately owned firms in joint ventures and to bid for overseas business. This freedom is designed to allow a company like Oil and Natural Gas Corporation (ONGC) to compete more effectively with Chinese state-owned enterprises in Russia, Kazakhstan, or Nigeria.

If India's political system complicates liberalization, it also makes it impossible to fully pursue state capitalism. Russian and Chinese leaders care very much about the state's ability to provide for its people, but they don't answer directly to voters. India's political leadership is too busy improvising its way toward the next election to develop a coherent state approach to economic development, and local governments have more than enough political muscle to deny federal officials access to that much economic power. In fact, these factors limit state capitalism's ability to take root within any truly representative democracy. However tentative the reform process, the state's hand in strategic sectors of the domestic economy represents nothing like the ambitious and lavishly financed state capitalism found in China. India's government runs large budget deficits even in good times. It has enough money to help state-owned companies roll over their debts or to share the burden of losses from subsidies, but it can't provide them with the enormous sums available to their Chinese counterparts.

India hasn't fully embraced globalization; foreign trade still accounts for just 25 percent of GDP, among the lowest levels of any of the world's largest economies. The state continues to use state-owned com-

---

* They were called *navratna* because there were originally just nine such companies.

panies to wield heavy influence in strategically important political sectors. But over the past two decades, India's entrepreneurs and its small and medium-size businesses have demonstrated a level of dynamism and strength that the Indian government couldn't suppress—even if it wanted to.

Africa

State capitalism also plays a role in some of Africa's largest developing democracies. In South Africa, the African National Congress (ANC)–led government uses elements of state capitalism to try to right centuries of historical wrongs and to preserve the ruling party's political capital as endemic social and economic problems fail to improve at a fast-enough pace. The ANC didn't invent South African state capitalism. During the apartheid era, increasingly isolated white governments found global markets closed to them and were forced to rely on direct management of many aspects of a resource-rich domestic economy. The oil crisis of the mid-1970s and growing international criticism of apartheid forced the country toward deeper self-reliance and active state promotion of companies like Eskom (the state-owned power utility), Iscor (a steel producer), and Sasol (a developer of coal-to-fuel technology).

With the end of apartheid in 1994, Nelson Mandela's government took up the challenge of reversing decades of institutional racism and its impact on an undereducated, underemployed black majority. Knowing that South Africa's new government needed to avoid large-scale capital flight, Mandela worked to persuade white businessmen and landowners to remain in the country and to create favorable terms to attract foreign investment. At the same time, his government's first major policy document, the 1994 Reconstruction and Development Program, called for stimulating growth through redistribution of wealth, a plan that included an ambitious social-welfare program. In 1996, as investors lost confidence in a still-stagnant economy, the plan was replaced with the more market-friendly Growth, Employment, and Redistribution (GEAR) program. GEAR proposed ideas designed to reduce the government's fiscal deficit, relax currency-exchange controls, and lower tariffs on imports.

But in recent years, the government has tried to address chronic development problems by spending much more on education, water, sanitation, and welfare grants. To narrow the wealth gap between white and black South Africans and to create a black middle class, it instituted a Black Economic Empowerment program, which supporters call a growth strategy and detractors label affirmative action. According to the program, all companies are required to comply with specific targets on black ownership, procurement, and employment equity.[*] Many government tenders give preferential treatment to BEE-compliant firms. In 2004, it scrapped plans to privatize state-owned companies like Eskom and decided instead to use them to help generate stronger growth. More recently, the government, unions, and even the business community, disappointed that its embrace of free markets at the expense of more focused state efforts to alleviate poverty and improve living standards has managed only mediocre growth rates, have begun to turn toward Asia's state capitalists as a model for development. That's an unrealistic plan. South Africa's ruling party has much less domestic political power and many more checks on its ability to direct investment and growth than China's Communist Party, and South Africa's relatively unskilled and poorly educated workforce is a long way from competing with its Chinese counterpart. But these factors haven't kept some within the ANC from charting a more state-capitalist course.

In June 2007, delegates to the ANC national policy conference publicly embraced the idea that the state, not the invisible hand, should play the primary guiding role in the economy. The ANC government,

---

[*]   According to South African law, the word *black* includes South African citizens who are Chinese, Indian, or of mixed race.

it said, should stimulate economic development, by "directly investing in underdeveloped areas and directing private sector investment." The resolution also called for construction of an "effective, democratic, and developmental state," which will "intervene in the interest of the people as a whole." Central to this plan is continuation of a state-led infrastructure investment program.

The financial crisis and global recession pushed the government further in this direction, encouraging efforts to prop up failing industries and to prevent the loss of huge numbers of jobs—particularly among black citizens, who still suffer an unemployment rate of about 30 percent. South Africa remains a relatively open economy and receptive to foreign investment. The legal system is independent, and foreign investors can expect a fair hearing in the country's courts. But though radical policy changes are unlikely, President Jacob Zuma and the ANC leadership have emphasized industrial policy as a cornerstone of the new administration. Zuma's political allies within South Africa's Communist Party and the Congress of South African Trade Unions insist that it's time to put workers first if the country's wounds are to finally heal.

Nigeria's government uses state-capitalist tools to preserve a delicate balance between majority Muslim northern provinces and the Christian-dominated south. Oil was first discovered in the marshlands of the Niger Delta along the country's southern coast in the 1950s. But when the country gained independence from Britain in 1960, its federal government was relatively small, individual provinces had greater autonomy, and farming still dominated the national economy. A civil war in the late 1960s dramatically expanded the power of the state. In 1971, Nigeria became a member of OPEC, and the dramatic rise in oil prices in the years that followed allowed its central government to essentially bribe provincial governments into submission with payments from the proceeds of oil exports.

Today, Nigeria is one of the world's ten largest oil producers and a key supplier to the United States. The poorer Muslim provinces continue to depend on monthly cash transfers from oil production in the Delta region. The service-based economy of the southern provinces also depends heavily on the energy sector. The federal government, grown fat from decades of profits generated by the state-owned Nigerian National Petroleum Corporation (NNPC) and taxes levied on foreign energy companies, largely controls the national purse. This massive state effort to keep the peace by redistributing wealth has fueled militancy in the Delta, where armed gangs, angry over the diversion of oil profits to other parts of the country, have launched attacks on foreign oil companies, government troops, and oil infrastructure—shutting in up to 30 percent of Nigeria's peak output. In 2003, governments in the Delta began receiving a 13 percent share of oil revenues before the rest was divided among states, but local corruption ensures that little of this money is invested in improving the lives of the people who live in the area, and the militant attacks that threaten to strangle the central government's cash cow have only intensified.

Elements of state capitalism also distort the politics and economies of a diverse range of countries in Latin America, a region that has been through enough booms and busts to believe in both the power of free markets to generate long-term growth and the need for a strong state to limit the damage when things go badly. From state-driven systems like those in Venezuela, Ecuador, Bolivia, and even Argentina, governments have created tools that allow them to dominate certain markets for political purposes. In fact, government can control a key economic sector even in relatively market-friendly Mexico.

Mexico

The one significant element of state capitalism in Mexico—and it's a big one—is Petróleos Mexicanos (Pemex), the country's state-owned oil company. Pemex, which ranked thirty-first on the 2009 Forbes Global 500 list of top companies by revenue, holds a monopoly on all upstream and most downstream operations.[10] The company's privileged position has everything to do with how it was created. In 1938, foreign oil companies operating in the country refused demands from local employees for higher pay and better working conditions. The workers went on strike, and President Lázaro Cárdenas del Rio secured his legacy as a national hero by seizing the foreign companies' assets in the name of the Mexican people. From this expropriated property he founded Pemex, and Article 27 of the country's constitution still guarantees the company's monopoly. Though its production is in decline and efforts to reform its operations have become a perennial political football, Pemex remains a symbol of Mexico's independence and a source of national pride.

Yet there are two major factors that prevent Mexico from a fuller embrace of state capitalism. First, like India, Mexico is a vibrant multiparty democracy. The party currently in power, President Felipe Calderón's National Action Party (PAN), strongly favors free-market capitalism. To move anything through Mexico's legislature, the PAN depends on support from the relatively more centrist Institutional Revolutionary Party (PRI), which is split between those who favor open markets and those who support a stronger role for the state. The opposition, left-leaning Democratic Revolutionary Party (PRD) favors a more state-interventionist approach, one that would redistribute income and manage markets in certain economic sectors, but even this party favors some level of foreign investment in Mexico's economy. No party holds a congressional majority, and any legislation that would swing the country toward or away from a greater government role in the economy can only succeed as a product of compromise.

Second, there is Mexico's mutually profitable relationship with its neighbor to the north. If globalization is the movement across borders of ideas, information, people, money, goods, and services at unprecedented speed, Mexico is a truly globalized country, because its economy depends so heavily on the foreign currency it earns from oil exports, tourism, and the cash remittances that Mexicans working in the United States send home to their families. In all three cases, it's clear that Mexico relies on access to U.S. markets. Even if the country were to undergo a profound philosophical shift—the kind that only a catastrophic, history-changing event could produce—Mexico's government would have to withdraw completely from the North American Free Trade Agreement (NAFTA) to move toward a new economic system.

Brazil

Given the dynamism of its economy and the trajectory of its development, the most interesting of Latin America's emerging markets is Brazil, a country that has undergone a remarkable transformation over the past two decades. In the 1970s and 1980s, state-owned enterprises dominated the country's economy, and a few wealthy families with ties to the political elite controlled most of the largest privately owned companies. To jump-start lagging growth, successive Brazilian governments privatized telecommunications, mining, aviation, and utilities companies and ended the state monopoly on oil and gas. Beginning in the 1990s, governments throughout Latin America opened their economies, and Brazil followed suit, mainly to attract cheap imports to help keep inflation in check. Since 2000, foreign trade has grown as a percentage of GDP by about 10 percentage points to around 25 percent, and Brazil's government has taken an active role in international trade talks.

When voters first elected Luiz Inácio Lula da Silva (known as Lula) Brazil's president in 2002, many foreign investors feared he would follow the lead of Venezuelan President Hugo Chávez and push the country sharply to the left. Despite campaign pledges to maintain his predecessor's disciplined, market-friendly economic policy, some feared he would reverse himself at the first sign that profligate state spending might boost his popularity. It didn't happen. Western media routinely refer to Lula as leftist, mainly because he rose to fame decades ago as a tough-minded labor negotiator. But Lula is not a Chávez-style revolutionary ideologue. He's a pragmatist and deal maker who understands the value of compromise. His leftist reputation has helped him build a left-right political consensus in favor of free-market capitalism—within certain limits. As his presidency draws to a close, he remains enormously popular in Brazil.

Lula is no Margaret Thatcher. He believes his government has a responsibility to Brazil's long-neglected poor to bolster the state by strengthening (rather than privatizing) most of the remaining state-owned companies and by fostering privately owned national champions, especially in sectors like mining and telecoms. But these state interventions are not nearly as intrusive as in Russia or China. State-owned companies like Petrobras (Petróleo Brasileiro, oil) and Eletrobrás (Centrais Elétricas Brasileiras, electricity) will play a larger role than in the past, but government will work to attract more private investment, even into the energy sector.

Two important developments threaten to push Brazil's government toward a much larger state role in its domestic economy. First, in November 2007, Petrobras announced the discovery of enormous offshore oil deposits buried deep beneath the Atlantic seabed off the country's southern coast. Further exploration suggests the area could eventually yield between 50 and 70 billion barrels of oil, enough to make Brazil an energy export powerhouse. It's also enough to tempt the state to tighten its grip, because it's an asset that could finance politically inspired spending projects for many years to come—with potentially serious long-term consequences for Brazil's private sector. The government has already proposed changes to a 1997 law that allows foreign companies an important role in exploration and production. Lula has acknowledged that Brazil needs foreign oil companies to help develop the new reserves, but he also wants to increase the government's share of the profits and to ensure that Petrobras doesn't lose its leadership role in the sector. Under heavy pressure from Lula's government, Petrobras announced an ambitious five-year plan in January 2009 to invest $174 billion in Brazil's oil infrastructure, a 55 percent jump from its previous program.

The second potential game changer was the impact of the 2008 financial crisis on Brazil's domestic economy. As commerce slowed and credit became scarce, the government used the National Development Bank (BNDES), the federally owned Bank of Brazil, and the National Savings Bank to inject cash into Brazil's private sector—increasing the state's stake in some of Brazil's largest companies. Oil prices fell sharply in the second half of 2008, and Petrobras officials warned that the company could not afford the spending Lula wanted. But his government sees state investment via Petrobras as a means to stimulate growth without blowing up the government's own budget. It has also been working with Petrobras to secure loans from other countries—especially China, which has agreed to a $10 billion loan from the China Development Bank in exchange for Brazil's commitment to guarantee oil exports of up to 150,000 barrels per day.

Beyond Petrobras and its various development banks, Lula has worked to help create private national champions capable of competing internationally in some sectors. But because these companies have financing from other sources, the state can't fully control them. Mining giant Vale is a prime example. For the company's leadership, strong relations with government are a must, because the state holds a "golden share" in the company that allows it an authoritative voice in Vale's most important strategic decisions. At the same time, Vale remains competitive internationally and doesn't rely on state subsidies and financing to meet its payroll.

The Lula administration also announced plans in December 2008 to create a sovereign wealth fund. The original idea was to use the fund to help finance Brazilian companies abroad and to devalue Brazil's currency to help promote exports. The government would borrow in Brazilian reals and buy dollars to finance Brazilian companies' purchases of assets abroad. The economic slowdown changed the government's plan. Now it wants the fund's capital (just under $7 billion) to finance state investment in Brazil and to ensure that federal financial institutions have the cash they need to weather the financial crisis.

In October 2010, Brazilian voters will return to the polls to elect Lula's successor, and they're likely to face a relatively stark choice. Opposition candidate and governor of São Paulo state José Serra is well known as a champion of free-market capitalism. His likely opponent, Lula's chief of staff and favored candidate Dilma Rousseff, favors a newly strengthened role for the state in Brazil's development. Brazil is not a state-capitalist country. Its democracy provides checks on state power, popular opinion welcomes trade and foreign investment (even in the energy sector), and its sovereign wealth fund is tiny compared with those in China or the Persian Gulf. But even if voters decide the elections on other issues, Brazil's next president will have considerable influence in determining how the country develops one of the world's largest oil discoveries of the past several years, how open Latin America's most dynamic economy remains to foreign investment, and what kind of example it offers for other countries in the region.

Southeast Asia

In Southeast Asia, there are several countries that practice elements of state capitalism. As early as 1986, nominally communist Vietnam launched its *doi moi* ("renovation") program to move the country from a command economic system toward state capitalism. As in Russia and China, the goal remains to bolster the state's political power by empowering the private sector to generate growth in some economic sectors while maintaining tight control of others.

In Indonesia, thirty-one years of Suharto's authoritarian rule (1967–1998) produced dozens of state-owned companies, and it will take time for even the most powerful and determined advocate of free markets to strip the business elite of its advantages. Suharto supported the creation of state-owned banking, power, utility, and telecommunications companies and a complex network of politically connected private companies in timber, oil, gas, mining, textiles, cigarettes, and agriculture. Even today, many of the country's best-connected businessmen use close personal ties with powerful political officials to block the market reforms that would burden them with genuine competition. In addition, the 1997 Asian financial crisis forced even greater state intervention after the government had to bail out most of the country's largest banks. A decade later, the state still owns majority or large minority shares in many of them. Current President Susilo Bambang Yudhoyono has worked to ensure that his economic team includes committed free-market-minded professionals, and he has risked public anger by reducing government subsidies for fuel and sugar. But as in Russia, he has also embraced state control over the oil, gas, and mining resources and hasn't hesitated to use state institutions to favor state-owned companies and privately owned favorites over foreign competitors.

For forty years, Malaysia's government has used state capitalism to serve its political interests by establishing and enforcing a kind of majority affirmative action—empowering Bumiputeras (Malays and other native ethnic groups) at the expense of commercially successful Chinese and Indian minorities. In 1969, the ruling United Malays National Organization (UMNO) capitalized on nationalist rage stirred by "race riots" between Malays and minority Chinese to create the New Economic Policy, which guarantees Bumiputeras a fixed share of Malaysia's national wealth. In recent years, support for the policy has fallen as it's increasingly seen as a drag on economic development. Yet forty years later, the UMNO-led government still wins votes by pandering to the ethnic majority with promises to use state power to send a guaranteed share of the country's wealth their way.

The national oil and gas company Petronas owns all of Malaysia's natural hydrocarbon resources and manages them through production-sharing contracts with foreign investors. Petronas has investments in more than thirty countries, from Argentina to Algeria to Mozambique to Uzbekistan to Australia. During the Asian financial crisis, Petronas acted on government instructions to bail out several state-owned or state-linked companies, one of which reportedly belonged to former Prime Minister Mahathir Mohammad's son Mirzan Mahathir. Khazanah Nasional, Malaysia's sovereign wealth fund, owns a substantial stake in the CIMB (Commercial International Merchant Bankers) Group of banks and other large companies. CIMB Group is headed by Nazir Razak, brother of Malaysian Prime Minister Najib Razak. UMNO's power isn't what it used to be. In March 2008, opposition parties did well enough in national elections to deprive the ruling coalition of its two-thirds supermajority in parliament—and therefore of its power to unilaterally amend the country's constitution in ways that serve its political interests. The ruling party's new vulnerability only makes it more likely to use the tools that state capitalism provides to control as large as possible a share of the country's wealth and to use it for political gain.

But China is the world's leading practitioner of state capitalism. Were it not for China's emerging wealth and its economic dynamism, this system would pose a far less patent global challenge to free-market capitalism.

China

In September 2008, just as the Western financial crisis was beginning to dominate the world's attention, Chinese Premier Wen Jiabao sat down for an extraordinary interview with CNN's Fareed Zakaria. During their conversation, Wen provided what amounts to a precisely worded definition of Chinese state capitalism: "The complete formulation of our economic policy is to give full play to the basic role of market forces in allocating resources under the macroeconomic guidance and regulation of the government. We have one important piece of experience of the past thirty years, that is to ensure that both the visible hand and invisible hand are given full play in regulating the market forces."[11]

Three decades ago, the invisible hand was truly invisible in China. When Mao Zedong died in 1976, he left behind a society in turmoil, an economy in ruins, and a ruling party in real danger of irrelevance. Within two years, paramount leader Deng Xiaoping and his premier, Zhao Ziyang, overcame considerable resistance from senior Communist Party officials to launch a slow but deliberate plan to experiment with capitalism. For China's economy and the ruling party's future, it was a matter of necessity, and without Deng's personal and political talents, the changes might never have been made.

Years before Mikhail Gorbachev first charmed a Western audience, a willingness to move beyond Mao and an openness to Western culture transformed Deng into one of the American media's most improbable celebrities of all time. Not long after the United States and the People's Republic of China established formal diplomatic relations in 1979, the barely five-foot-tall Deng visited the United States, famously donning a cowboy hat while watching a Texas rodeo. At home, Deng's forceful leadership ensured that no officials dared challenge him publicly as he and Zhao pushed China into the treacherous crosscurrents of uncharted capitalist waters. Deng himself described the pragmatic experimentalism of his plan as "feeling for rocks while crossing a river."

The first decade of reform yielded promising preliminary results. Deng's increasingly ambitious plans, which came to be called "reform and opening up," began with the establishment in several cities along China's east coast of "special economic zones" (SEZs), isolated laboratories of carefully managed capitalism, where foreign firms were invited to invest on highly attractive terms. Success in these zones led to the creation of many more. The state abandoned hopelessly inefficient collective farming and created a "household responsibility" system that allowed farmers who had fulfilled their production quotas to sell any extra produce at market prices. Agricultural yields exploded. Deng and Zhao developed other policies that encouraged the growth of private commerce. In the countryside, township and village enterprises bloomed. In cities, small privately owned businesses began to flourish. Entrepreneurialism expanded, and average incomes began to rise. Along the coast, the special economic zones helped cities like Shenzhen and Guangzhou transform almost overnight from stagnant backwaters into modern manufacturing powerhouses.

Behind all this experimentation was a determination to go slow, to avoid the kind of "shock therapy" that might destabilize the country. The state tinkered with various sets of incentives and restrictions to determine what worked and what didn't. The carefully managed pace of change ensured that much of the nation's industrial base remained in state hands and that much of its urban workforce depended on gigantic state-owned enterprises for food, housing, salaries, and social benefits. Beyond fears of doing too much too fast, Deng knew that his battle with opponents of reform within the leadership was never fully won and that any substantial setback might encourage them to more actively resist his plans. This explains in part why Deng and Zhao cast reform as a bid to build "socialism with Chinese characteristics." China would have to find its own way toward prosperity, but the state's guiding role in leading industries could never be completely abandoned. Deng also worked to try to ensure that economic "opening up" did not trigger demand for a liberalization of China's one-party politics.

But reform created an entirely new set of problems. With so much more money to fight over, official corruption reached new heights, especially at the local level, stoking public anger. Worse still, China's rigid state bureaucracy was unable to keep pace with reform, hobbling government efforts to respond to the problems created by sweeping changes in Chinese society—like the huge population shift as millions of migrants abandoned the countryside to search for a better life in the country's fast-growing cities. Reform reached a crossroads in the late 1980s, as an aging Deng could not prevent pro- and anti-reform factions from emerging within the party leadership. Leading the fight against further reform were powerful party elder Chen Yun, who directed the state's economic management in the early years of Mao's rule, and Premier Li Peng, who warned that economic reform would deprive the party of political power. The leading voices for reform included Zhao and the publicly popular Party Secretary Hu Yaobang. It appeared for a time that opponents of reform had the upper hand. Hu was forced to resign his position, and Zhao faced intense criticism over his support for relatively modest political reform. These problems generated enough social upheaval to set the party leadership on a collision course with the public expectations it had yet to fulfill, a conflict that came to a head in the spring of 1989 in Tiananmen Square.

In the spring of that year, a group of students gathered in central Beijing to mourn the sudden passing of Hu Yaobang. When steadily growing crowds pushed the show of respect toward large-scale protest and demonstrations took on a life of their own, the battle within the leadership over reform reached the breaking point. Zhao urged the Politburo Standing Committee, China's most powerful decision-making body, to placate the students, but the more conservative faction persuaded Deng that the movement gathering just outside the party's leadership compound threatened China's national security and the party's survival. Deng gave the order, tanks crushed the student-led uprising, and Zhao Ziyang spent the rest of his life in political exile.

As communist governments fell throughout Eastern Europe in 1989 and Gorbachev's government reformed its empire out of existence in 1991, China's economic reform effort lost plenty of steam. But Deng, then eighty-eight years old, breathed new life into market liberalization in 1992 during an unexpected tour of several of his special economic zones. The entire country, including senior members of the bureaucracy and anointed successor Jiang Zemin, got the message that market reforms must continue—and at a faster pace. Once in charge, Jiang accelerated the process of capitalist experimentation, but he also helped create and exacerbate some of the social and environmental problems that plague China today. The former Shanghai party boss focused on the development of China's east coast, widening the growing wealth gap between the country's increasingly affluent cities and its neglected countryside. Though China's political leadership has fewer direct personal ties to state-owned companies and banks than we find in Russia, Jiang ensured that China's business elite developed a stake in the state's success. He called on the party to grant membership to favored businessmen, "red capitalists," to bolster the regime's popular legitimacy and to bring a better understanding of capitalism into the party bureaucracy. Career paths have since become linked more closely than ever to party membership, because it's within the political elite that so many business relationships are now formed. A growing number of college students now join the party to improve their job prospects.

Fortunately for the coherence of reform, Jiang empowered a capable economic manager, Premier Zhu Rongji, to play a central role in professionalizing large state-owned enterprises and in rescuing an antiquated banking system overwhelmed by a blizzard of bad loans. Zhu's greatest lasting achievement may well prove to be the negotiation of China's entry into the World Trade Organization in 2001, a move that committed China's future political leadership to market liberalization and compliance with established international trade practices and investment rules.

In the years since China joined the WTO, its trade with the rest of the world—particularly Europe, the United States, and Japan—has skyrocketed, and the country has become crucial for the global production chain and the future of the global economy. By engineering an economic system that relies on huge export volumes for economic growth, China's leadership created the most prosperous period in the country's history. But it also left China dangerously vulnerable to conditions outside the country, as we saw firsthand in 2008 and 2009, when recession in Europe and America took a large bite out of global demand for the products that Chinese manufacturers sell.

Since 1978, the Chinese Communist Party leadership has, by fits and starts, enabled market forces to shape the country's domestic economy and opened China to foreign trade and investment. In the process, it has leveraged its enormous population and low labor costs to become a fast-emerging economic powerhouse. But it has also created internal vulnerabilities that Mao Zedong–era bureaucrats could never have imagined. Over the centuries, China has endured extended periods of chaos and self-destruction. It's possible that as Deng Xiaoping weighed the decision to send tanks into Tiananmen Square, he thought of the Cultural Revolution, the Mao-inspired decade of violence that crippled his son, drove his brother to suicide, and temporarily cost him his freedom. When future Chinese leaders face the threat of large-scale disorder, they may well remember the costs of Tiananmen Square itself. The Chinese leadership's fear of anarchy is not abstract; it's a powerful force that prevents China's state capitalists from fully embracing free markets. Then again, why should Chinese leaders abandon a system that has profited them so handsomely?

Chinese State Capitalism Today

To legitimize its monopoly control of domestic political power, the Chinese Communist Party leadership believes it must create millions of new jobs each year. That's the only way to ensure that rising expectations for prosperity can be met and that citizens moving from poverty into the workforce can spur further growth and won't become a threat to social order. Chinese officials know from bitter experience that a command economy can't consistently meet that challenge and that only market forces can spur innovation and generate a sustainable economic expansion. They also believe, as Wen Jiabao told Fareed Zakaria, that they can build an economic system that ensures that market forces serve the state's development goals and not simply the financial interests of those that Mao once denounced as profiteers. Finally, they know that to sustain high growth in years to come, Chinese companies, backed with every advantage the state can provide, must venture out into the world to lock down long-term access to the crude oil, natural gas, metals, minerals, and other commodities needed to fuel a still-vulnerable developing economy. In other words, China isn't simply open for business. Its political elite embarked years ago on a strategy to *engineer* China's development, and it is using state-owned companies, sovereign wealth funds, and domestic political control to do it.

China's version of state capitalism begins at the very center of its government, within the State Council, the country's main administrative authority. The council is chaired by Premier Wen Jiabao and includes the heads of every government ministry, from national defense to finance to ethnic affairs to water resources. The most important of these bureaucracies for day-to-day management of the domestic economy is the National Development and Reform Commission, which guides macroeconomic planning and intervenes in markets, particularly by setting prices for many products and by influencing national oil companies and other state-owned enterprises.

The state also plays an active role in China's banking sector. There are many reasons why the challenge of dominating a domestic economy is more difficult for China's leadership than for Russia's, but the most obvious is that Russia draws so much of its state revenue directly from oil and gas exports. China must rely on a much more broadly diversified economy if it hopes to create jobs for a population that outnumbers Russia's by nearly ten to one. To manage this more complex system, Chinese officials believe they must exert heavy influence over the country's banks, especially in deciding how much money they loan, to whom, and on what terms. In the late 1990s, China's banking system needed a major overhaul to ensure that it was competitive and efficient enough to power continued growth. To improve their performance in recent years, Beijing has slowly transformed three of four state-controlled banks into market-driven, publicly listed companies, while keeping a majority ownership stake. The remaining fully state-owned bank, Agricultural Bank of China, is slated to soon follow the same path. But though the state has loosened its grip on the banking system, it has no intention of releasing it altogether. China's central bank continues to dictate terms for new lending, especially when state-owned companies are doing the borrowing.

As for the state-owned companies themselves, there is no single Chinese model. The largest of them tend to be majority owned by the state, while drawing their profits from subsidiaries listed on equity markets in Hong Kong. Many of them, including the big national oil companies—China National Petroleum Corporation (CNPC), China Petroleum and Chemical Corporation (Sinopec), and China National Offshore Oil Corporation (CNOOC)—conduct most operations through these subsidiaries. The state exerts considerable influence over their policies by, for example, setting domestic energy prices and controlling the selection of personnel for key positions. Yet most are allowed a certain degree of autonomy in deciding where and how much to invest. At times, the three companies even bid against one another for foreign contracts. To make them more efficient and competitive, the state has even laid off workers, as many as 50 million during the 1990s, a number larger than the entire population of Spain.

The state sends these state-owned energy companies out into the world to bring home the oil and gas reserves that China will need in years to come, a development that has already had considerable impact on the global economy. These firms are not merely appendages of the state, and they sell some of their product to other buyers at market prices. But they must also ensure that the state gains access to the energy it needs. They are armed with three crucial competitive advantages. First, they are lavishly subsidized by their government, which allows them to outbid privately owned competitors and to pay above-market prices for long-term contracts. That adds upward pressure on the prices that everyone else pays for energy and other commodities. Second, they arrive in Africa, Latin America, Southeast Asia, and other parts of the world with the full political backing of the Chinese state. For developing world governments eager to curry favor with deep-pocketed new friends in China ready to extend credit, awarding contracts to state-owned Chinese companies makes good sense. Third, these state-owned enterprises can do business in countries where Western multinationals can't go. The governments of Iran, Sudan, Burma, Zimbabwe, and others face U.S. and European pressure to change their political behavior. But China, which has never welcomed Western criticism of its own political system or human-rights practices, has the cash, the influence, and the willingness to do business to lock up investment contracts in all these places. Having invested in these countries, China then has a material interest in blocking U.S. and European efforts to pressure them.

For example, though the West has shunned Sudan's government in recent years for refusing to end state-sponsored violence in the country's Darfur region, China and its state-owned energy companies have been doing business inside the country for more than a decade. CNPC has invested in oil exploration and production and in transportation infrastructure. Sinopec has been hard at work for years on a thousand-mile pipeline. Chinese mining companies have been active in Algeria, Tunisia, Chad, Mali, Zambia, Niger, and other states. A $2 billion dollar loan from China's export-import bank helps Sinopec win oil contracts in Angola. China's oil firms are also active in Nigeria, Mauritania, Gabon, and Equatorial Guinea. Chinese companies have energy investments in Canada, Kazakhstan, Brazil, Venezuela, Ecuador, Argentina, and many other countries around the world. They've signed deals for copper in Chile, iron ore in Peru, and nickel in Cuba.

In addition, few in the West worried very much when Deng Xiaoping began bragging in the early 1990s that the Middle East had oil but China had "rare-earth minerals." In 1994, China reportedly controlled about 46 percent of the world's so-called rare earths. Today, industry estimates suggest it supplies between 90 and 95 percent of them. The Chinese government has accomplished this by investing billions in mines and processing plants at home, in manufacturing technology abroad, and by bankrolling the world's most ambitious rare-earth research-and-development program. Business media still pay these minerals little attention, because for the moment the market for them is worth only about $1 billion, a tiny sum when compared to the daily buying and selling of crude oil or iron ore. Unless you're a geologist, you've probably never heard of yttrium, scandium, or dysprosium. But these and a couple of dozen other such minerals are essential for the production of a wide variety of twenty-first-century consumer products—like miniaturized electronics, batteries for hybrid cars, computer disk drives, display screens, and iPods. For privately owned foreign companies competing with Chinese state-owned giants, the worry is that China is actively cornering the market. For the United States government, the added worry is that rare earths are a key ingredient in the manufacture of lasers and precision-guided missiles. Both political and business leaders fear that China's State Council will impose new restrictions on the export of rare earths—as it did in 2007, 2008, and 2009—stockpiling them instead within a strategic reserve.[12]

Financing all its various projects will cost China huge amounts of money. Having amassed more than $2 trillion in foreign-exchange reserves from the success of its export strategy, China created its first sovereign wealth fund, the China Investment Corporation (CIC), in 2007 with $200 billion in assets under management. A government agency known as the State Administration of Foreign Exchange (SAFE) had been behaving like a sovereign wealth fund for years, but many within the leadership believed it needed to create a more broadly diversified portfolio to bring a better return than the more conservative SAFE could provide. Both institutions sometimes appear to make commercial decisions with political goals in mind—as when SAFE bought $300 million in government bonds from Costa Rica in September 2008 to persuade that country's government to end its diplomatic recognition of Taiwan in favor of China.

Reflecting China's broader management strategy, CIC is led by a combination of political officials and experienced fund managers. Its chairman is longtime party member and former Finance Ministry official Lou Jiwei, but day-to-day operations are thought to be run by CIC President Gao Xiqing, a graduate of Duke University's School of Law, a veteran of Wall Street, and reportedly the first Chinese citizen to pass the New York State bar exam. This team hasn't always performed well. By some estimates, CIC lost more than $4 billion in its first two years of existence, prompting sharp criticism from senior Chinese officials. CIC's investment is certainly useful for the foreign companies and investors who need the capital. But the fund distorts markets in several ways. CIC's investments in energy and other commodities add upward pressure on prices. Its capital strengthens China's domestic banking system, which helps keep foreign banks at a competitive disadvantage. Its funding for Chinese firms helps them stay ahead of foreign competitors.

State Capitalism at Home

The special economic zones that Deng Xiaoping launched in the late 1970s would not have succeeded if foreign investors hadn't been willing to take a chance on China. In essence, foreign companies were invited to bet on the future of Deng himself. If opponents of reform within the party had toppled him, outside investors could have sustained heavy losses. Just two years after Mao's death, the long-term political survival of a man who had once been disgraced by Mao's government seemed less than a sure thing. But more than a few were willing to gamble for much the same reason that foreign companies look to China today: Its labor force and potential consumer base is so enormous that the country appears capable of single-handedly keeping many a Western multinational in profits for decades. Foreign direct investment has grown from nearly nothing in 1978 to $92.4 billion in 2008, according to China's commerce ministry.

China has needed that investment to create jobs and to gain exposure to new sources of capital, new products, new technologies, and Western business practices. Foreign companies have made huge amounts of money by using Chinese labor to build their products less expensively than is possible in the United States or Europe and by selling to shoppers back home—and to a fast-growing number of Chinese consumers. But how long will China's openness last? In recent years, a growing number of domestic Chinese companies, many of them state-owned, have lifted their game to a level at which they can compete with foreign rivals within the Chinese marketplace. As state-owned companies become ever more important to their country's political and economic development strategy, they build more leverage within the state bureaucracy, gaining influence they can use to persuade political officials to create new rules and regulations that advantage Chinese companies at the expense of their foreign competitors.

State officials have their own reasons for favoring domestic companies. Many emerging Chinese companies have gained valuable managerial experience in recent years. In some cases, Chinese officials have allowed foreign companies access to local consumers in exchange for transfers of technology and intellectual property, assets that local firms have used to become much more competitive. As in Russia, officials in

Beijing have carved out strategic sectors, including telecom, shipbuilding, oil, petrochemicals, and steel, that are now virtually closed to significant levels of foreign investment.

In addition, a surge of national pride throughout China in recent
years powers the rise of both state-controlled and privately owned
Chinese companies, some of which have skillfully manipulated public
opinion to build a competitive edge against foreign commercial rivals.
Companies like consumer electronics firm Aigo (which translates literally as "patriotism") have used this tactic less subtly than others. Those
within the Chinese government with political or financial interests at
stake can sometimes incite nationalist passions to block the foreign purchase of domestic companies. In 2009, Coca-Cola was hoping its lead
role as a sponsor of the Beijing Olympics the year before would warm
official attitudes toward its $2.4 billion bid for Chinese juice maker
Huiyuan. During the negotiation process, Huiyuan owner Zhu Xinli
exploited popular anger over the proposal, even as he courted the bid
in case the state approved it. The Chinese government ruled that the
proposal violated antitrust legislation, and Coke came away empty-
handed.

Pressure on government to defend Chinese interests from perceived
encroachment by foreigners is also coming directly from the Chinese
public. In July 2009, the *New York Times* published an article on the
public backlash inside China against foreign players competing in the
country's professional basketball association. In 2008, league officials
had moved to generate more excitement for Chinese fans by attracting larger numbers of high-quality foreign players. The league eased
restrictions on the amount of money these players could earn and removed limits on how long they could be on the court. Within one sea-
son, the game had won a wider audience throughout China, but the
foreign players had begun to take charge on the court. American stars
were reportedly earning six-figure salaries as Chinese players warmed
the bench for $14,000 a year. The league's top fifteen scorers were non-

Chinese, and local fans began grumbling that outsiders had stolen their game. "Foreigners should play supporting roles, not dominate the game," griped the league's director of operations. Chinese state-run media called the foreign athletes a "malignant tumor." The Chinese market had opened, but once foreign players began to dominate, ordinary citizens called on their government to restore protectionist rules. More ominously, some of the league's less competitive teams simply stopped paying their foreign players, sending them home with worthless contracts when Chinese courts refused to intervene.[13]

This will become a growing problem for foreign companies and investors trying to find a place for themselves within China's state-dominated system, because the state itself now faces unprecedented public pressure to satisfy public demand for all kinds of things. Ironically, it's one of globalization's primary engines, the Internet, that is making this possible. Sometime in 2009, the number of Internet users in China surpassed the total number of citizens in the United States. Industry experts expect that by 2012, that number will double, and there will be 600 million Chinese online. In 2008, the Chinese Communist Party caught a glimpse of how twenty-first-century communications tools had forced the state to become more responsive than ever to Chinese public demand. On May 12, a tremendously powerful earthquake devastated a large area of China's Sichuan province. In the hours that followed, as the government monitored the fallout and prepared a state response, large numbers of ordinary Chinese took to the Internet to coordinate relief efforts and demand government help. Within hours, Premier Wen Jiabao was touring the affected area to help guide search-and-rescue operations. State officials felt compelled to respond publicly to grieving residents who demanded to know why the quake had leveled so many schools and so few government buildings.

Days later, China's blogosphere again demonstrated its power, this time with a direct impact on a Western company. When actress Sharon Stone told a reporter at the Cannes Film Festival that the quake might have been a result of "bad karma" following a Chinese crack-down in Tibet, a few of China's 70 million bloggers created a tidal wave of outrage. French fashion house Christian Dior averted disaster by quickly removing photographs of Stone from its stores throughout China and tearing up her modeling contract. The tumultuous path of the Olympic torch across Europe and the United States that spring also created large potential problems for foreign companies operating in China.

State power extends to the Internet, where the so-called Great Fire-wall prevents most Chinese Internet users from reading about politically sensitive topics. China's use of state-run media helps shape opinion on the Internet about many other topics. But the Communist Party can't control every wave of public outrage that arrives like an unexpected storm. In extreme cases, it can only hope to use other instruments of state power to ride the wave wherever it goes. Over the next several years, this emerging trend is likely to create all kinds of unforeseen problems for foreigners hoping to do business in China.

Lessons learned in "giving the people what they want" returns us to the primary reason that the country's leaders will continue to rely on state capitalism: They believe it's the surest way to produce a steady stream of jobs. Every week brings new reminders of why creating and protecting jobs is so important. In July 2009, the government of Jilin province was preparing to sell state-owned Tonghua Iron & Steel to Ji-anlong Group, one of China's largest private steel companies. Tonghua hadn't earned steady profits in some time, and privatizing made good economic sense. Jianlong then sent a man called Chen Guojun to run Tonghua as its interim general manager until the deal was done. Chen made few friends among Tonghua's fifty thousand workers, most of whom feared that privatization meant they would lose their jobs. Chen arrived for work one morning to find a crowd of Tonghua employees waiting for him. Tempers flared, and the mob beat Chen to death. Press accounts suggest that local police arrived to find thirty thousand riot-ers blocking the path of an ambulance dispatched to the scene. Hours passed before order could be restored.

In this case, a group of angry workers found a particularly dramatic way to make clear that decisions that eliminate jobs can never be taken lightly in any developing country. This is a version in miniature of the sort of whirlwind that many Chinese officials believe a Western-style relaxation of state control might one day unleash.

The Financial Crisis

Before 2008, Chinese officials had begun to loosen state control of some aspects of China's economic life. Bush administration Treasury Secretary Henry Paulson and his negotiating team engaged China in a "strategic economic dialogue," hoping to, among other things, persuade their Chinese counterparts to ease restrictions on China's financial sector. Progress was sharply limited by deep-seated Chinese fears that the country's financial and capital markets weren't ready for the reforms Washington wanted, but Beijing further liberalized some domestic markets. The Western financial crisis and the global recession that followed moved that trend into reverse, and Chinese state officials, who blamed the global market meltdown on Washington's unwillingness to properly regulate its own markets, have moved quickly to engineer a recovery.

A significant portion of the Obama administration's 2009 stimulus package took the form of tax cuts for individuals and businesses large and small. But policy makers in Beijing, anxious to create huge numbers of new jobs, responded with hundreds of billions of dollars in state-directed funding for the construction of roads, bridges, airports, power grids, and the reconstruction of earthquake-ravaged Sichuan province. To protect existing jobs, officials provided massive financial help for manufacturers in danger of closing their doors. They encouraged household spending by offering direct subsidies for many purchases. In December 2008, as many large Western banks were going bust, CIC agreed to buy publicly traded stocks in Chinese banks, using state funds to buoy their share prices. In the late 1980s, the Chinese used one airline to create three new ones. In 2002, a single power-generating firm became five separate companies. All these firms remain subject to state-imposed price caps, and all of them continue to lose money. But they remain protected by a Chinese Communist Party leadership that is now much more risk averse than it was just two years ago.

The main reason the financial crisis has reinforced state capitalism in China is that massive government stimulus spending strongly favors state-owned enterprises (SOEs) over the private sector.* Some privately owned companies have benefited from state largesse and will continue to. But China's leadership wants to do more than simply spend hundreds of billions to jump-start China's economy; it wants to control where that money goes next and how it's used. Many state-owned enterprises with newly strengthened balance sheets are now buying smaller private-sector competitors—and by directing state money toward state-dominated companies, China's government has deliberately helped accelerate that process. Some local business owners worry over a government policy known as *guo jin min tui,* "The state advances as the private sector retreats."[14]

China, which became the world's largest exporter in 2009, produces more than its people can consume, and before the financial crisis made landfall, U.S., European, and Japanese consumers were buying the excess production. As recession took hold in these countries, Beijing decided on a plan to use state funding to push for consolidation of many overproductive industries. These big fish will swallow up lots of little fish, making the marketplace less competitive. Some newly cash-rich state-owned firms will find themselves strong enough to crowd out investment from would-be foreign competitors. Beijing will also use

---

* The SOEs that have benefited most are those in the nine "crisis-stricken" industries that have been strategically targeted for support—electronics, petrochemicals, metallurgy, steel, automotive, light industry, textiles, shipbuilding, and telecommunications.

its financial muscle to transform energy- and commodity-based state-owned companies into globally competitive national champions, by allowing them to borrow directly from the state's massive foreign-exchange reserves to finance still more foreign acquisitions—and at a moment when cash-strapped multinationals can least afford to compete.

What will the Chinese economy look like ten years from now? The leadership appears to recognize that it will have to balance greater state control with the growth, technical innovation, and sustainable job creation that can only come from genuine competition—particularly among small and medium-size businesses. The State Council will probably work to accelerate the development of rural finance to boost consumption in the countryside. The leadership recognizes that China will remain dangerously vulnerable to economic downturns in the West if it continues to rely heavily for growth on its exporters. But we won't see a substantial enough spike in demand for Chinese products from Chinese consumers until the benefits of economic growth are spread more evenly across the country.

This state-capitalist model will rule the day for many years to come, because China's leaders believe it's the only system that can satisfy *their* long-term political needs. They know the private sector is indispensable for sustainable growth and that China's rise could not have happened and cannot continue without huge volumes of trade and foreign investment. But the financial crisis only further persuaded them that enlightened state economic management will protect them from the natural excesses of free-market capitalism. That's why both the visible and invisible hands will continue to guide the country's twenty-first-century development—and why Western governments and companies will be negotiating with China's economic engineers for many years to come.

CHAPTER FIVE

The Challenge

What we're seeing is not merely private foreign investment—it is
foreign government investment, which raises new policy questions for
which we do not have all the answers.

—SENATOR JIM WEBB (D-VA)

The Cold War is over, and it's not coming back. No government is using state capitalism to force a return to communist command economics. The emergence of state capitalism—particularly in China, Russia, and the Arab monarchies of the Persian Gulf—poses a variety of serious threats for international politics and the global economy, but before we look at those problems more closely, it's worth putting them in perspective. Twenty-five years ago, there was no end in sight to the conflict between capitalist and communist governments. Soviet leader and former KGB chief Yuri Andropov died and was replaced by the already gravely ill Konstantin Chernenko. The U.S. Defense Department began early testing of its strategic missile-defense program, popularly known as Star Wars. Throughout Europe, the placement of U.S. missiles provoked angry public protests. NATO and the Warsaw Pact staged war games, and China's experimentation with capitalism had barely begun. Anyone who predicted that Germans would dance atop the Berlin Wall within five years, that the Soviet Union would collapse within seven years, that most of Eastern Europe's communist countries would join NATO and the European Union, and that the world would turn to China, India, and Brazil to drive an increasingly large percentage of the global economy would have provoked more laughter than serious discussion.

Today, the primary armed threat to U.S. national security comes from terrorists armed with chemical, biological, or nuclear weapons. The Chinese and Russian governments know that zero-sum mercantilist thinking is a thing of the distant past. They want to protect their borders and extend their influence throughout their immediate neighborhoods, but neither has any illusion that it can use state-capitalist tools to establish global dominance. Russia's military is in no position to occupy Belarus, much less Berlin. It fought a five-day war with Georgia in August 2008 and conducts joint naval exercises with Venezuela, but it's hard for officials in Washington or Moscow to pretend that either is much more than an irritant for U.S.-Russian relations. The Kremlin draws a much greater sense of security from its hundreds of billions in foreign-exchange reserves than from its stockpiles of Soviet-era nuclear weapons.

China might one day pose a broader military threat than it does now, but its economy has grown so quickly and its living standards have improved so dramatically over the past two decades that it's hard to imagine the kind of catastrophic, game-changing event that would push its leadership to pose a Soviet-scale military challenge to America and Europe. In fact, China has become a status quo power, one that contributes twice as many troops to UN peacekeeping operations as the United States, Britain, and Russia combined.[1] If its leadership's primary goal is to bolster its political control by generating prosperity for the Chinese people, why would it allow anything short of the most dire and immediate threat to its territorial integrity to ignite a military conflict that would sever its complex web of commercial ties with countries all over the world—and, in particular, with its largest trading partners: the European Union, the United States, and Japan? Beijing's primary military concern is the risk of a direct or proxy conflict with the United States over Taiwan. But the Chinese leadership is well aware that no U.S. government will support a Taiwanese bid for independence, and why should the Chinese launch a self-defeating invasion of the island when it can co-opt most of Taiwan's business elite with privileged access to investment opportunities on the mainland? So far, globalization has been good to China's Communist Party, and wars are bad for business.

Certainly, China has ambitious military modernization plans. With 2.3 million soldiers under arms, its People's Liberation Army (PLA) is already by far the world's largest. The PLA has reportedly invested considerable time, effort, and money in cyberwarfare technology. Its total military budget is believed to have doubled between 2003 and 2009 to about $70 billion. But that's about 12 percent of what the United States now spends on its military each year—and an even smaller percentage if supplementary U.S. spending on the wars in Iraq and Afghanistan is included. For the projection of power around the world, no weapon is more valuable than an aircraft carrier. The United States has eleven carrier groups; China has none. In short, the gap between the U.S. and Chinese militaries is considerable, and widening in America's favor.

But though state capitalism's challenge to free markets won't generate the drama of the Berlin airlift or the Cuban missile crisis, it can compromise a country's security and the future of the global economy. With mercantilism a thing of the past, few now doubt that commerce can generate new wealth and expand more than one economy at a time. The end of the Cold War and the growth of emerging-market states like China, India, Russia, Brazil, and others have created new opportunities for precisely that kind of mutually profitable exchange. The willingness of politicians in a growing number of developing states to gamble on greater openness to foreign trade and investment has brought hundreds of millions of new players into the global economy.

Herein lies state capitalism's greatest threat: Opportunity can enable dependence, and it's clear that an expanding number of Western companies and their governments are becoming ever more reliant on the willingness of all these new players to remain open for business. What happens when the Chinese leadership decides that its development strategy no longer depends on so much foreign investment and prefers instead to use all the tools at the state's disposal to support local companies and shelter them from foreign competition? What happens when international politics produces the kind of conflict that moves large numbers of consumers in country A to punish companies they associate with government B—as when Chinese Internet users organized spontaneous boycotts of French companies following protests in France involving Beijing's Olympic torch or when Muslim leaders called on followers to boycott Danish companies following the publication in a Danish newspaper of cartoons they believed had insulted the prophet Mohammed? It's not just goods and services flying around the world at breakneck speed. Controversy moves at high speed as well. Reliance on international trade means vulnerability to political shocks, and the state's ability and willingness to use markets for political purposes increases both the risk and the stakes.

The Cold War created risks of nuclear conflict, but the purely economic threats it posed the free-market world were minimal, because decisions made by economic ministries in Moscow or Beijing had virtually no impact in Europe or the United States. In 2008, U.S.-Chinese trade totaled more than $400 billion. In 1979, before China opened its first "special economic zones," the figure was just $2.4 billion. U.S. trade with the Soviet Union that year amounted to just $4.5 billion, less than 1 percent of America's total. Americans and Soviets traded Pepsi for Stolichnaya, but it took the collapse of an empire to generate real commerce—and the vulnerabilities that come with it. Today, political choices made in Beijing and Brasilia, Moscow and Mexico City, Delhi, Abu Dhabi, and Ankara move markets twenty-four hours a day—with immediate implications for advanced industrial economies, governments, and multinational companies. Compared with Cold war–era threats, the challenges this emerging trend poses are less dramatic but just as far-reaching and much more complicated.

The Western financial crisis and global recession have left champions of free-market capitalism facing an increasingly skeptical international audience. Countries like state-capitalist China (and those with a relatively smaller stake in international trade, like India and Egypt) have taken a much less severe hit from the slowdown than free-market powers in America and Europe. With the "rise of the rest," these and other developing states have cut into U.S. political, economic, and cultural hegemony over the past several years, and Washington has seen its great-power advantages begin to shrink, at least on a relative basis.[2] If all these emerging powers embrace free-market capitalism, America might still hold a somewhat smaller piece of a much bigger pie. The risk for the United States—and for free-market democracies generally—is that distortions created by state capitalism will ensure that the pie isn't expanding quickly enough to accommodate all the new mouths it will soon be expected to feed. That will threaten not just standards of living, but eventually perhaps the security of the world's free-market democracies.

Economic Efficiency

How much state involvement in an economy is the right amount to generate long-term prosperity? In general, the more government intervenes in the processes of economic exchange, the more likely it is to burden them with political distortions, bureaucracy, waste, and corruption. Some suggest that prosperity flows from something called "consumer sovereignty," a system in which the consumer is king and producers compete to offer products of the highest possible quality at the lowest possible price. To thrive, producers must innovate. This is a key reason why free markets work: As producers invent new ways to push production costs lower, the consumer—and society as a whole—wins. When the state enters the game to limit competition, these gains are reversed. That's the theory.

But when the state fails to properly regulate market activity, it allows for a system in which players have every incentive to value cleverness more than prudence, short-term gains over longer-term investment. During the twenty-five-year period before the market meltdown of 2008, the conventional wisdom in corporate management theory favored an approach that privileged "shareholder value," a concept widely associated with former General Electric CEO Jack Welch, who was promoting the idea in speeches as early as 1981.[3] The assumption was that since company shares are bought and sold in a marketplace, shareholders will collectively allocate a company's resources more efficiently and intelligently than its management can. In other words, senior executives can only be sure they're managing the company well if more and more investors are pushing its share price ever higher. By forcing managers to maximize share price through cost-cutting, more capital and workers are released back into the marketplace to power other companies and sectors. This concept even earned the blessing of the Organisation for Economic Co-operation and Development.[4]

In this ultracompetitive environment, problems began to emerge once CEOs and company management became obsessed with maximizing quarterly profits at the expense of investment in a sound long-term growth strategy. Why should a corporate executive who wants to keep his job deny shareholders the largest possible quarterly dividend payment—especially when investment in the company's future will profit only his successor? Why should he ask the company's top performers to forgo this quarter's performance-related bonuses when they might earn more this year by working for a competitor? Adding to this epidemic of short-term thinking, many of today's largest shareholders are managers of large portfolios who buy and sell shares quickly in search of instant profit. Many of them care little about a company's multiyear prospects. As stock prices climbed, critics of this theory were dismissed. But when financial markets spiraled toward crisis in 2008, it became clear that the short-term thinking of the few had inflicted enormous damage on the many—including victims of the broader economic meltdown, the crisis's "collateral damage." By early 2009, even Jack Welch was denouncing the concept of shareholder value as "the dumbest idea in the world."[5] This is just one example of the sort of failure of imagination that sent markets into free fall in 2008. Reckless borrowing and lending, ill-conceived risk taking, poor risk management, and many other human failings played crucial roles, but the common denominator in all these mistakes is a lack of intelligent government oversight of all this activity. Any argument that the state should remove itself entirely from the marketplace is absurd, because markets have proven again and again over several centuries that they cannot and will not regulate themselves. On the other hand, few except those on the socialist fringe claim that the financial crisis argues for a return to command economics. The debate among members of the G20 group of leading industrialized and developing countries is about how to make capitalism work best, not whether it should be replaced.

But does the crisis argue for a shift toward state capitalism? Does the need for more rigorous government regulation of markets imply that the state should move to dominate them? No, because governments use the tools provided by state capitalism to accomplish *political* goals, not to serve the public welfare. This system allows them to minimize the political risks they face by maximizing their control over activities that generate substantial amounts of wealth. That's not a formula for producing more efficient or more equitable economic performance.

China emerged strong from the Asian financial crisis of the late 1990s at least in part because its leadership supplemented stimulus spending with measures designed to further liberalize the Chinese economy—especially by privatizing urban housing ownership, turning a government benefit into a market commodity. The result was increased corporate investment and a spike in consumer spending. To respond to the larger market meltdown in 2008, the Chinese government announced a $586 billion stimulus package to be invested largely in infrastructure and affordable housing. But some of the Chinese domestic economy's most profitable sectors, like mass transportation and communications, remain within the control of state-run giants. The privately owned companies that might force them to compete and operate more efficiently are left on the outside looking in. In less developed rural areas, small farmers and business owners struggle to access credit from state-owned banks, sharply limiting their ability to produce growth in areas of the country that badly need it. In other words, state capitalism is burdened with its own brand of shortsighted, short-term thinking, especially when powerful players within the system have their own set of incentives for earning short-term rewards. The injection of hundreds of billions of dollars can kick-start any developing economy, but the problems that threaten future growth continue to metastasize.

In addition, as we've seen, the ties that bind political and business elites in state-capitalist countries shape the environment in which some of their largest companies operate. In China, the leadership reserves the right to select the heads of all major banks and large industrial enterprises. Answering the immediate demands of fickle shareholders creates one set of problems; satisfying the needs of political officials poses another. In Russia, conflicts of interest are more obvious. That Viktor Zubkov moved from prime minister to chairman of Gazprom, Russia's gas monopoly, when Dmitry Medvedev left Gazprom to become Russia's president reveals all we need to know about government control of an internationally powerful state-owned company. This problem brings political bureaucrats into economic decision making to an extent we haven't seen since communism collapsed.

In general, the political officials who run many of these institutions have neither the education nor the training to make the sound commercial decisions on which long-term productivity and financial stability depend. Aware of this problem, some governments entrust business professionals with day-to-day management of some of these companies and institutions. But the best of the professionals are hard to come by, and being human, they sometimes make bad bets. When they do, political officials may decide they can no longer trust them, a trend we've seen in several sovereign wealth funds that have taken the same large losses from the financial crisis that have plagued so many privately owned financial institutions. In addition, however they were chosen, those who manage these companies and institutions must ultimately answer to a political patron, someone who measures performance by how well it satisfies the state's political goals. Those that succeed are rewarded with generous state subsidies and a dominant (and protected) position within a particular economic sector, further tilting the playing field by allowing these companies to crowd out competition from privately owned foreign and domestic potential rivals that operate on a purely commercial basis. In the process, politics trumps efficiency, entrepreneurship, and innovation.

Finally, the financial crisis helped popularize an especially frightening phrase in America and other free-market countries: "too big to fail." But how many American companies really fit that description? In a country where the government practices large-scale state capitalism, many state-owned enterprises were created in part to provide jobs for large numbers of people who might otherwise find themselves on the street demanding change from their government. The Obama administration and the Democratic majority in Congress bailed out a handful of very large privately owned companies in 2009. But their number pales beside the number of state- and privately owned companies that received emergency funding from China's government or the number of factories, plants, and banks that the Russian government and loyal oligarchs have infused with new cash. In many cases, these political officials are throwing good money after bad.

Protectionism

In general, those who rule in authoritarian states have more to fear from their own people than from other governments or their militaries. That's especially true in a post–Cold War world in which the threat of global military conflict has decreased sharply. In 2010, U.S. troops are still fighting in Iraq and Afghanistan, but they're struggling to overcome militants and insurgents, not foreign military powers. The Chinese leadership fears the social implications of a sharp economic slowdown far more than it fears U.S. warships patrolling the Taiwan Strait. Russia's political elite worries much more that a run on domestic banks will trigger a financial crisis than that NATO will launch an invasion. Saudi royals fear the power of domestic terrorist cells to sow disorder more than any attack from a neighboring state. That's why, though state-capitalist governments have no monopoly on protectionism, they are far more willing to use it. Their first concern is domestic, and their primary goal is to buttress the power of the state. Concerns for relations with other states are important, but secondary. They are also better able to use protectionism, because they're much less likely to face rival political parties, courts, or an independent press that can check the government's power to do what it wants.

Many protectionist weapons are familiar. To shelter domestic producers from foreign competition, governments can impose quotas, which limit the amount of a particular good that enters the country, and tariffs, which discourage consumers from buying imports by making them relatively more expensive than similar goods produced at home. They can help local exporters by providing subsidies or loan guarantees that allow them to produce goods more cheaply. But there are also more subtle ways of tilting the playing field in favor of local companies. The state can require licenses that apply mainly to imported goods, limit imports to a small number of ports of entry, impose difficult- (or impossible-) to-meet public-health or safety standards on particular imported products, or block them on environmental grounds. It can direct local banks to favor domestic over foreign borrowers. It can move money through state-owned banks to hide subsidies for exporters or require that domestic companies receive a fixed share of the largesse from state spending sprees, as when the Obama administration and Democratic lawmakers included a "Buy American" provision in the 2009 stimulus package. Or a government can simply refuse to enforce existing laws and regulations. The inability or unwillingness of Chinese officials to protect intellectual property rights of foreign firms has undermined Beijing's relations with several other governments, but it accomplishes the state's domestic political goal. Protectionism is essentially a remnant of mercantilism, an effort to protect domestic wealth at the expense of outsiders. For those who believe that trade and investment spur competition and innovation, generating new wealth that can't be created in any other way, protectionism undermines the ability of free markets to produce a general prosperity.

The protectionist measure that has arguably done more harm to the global economy than any other—the Smoot-Hawley Tariff Act of 1930—illustrates two important points: that protectionist temptations are at their most intense when times are hard and that bastions of free-market capitalism are not immune to them. Every government fears that an economic crash will put large numbers of people out of work, unleash social unrest, and threaten the government's hold on power. Politicians of all stripes are apt to pander to the crowd. About eight months after the stock market crash of 1929, President Herbert Hoover signed Smoot-Hawley into law, sharply increasing already high tariffs on more than twenty thousand imported items to support struggling farmers and manufacturers who had just begun to learn how to collectivize their influence and to pressure lawmakers.[6] Canada answered Smoot-Hawley's import duties with tariffs of its own. The British Empire and other European traders followed suit. Between 1929 and 1934, the volume of both U.S. and global trade fell by two thirds. Some historians have argued that the collapse in international commerce and the hardships it imposed helped speed the slide into World War II.

Over the past six decades, much of the growth that has lifted so many new players onto the global economic stage flowed from the willingness of governments to restrain the most potentially damaging of their protectionist impulses. When World War II came to an end, international trade negotiations focused mainly on untying the protectionist knot that Smoot-Hawley had helped tie—and that war had tightened further by forcing governments to control production for the war effort. The long and winding road away from prewar protectionism passed through eight rounds of trade talks under the General Agreement on Tariffs and Trade (GATT) between 1948 and 1994, providing ample evidence that protectionism is that rare creation that takes much longer to destroy than to construct. But the rewards were priceless: The wealth generated by successive international trade agreements helped free-market democracies outlast communism's command economies. After a final round of talks, GATT gave way to establishment of the World Trade Organization (WTO) in 1995, and rules governing trade in services and intellectual property rights were added to existing regulations covering trade in goods. The WTO, also a forum for the settlement of commercial disputes, now has 153 members, including every country profiled in this book except Russia and Algeria. Collectively, these states account for more than 95 percent of total world trade. In late 2009, there were also about two hundred current and another two hundred planned bilateral or regional trade agreements.

The WTO was not designed to serve governments. In the words of its directors, "Although negotiated and signed by governments, the goal (of the rules) is to help producers of goods and services, exporters, and importers conduct their business, while allowing governments to meet social and environmental objectives. The system's overriding purpose is to help trade flow as freely as possible—so long as there are no undesirable side-effects—because this is important for economic development and well-being. That partly means removing obstacles. It also means ensuring that individuals, companies and governments know what the trade rules are around the world, and giving them the confidence that there will be no sudden changes of policy."[7] Despite the organization's many shortcomings, it invites governments to acknowledge publicly that protectionism and trade wars are self-defeating, and it has the power to enforce its rulings.

In April 2009, heads of state at the G20 summit in London formally pledged to "not repeat the historic mistakes of protectionism of previous eras" and to "refrain from raising new barriers to investment or to trade in goods and services, imposing new export restrictions, or implementing World Trade Organization (WTO) inconsistent measures to stimulate exports."[8] But the World Bank has found that during the five months leading up to that meeting, seventeen of the nineteen group members implemented forty-seven measures that restricted trade at the expense of other countries. It concluded that "if there is one lesson from the experience of the 1930s that is suddenly relevant, it is that raising trade barriers merely compounds recessionary forces—and risks pushing the economy into prolonged contraction." The bank has estimated that governments had provided struggling domestic automakers with tens of billions of dollars in subsidies by mid-2009, with the United States accounting for about one third of that total. The German, British, Canadian, Swedish, and Italian governments responded by protecting their own automakers. French President Nicolas Sarkozy conditioned state loans to Renault and Peugeot-Citroën on the preservation of jobs in France, even if it meant closing relatively more productive factories in the Czech Republic and Slovakia. Then there's the banking sector. In Europe, competition policy was effectively suspended in 2008.

A number of the largest European banks were nationalized in all but name. The injection of state money into banks and the addition of state-appointed officials to their boards gave those governments substantial new influence over the lending process—leverage that some of them might use to direct loans toward national champions or other domestic firms at the expense of companies in other countries.

But the extraordinary circumstances of the financial crisis aside, state-capitalist governments are much more susceptible than free-market democracies to protectionist temptations, for three reasons. First, there's an important qualitative difference between short-term measures meant to protect jobs and jump-start growth, on the one hand, and the institutionalization of protectionism as a key component of state-capitalist development strategy, on the other. While bailing out U.S. automakers and banks, the Obama administration used every available public opportunity to assure anyone who would listen that the measures were temporary. China's government feels no such impulse as it extends state control into new areas of the domestic economy.

Second, elected leaders of free-market countries know that private-sector firms that depend on international trade relationships have the political influence and financial clout to defend their interests. Companies that have benefited most from globalization, especially those that import large quantities of production material and equipment or have supply chains that extend across multiple countries, tend to lobby against protectionism. In state-capitalist countries, private firms often find themselves squeezed between a government that dominates key economic sectors and the relatively stronger and better connected state-owned companies and privately owned national champions that have a clear interest in protecting the status quo. In addition, the supply chains of state-owned and state-favored companies tend to cross fewer international borders, in part because their governments use them to create work for domestic suppliers. They're more likely to seek the protectionist advantages their government can provide because they're competing with established multinational companies with access to more sophisticated technologies, more and better management experience, established client contacts, and much greater experience in developing, branding, and marketing their products.

Third, state-capitalist governments can afford to be more secretive than free-market democracies and are better able to disguise subtle forms of protectionism. In Washington, the debate over the "Buy American" provision in the stimulus package played out under klieg lights in congressional hearing rooms. Lobbyists debated the plan's merits on cable television, and anyone with an Internet connection could read the text of the various versions of the provision under discussion. A company seeking legal remedy against this or that aspect of the legislation could count on a fair hearing in court. Authoritarian state-capitalist governments dominate their domestic economies, but they also exercise enormous influence over how their plans are implemented, how they are legally interpreted, and how they're portrayed by domestic media. Their citizens have much less access to information about what government is up to. In effect, the state referees the game, controls many of the biggest players, pressures the others, and directs the TV coverage to ensure that fans at home feel a surge of national pride from the winning team's accomplishments. Protectionism is especially easy to practice and enforce in countries where courts rarely rule against the state or in favor of a foreign company or investor at the expense of a domestic one.

Decoupling

The rise of state capitalism undermines both America's singular international influence and the global economic interdependence that encourages governments to work together in ways that bolster growth. The 2008 financial crisis exacerbated both trends. This development wasn't immediately obvious. In the short term, the global market slowdown reinforced the centrality of the U.S. economy and the importance of U.S. leadership for global growth.

Many around the world blamed Washington and Wall Street for creating the problem. Fairly or unfairly, they charged that the U.S. government had singlehandedly pushed the world into recession by failing to properly regulate financial markets and by allowing U.S. lenders and retailers to encourage the American public to borrow and consume too much while saving too little, thereby creating huge imbalances in the global economy. But in a perverse way, the claim that America's failures could inflict such widespread damage is itself recognition of the country's continuing importance. Whatever the merits of these accusations, the crisis made clear that much of the world still looks to Washington to make things right—by correcting its own mistakes, providing a relative safe haven for investment when markets in other countries begin to wobble, and by fueling the next stage of the global economy's rise by reinvigorating U.S. consumer demand for the world's exports.

In the years before the crisis, the idea of "America in decline" had reached the status of cliché. The growing weakness of the dollar generated anxiety among those who held U.S. currency in large quantities, particularly in China, that a lack of confidence in Washington's judgment was eroding the value of their dollar holdings. Talk of *decoupling*, the process by which emerging-market countries, particularly in Asia, sharply reduce their dependence for growth on U.S. markets, became commonplace. An internationally unpopular Bush administration had become a focal point for anger among those ready to dismiss the importance of U.S. global leadership. But events in 2009 helped restore confidence in America's vitality.

First, the impact of the financial crisis on China's economy demonstrated that decoupling has a long way to go. Though China's banks had little exposure to the toxic assets that inflicted so much damage on financial institutions in the West, the impact of the slowdown on China's best customers in America and Europe closed thousands of

Chinese factories and aroused fears within the leadership of a sharp spike in unemployment. Officials on both sides of the Pacific saw that a bad day for America's economy is still a bad day for China's, and Beijing's bid to restructure its economy to rely much more for growth on domestic consumer demand remains a long-term project. Second, as the crisis metastasized around the world, risk-averse investors again turned to U.S. treasuries as a hedge against turmoil in developing states, helping Washington protect the advantages that come with the dollar's status as the world's reserve currency. Finally, the same polls that underscored the Bush administration's international unpopularity revealed that the election of Barack Obama had inspired much more positive attitudes toward America and its role in the world in almost every country surveyed.[9]

Yet over the longer term, the financial crisis *has* done considerable damage to America's ability to lead by example as a champion of free-market capitalism. The "rise of the rest," including several governments that practice state capitalism, will erode America's great-power advantages. For more than six decades, the United States has symbolized capitalist muscle and material success. In 1945, Europe lay in ruins. Japan was a defeated and occupied country. Russia and the other captive nations of the Soviet Union remained burdened with an unsustainable political and economic system. China stood on the brink of civil war, and India was still a British possession. Africa and Latin America had not yet shed the shackles of colonialism. America set aside an isolationist past to take on global leadership and to preach the gospel of free-market capitalism. With the end of the Cold War and the collapse of communism, America appeared to have no credible rival. But the fall of the Berlin Wall did not signal the end of authoritarian government, and those who rely on tight political control still need an economic system they can use to ensure that they don't join the Bolsheviks atop the ash heap of history.

Successive U.S. presidential administrations have used the power that Washington wields within international financial institutions like the World Bank and International Monetary Fund to condition much-needed aid packages on the willingness of recipient governments to swallow America's medicine and to emulate its economic model. During the 1990s, the Clinton administration worked to shape post-Communist reconstruction in Eastern Europe and the former Soviet Union. Some within those countries complained that the help came with generous helpings of post–Cold War American self-satisfaction, and many citizens struggled to adapt as U.S.-endorsed shock economic therapy generated hardship not seen since the end of World War II. Now that the excesses of free-market capitalism have generated a market meltdown at home and a crisis abroad, the world's state capitalists find a more sympathetic audience, and the governments of other developing states now have a credible alternative model for success—one that appeals to their drive for political control.

After all, if Washington must spend hundreds of billions to bail out American-style capitalism and if a majority of Americans tell pollsters they favor a substantial government-led overhaul of the country's health-care system and its energy policy, how can U.S. officials argue with a straight face that foreign governments should intervene less in their domestic economies? With all the political upheaval inside the United States, why should other governments look to America to lead in the creation of new rules that govern global financial flows and to reform multinational financial institutions that no longer reflect the true balance of international power? The leaders of developing states know that China's government will offer them no advice on how best to mature their politics or grow their economies. But the Chinese will make deals. They offer investment, and in some cases political cover, in return for access to the resources they need to achieve their domestic goals. In other words, cash-strapped developing world governments know they now have a choice in lenders. They can accept IMF loans if they're willing to promise to impose the kinds of belt-tightening measures that make governments unpopular. Or they can accept loans from China that come without political strings attached.

In addition, though China's economy suffered serious damage during the global economic slowdown, it rebounded strongly and quickly. Russia remains burdened with a fragile banking system, but the foreign reserves amassed from years of high oil prices provided enough money to maintain the stability of the state and the popularity of the men who run it. India weathered the crisis, thanks largely to its relatively limited reliance on foreign trade. Thus, the lesson that many emerging-market governments took from the crisis is that free-market capitalism had ignited a wildfire and that those who depended on it most had suffered the worst burns. Others had used national oil companies and sovereign wealth funds to build themselves a firewall—by amassing deep financial reserves, bailing out struggling domestic companies and banks, and investing abroad where crisis created opportunities.

A growing number of governments appear to believe they will soon depend less on America for stability, security, and prosperity—complicating Barack Obama's bid to translate global popularity into geopolitical leverage. When the global recession was at its worst, he was not able to persuade others that coordinated stimulus would revive global growth. He has not won new commitments from the governments of NATO allies for substantial numbers of new troops to support the U.S. war effort in Afghanistan. He has not earned support from Moscow or Beijing for sanctions tough enough to force Iran's government to renounce its nuclear ambitions. Finally, without a substantial international crisis to divert his attention, most of his administration's time and energy will be spent on the domestic reform issues that will likely determine his chances for reelection. For those around the world who believe that U.S. leadership is essential for geopolitical stability, that trend will fuel fears that Washington will accept responsibility for only the most pressing of international problems—and that it will respond to events rather than shape them. Finally, if history is any guide, Congress will likely impose unnecessarily heavy regulatory burdens as part of financial-sector reforms intended to avoid a repeat of the financial crisis. In other words, having allowed American capitalism to swing too far to the right along the market spectrum, Washington will likely respond by pushing too far to the left. All of these problems will empower governments that practice state capitalism to play a larger role on the international stage—often in ways that undermine free markets.

The Threats

State capitalism poses a variety of threats. Here's one you might not imagine. When longtime dictator Lansana Conté of Guinea died in December 2008, a group of military officers led by Moussa Dadis Camara seized power in that West African nation. In this mineral-rich country, multinational mining firms like Rio Tinto, Anglo Gold Ashanti, and others compete for access to supplies of gold, iron ore, and bauxite (aluminum ore) with companies from China and Russia that have complex (sometimes hidden) ties to their home governments. On September 28, 2009, thousands of unarmed prodemocracy demonstrators gathered at a sports stadium in the capital city of Conakry. Soldiers opened fire on the crowd, killing 157 people and wounding more than 1,000, according to a local human-rights group. Given the threat of instability and the reputational risks that companies face in shaking hands and making deals with such a regime, it's all the more striking that just fifteen days after this massacre, the Guinean government announced agreement on a $7 billion mining contract with an unnamed Chinese company, a firm that Mining Minister Mahmoud Thiam said would become a "strategic partner in all mining projects" in the country. Companies with ties to authoritarian governments like China's, whether state owned or simply state supported, achieve success by helping their government meet its economic (and political) needs. They don't answer to shareholders and international opinion as a Western multinational would and can go places that multinationals can't afford to go. This tilts the commercial playing field away from privately owned companies, but it also enables a repressive government like Guinea's to make the deals that raise the cash that enables the regime to maintain its hold on power. Details of these deals are often treated as state secrets. As China develops more extensive commercial ties throughout Africa, it will have to care more about political instability. Social unrest is bad for business in all sorts of ways. But for the moment, these sorts of deals will continue to distort market competition and to feed unrest in politically volatile countries and regions.

In fact, the secrecy with which many state-owned companies and sovereign wealth funds operate creates many different kinds of risks and challenges. The governments that control SWFs, for example, insist that they created them to maximize return on investment, not to advance political goals. Yet, because so many of them operate behind a veil of secrecy, the rest of the world is essentially expected to take their word for it. In 2008, the IMF invited the world's largest sovereign wealth funds to discuss new rules that would make their operations more transparent. The result of this summit included agreement on a voluntary code of conduct, but no new rules that would compel funds to disclose what they hold and how they operate. In short, the leaders of free-market countries who worry that foreign governments can exploit the openness of their economies to weaken their companies, steal their secrets, or gain new political leverage have no solid evidence that their fears will be realized. But they don't have evidence to the contrary either, and they find themselves weighing the cost of shutting out much-needed investment to guard against hypothetical threats.

Fear of state capitalism comes from many sources, some more reasonable than others. First, its leading practitioners are China, Russia, and the Arab monarchies of the Persian Gulf. For Americans, China and Russia are former Cold War adversaries. The oil embargo of the mid-1970s and the fact that all nineteen of the September 11 hijackers were Sunni Arabs makes it easy to demonize Sunni Arab governments—as we saw in 2006 when political attacks in Washington blocked a bid by Dubai Ports World to operate U.S. ports. It takes little imagination for politicians to portray any of these governments as a potential threat. Second, state-run enterprises and investment funds tend to labor under the same bureaucratic burdens that plague the governments that own them. Given that state-owned companies control three quarters of the world's known oil reserves, the mismanagement, corruption, and inefficiency that distort their operations drive up energy costs for everyone. Third, governments that practice state capitalism are making risky investment bets inside other emerging markets. When a Chinese state-owned firm buys long-term access to oil, gas, metals, or minerals inside a potentially unstable country, it exposes Beijing to risks of heavy financial losses, with potentially serious consequences for its own still vulnerable economy.

In addition, the advantages provided by state capitalism encourage some countries to pursue high-risk political strategies and reduce the ability of free-market democracies to pressure them to change their ways. Iran's government uses the cash generated by its control of domestic oil production to build a nuclear program, secure in the knowledge that governments that need access to its energy (like China and India) will refuse to support tough sanctions on its government. There's also the risk that an energy-rich state like Russia will turn off the taps for political gain—as many accuse Moscow of doing whenever Gazprom and the government of Ukraine come to blows over natural-gas prices. A threat from Moscow to slow gas supplies to the West already strikes fear in European capitals. Finally, there is the fear that foreign governments can use state-capitalist tools to undermine directly the national security of free-market democracies. Might Russia, China, and others use stakes in Western financial institutions to deliberately destabilize Western economies or as leverage with which to pressure Western governments into relinquishing some of their power within international financial institutions? Could they use their acquisitions to gain access to classified information, defense technologies, or trade secrets?

On the other hand, as the world recovers from the global recession and investors regain their appetite for risk, what if we discover that state-capitalist governments mean what they say about diversifying away from the dollar to diminish its status as the world's reserve currency? In other words, what if they slowly but steadily reduce their willingness to finance America's debt by buying U.S. Treasury bills? In 2008, as America's subprime mortgage mess generated an international crisis, sovereign wealth funds from Asia and the Middle East rode to the rescue with tens of billions of dollars for Citigroup, Merrill Lynch, and other financial institutions. They were bargain hunting, not trying to save American free-market capitalism, but these U.S. firms badly needed the money. Still, U.S. lawmakers reacted with suspicion. What if sovereign wealth funds decide *not* to invest in America, choosing instead to invest at home or to profit from higher returns from other emerging markets? In 2008, the Kuwait Investment Authority, stung by the loss of 10 percent of its $3 billion stake in Citigroup, redirected about $4 billion toward Kuwait's own collapsing stock market. Maybe the risk is that these funds will *stop* investing—and that America will have nowhere to turn the next time it needs cash to refloat a struggling economy. This threat is much less fanciful than the idea that China will use a sovereign wealth fund to try to destroy Western capitalism.

In fact, what happens if a patriotic backlash against Chinese or Arab investment in the United States closes the door on billions of dollars that could fuel the next stage of America's rise? One likely consequence: China, Russia, India, Brazil, the United Arab Emirates, and others will begin to do much more business with one another—and at the expense of Western countries' global market share and access to foreign markets for multinational companies. If America closes its doors, won't others do the same, reversing the gains from trade and investment of the past several decades? In particular, what if China finally succeeds in cutting its economy loose from America's as Chinese companies sell to a fast-growing Chinese middle class that becomes much larger than America's? In fact, what happens when China no longer needs huge volumes of foreign direct investment from America, Europe, and Japan, when Chinese companies use their growing influence to lobby for greater support against foreign competition, and when the Chinese public runs out of patience with an America less and less open to Chinese investment? What happens to the long-term plans of American and other multinational companies who have counted on decades of ever-growing profits from selling their products to hundreds of millions of Chinese consumers? In other words, what happens if China closes the door?

There's no new Cold War here, but free markets now face a whole new kind of challenge. In the final chapter, we'll consider what those who believe in free-market capitalism can do to meet this challenge.

CHAPTER SIX

Meeting the Challenge

I'm very optimistic about the future of free-market capitalism.
I'm not optimistic about the future of state capitalism—or rather I
am optimistic, because I think it will eventually come to an end.

—MURRAY N. ROTHBARD[1]

I agree with Murray. Not on everything, of course. Rothbard, a self-proclaimed anarcho-capitalist, argued that it made more sense to abolish government than to reform it. The economic meltdown of 2008–2009 made clear the need for *better* government, not less government, because it reminded us that investors and commercial strategists too often play for short-term gains and ignore longer-term risks. That's one reason why we shouldn't expect markets to regulate themselves and why intelligent (and limited) government intervention can help prevent market failures from generating shock waves through entire societies. In addition, the "state capitalism" Rothbard had in mind nearly four decades ago was the command economics of the communist bloc, not the more recent phenomenon described in this book. But free markets will probably outlast state capitalism as it is now practiced in China, Russia, the Gulf States, and elsewhere—just as they bested Soviet-style communism, because state capitalism has several important weaknesses.

First, state capitalism will never match the hold that communism once had on the popular imagination, because it isn't really a response to social or economic injustice. Early popular support for communist parties in Russia, China, and elsewhere was in many ways a rejection of the reactionary governments that had come before and the chaos of civil war. It's true that resource nationalism, one aspect of state capitalism, still has an ideological element. As Bolivia's Vice President Álvaro García Linera told the *Christian Science Monitor* in March 2007, "We are searching for a road to post neo-liberalism, for ways to disassemble the process of financial colonization and public resource privatization of the 1980s and 1990s." Russian political officials likewise often talk up their country's energy reserves with a healthy dose of nationalist resentment.

Yet state capitalism was created to maximize political leverage and state profits, not to combat injustice, and its lack of popular appeal makes the system much harder to export. State capitalism is less a coherent political philosophy than a set of management techniques. Communism wasn't rigid. The states that practiced it freely adapted the teachings of Marx and Lenin to fit their needs, but a core belief in collective ownership provided communism a basic consistency and an appeal for potential converts. The Chinese, Russian, or other state-capitalist governments don't need others to join their ranks—and they want to profit from the global economy, not dismantle it.

Second, China, Russia, the Gulf States, and other state capitalists have good reason to extend their political influence within their respective regions, but they're far too busy coping with headaches at home to spend time and resources on quixotic bids for global domination. This is the central reason they've chosen state capitalism in the first place. China's political leaders use state resources to buy long-term access to the crude oil, natural gas, and other commodities needed to fuel China's economy, create jobs, and safeguard the Communist Party's long-term survival. Russian officials micromanage the economic sectors that employ the largest numbers of workers to help keep them off the streets. The Saudi royals keep the kingdom's most lucrative assets in loyal hands to ensure they aren't used to finance challenges to their absolute political authority. All these governments see domestic problems as a far more immediate threat than anything coming from abroad.

Because state capitalism is more a set of governing principles than a coherent political ideology, no two state-capitalist governments can ever fully align their interests. By its very nature, it's exclusionary; it promotes state goals at the expense of outsiders. Just as Cold War–era rivalries between Beijing and Moscow left them unwilling and unable to partner at U.S. expense, so today's Russian and Chinese governments, the world's most influential practitioners of state capitalism, have competing sets of economic interests. Russia remains one of the world's leading resource exporters, and its government must manage the many problems that flow from a declining population. China is the world's fastest-growing resource consumer. Its government must cope with the challenges that come with an enormous population constantly on the move between the countryside and the fast-growing cities of the east coast and environmental problems that limit China's access to vital resources like clean drinking water. Russian officials know well that Chinese migrants are flowing in large numbers into Russia's thinly populated eastern provinces, provoking all sorts of tensions in local Russian politics. The two governments also compete for influence within the Central Asian countries that lie between them. Russia and China have plenty of opportunities for cooperation—on energy trade, for example. They'll find many more. They can sometimes work together to limit U.S. influence in their neighborhoods. But in crucial ways, their interests run in opposite directions. State capitalism wouldn't pose much threat to free-market capitalism if its most important actors didn't include the world's leading energy exporters and its largest emerging-market power. But for the foreseeable future, natural rivalry will limit their ability to work together or to project power far beyond their borders—and that's true of all state-capitalist governments.

Finally, some believe that the trend toward greater government involvement in domestic economies and state management of valuable assets is irreversible, because governments will never willingly surrender control of any instrument of wealth or power once they've grabbed hold of it. For example, commentator George Will has expressed deep skepticism that Obama administration officials and U.S. lawmakers would voluntarily withdraw from management of failing companies and their assets. Will argued that we must never underestimate "the pleasure politicians derive from using their nations' wealth as a slush fund for purchasing political advantage."[2] He's right about that. But governments *do* sometimes relinquish control of valuable assets. Sometimes they do it to raise cash. Sometimes it's because they don't want the responsibility. Sometimes it's to spur longer-term growth.

Prompted by the Thatcherite revolution in the early 1980s, most Western European governments began to divest themselves of many state-owned companies in order to produce a short-term spike in government revenue and to generate higher growth rates. Since the fall of communism, they've urged their Eastern European counterparts to do the same. The result over the past two decades has been the largest voluntary state surrender of economic control in modern history. Emerging-market states around the world have "emerged" precisely because they have liberalized and/or privatized key companies, industries, and economic sectors. China, India, and many others have grown their economies by expanding the size and scope of their private sectors to a degree that will prove extremely difficult to reverse. Governments practice state capitalism because it enriches them—and reinforces their ability to preserve political control. But if policy makers within these states decide that liberalization would better serve their interests, as they sometimes do, they will liberalize their economies.

In other words, though obituaries for dictatorship, the nation-state, and heavy state involvement in markets have proven premature, the free market isn't dead yet either. The Great Depression of the 1930s did not destroy free-market capitalism, even as communist and fascist alternatives captured imaginations around the world. Free-market capitalism defeated fascism, shed colonialism, and outlasted communism. It has also survived many crises of its own making. Why is it so resilient? Because virtually all people value an opportunity to create prosperity for themselves and their families and because free markets have proven again and again that they can empower virtually anyone. As hundreds of millions of people become more aware of how others live—across the road and across the planet—they see that some have much more than others. But many of them also see that wealth, however they define it, is no longer beyond their reach. They see that prosperity can be contagious as once-isolated nations and peoples join the global economy, creating new markets for the goods and services they produce.

Foreign trade and investment also offer the surest path toward the alleviation of poverty. The past three decades have proven that access to free markets—not financial aid alone—can lift huge numbers of poor people into the global economy. Development aid saves lives and rebuilds communities. At times, only an emergency infusion of cash can pull those with nothing from disaster. But handouts have never helped Cuba or North Korea stand on their own, and it isn't bailout packages that are raising the living standards of hundreds of millions throughout China and India.

Free markets provide those who participate in them with long-term advantages that state capitalism can't match. First, political officials have engineered state-capitalist systems to produce wealth, but mainly as a means of maintaining political control and of projecting state power. Forced to choose between the prosperity of their people and the security of their governments, state capitalists will choose security every time. In other words, if commercial activity depends on access to information, if the Internet provides the best, fastest, and most efficient access to that information, if the Internet also enables popular resistance to an authoritarian government, and if political officials have the means to (even temporarily) shut the Internet down, they will shut it down. This lowers the trajectory of long-term growth. Western governments sometimes allow security concerns to trump growth potential. But governments that practice state capitalism have many more levers to pull and buttons to push when it comes to shutting down the free exchange of just about anything.

Second, there is the concept of "creative destruction." Economist Joseph Schumpeter coined this phrase in his 1942 book, *Capitalism, Socialism, and Democracy,* to describe a process by which dying ideas and materials fertilize new ones, endowing capitalism with a self-regenerating dynamism. As industries become obsolete and die, the workers, assets, and ideas that once sustained them are freed to recombine in new forms to produce goods, services, and ideas that meet the evolving wants and needs of consumers. This process sustains an ever-expanding economic ecosystem. It's not the product of political whim. It's as organic as human evolution.

Those who administer state capitalism fear creative destruction— for the same reason they fear all other forms of destruction: They can't control it. Creative destruction ensures that industries that produce things that no one wants will eventually collapse. That means lost jobs and lost wages, the kind of problem that can drive desperate people into the streets to challenge authority. In a state-capitalist society, lost jobs can be pinned directly on state officials. That's why the ultimate aim of Chinese foreign policy is to form commercial relationships abroad that can help fuel the creation of millions of jobs back home. That's why Indian officials forgive billions in debt held by farmers on the eve of an election and raise salaries for huge numbers of government employees. That's why Prime Minister Putin travels to shuttered factories with television cameras in tow and orders them reopened. Of course, workers in a free-market system blame politicians for lost jobs and wages all the time. That's why candidates Barack Obama and Hillary Clinton tried to outpopulist one another in the hard-hit states of Pennsylvania and Ohio during the 2008 presidential campaign. But when the government owns the company that owns the factory, its responsibility for workers is both more direct and more obvious. Political officials don't want responsibility for destruction, creative or otherwise. Inevitable economic volatility will eventually give state capitalists ample incentive to shed responsibilities that become too costly.[3]

It is not my intent to argue that economic growth is an absolute good. Throughout much of both the developed and developing world, there's an increasingly obvious toxic downside to all this wealth creation. Governments are coping (or failing to cope) with severe environmental damage wrought by rapid industrialization. To slow the advance of global warming, political leaders of the world's wealthiest governments have called on major developing states like China, India, and Russia to commit to limits on the levels of carbon emitted within their borders. That's not likely to happen, because policy makers and entrepreneurs in developing states know that industrialization in the West did plenty of damage to the planet, and they won't postpone their own prosperity simply to appease those who already enjoy it. Yet free markets are not incompatible with environmentally responsible economic growth. Investment in green technologies can make an enormous difference for clean air and drinking water, even as it creates jobs and generates substantial profits for investors. Compromise on the regulation of carbon emissions is entirely possible and could help slow the warming of the planet, but a free market in green technology is far more likely than voluntary limits on carbon emissions to make a measurable long-term difference in pollution standards.

Now for the Bad News

Even if state capitalism isn't around a century from now, the financial crisis and the global recession have ensured that it will enjoy many more years of robust health. American-style free-market capitalism and the idea of globalization have taken plenty of blame for the meltdown. Developing states that opened themselves to trade and foreign investment took an especially tough hit, while those like India, Poland, and Egypt that are less dependent on cross-border financial flows weathered the storm with fewer lasting problems. Outside of these exceptions, international investment in the developing world slowed considerably during the crisis. In 2008, emerging markets took in $461 billion in net positive capital inflows. As of this writing, 2009 figures were expected to fall to about $165 billion.[4] A February 2009 World Bank report estimated that 53 million people in emerging-market countries would slide back into poverty over the course of that year.[5] Trade barriers have risen, protectionism has intensified, and large numbers of immigrant workers have returned to their home countries. Meanwhile, state capitalists, particularly in China, continued to invest. In 2008, for example, national oil and gas companies and emerging-market-based sovereign wealth funds accounted for a record 15 percent of global mergers and acquisitions and six of the ten largest asset deals.[6]

There is more than one model of free-market capitalism—and Americans and Europeans often argue over the relative merits of their own versions. The U.S./Anglo-Saxon model grew from mistrust of any system that gives government too much power. The European social-democratic model relies more on the state as guardian of the rights of the individual. Relatively speaking, it favors safeguards for workers over protections for employers. This can slow growth rates over time, but it provides a wider social safety net when things go wrong. Different as they are, the two models share a core assumption: that the private sector, not the state, must be the primary engine of economic expansion if growth is to be strong and sustainable. Yet the difference between free-market capitalism and state capitalism is a fundamental one. The former recognizes that government can help enable growth, while the latter asserts that government-managed growth can further empower government. For all the reasons outlined in this book, state capitalism limits the global free-market system's productive potential. That's why it's important that those who believe in free-market capitalism continue to practice what they preach.

There are political stakes in this contest. Free markets thrive in open societies because they depend on the relatively free flow of capital, ideas, and people. Independent courts and a free press bolster these processes by limiting the government's ability to regulate all this traffic. State capitalism helps authoritarian states resist demand for political reform by allowing their leaders to micromanage political and economic risks to their monopoly hold on power. Running a police state isn't cheap, and direct control of much of a nation's wealth can make all the difference. So can an ability to use courts and the media as instruments of state power. To invest in the power of free markets is to help large numbers of people build a stake in a system that shifts wealth and power from authoritarian governments into the hands of private citizens.

The clash between champions of free markets and state capitalists is playing out in multilateral institutions. The financial meltdown of 2008 revealed two things about international leadership. First, the G7 group of industrialized nations no longer reflects the world's true balance of power. Until recently, annual G7 summit meetings allowed the governments of the United States, Japan, Germany, Britain, France, Italy, and Canada to chart an economic course that most other countries had little choice but to follow. Differences among the leaders of these countries over the role of government in an economy were relatively small. But the financial crisis made clear that no institution that excludes China, India, and other emerging-market countries can speak with much authority on solutions to global problems.

Second, the meltdown also revealed that the G20, comprising the finance ministers and central-bank governors of nineteen of the world's largest economies (plus a representative of the European Union), has too many members. In 2009, a G20 summit featured talks on the world's central political and economic challenges that included U.S. President Barack Obama, Chinese President Hu Jintao, German Chancellor Angela Merkel, Indian Prime Minister Manmohan Singh, Russian President Dmitry Medvedev, Brazil's President Luiz Inácio Lula da Silva, French President Nicolas Sarkozy, Japanese Prime Minister Taro Aso, British Prime Minister Gordon Brown, Canadian Prime Minister Stephen Harper, Turkish Prime Minister Recep Tayyip Erdoğan, Italian Prime Minister Silvio Berlusconi, Indonesian President Susilo Bambang Yudhoyono, Mexican President Felipe Calderón, Australian Prime Minister Kevin Rudd, Argentine President Cristina Fernández de Kirchner, South African President Jacob Zuma, South Korean President Lee Myung-bak, and King Abdullah bin Abdul Aziz al-Saud of Saudi Arabia.

That's a big table, and it's much more difficult to build substantive compromise among twenty negotiators than among seven. It's also a forum that includes governments with fundamentally different ideas about the role of government in boosting economic growth, energy and climate policy, financial regulatory changes, the dollar's role as international reserve currency, and relations with the governments of countries like Iran and Sudan, which provide China with energy supplies and the West with headaches. A similar power shift is under way within other institutions—like the International Monetary Fund, where China, Russia, India, and Brazil demand larger voting shares to reflect their growing economic clout and the size of their financial contributions to the fund.

China Holds the Key

Western commentators have been writing the Chinese Communist Party's death notice for the past twenty years. In June 1989, the Chinese leadership essentially admitted that only brute force could hold the regime together when tanks crushed peaceful demonstrations in Tiananmen Square. With the stunningly quick collapse of authoritarian regimes throughout Eastern Europe later that year and the implosion of Yugoslavia and breakup of the Soviet Union two years later, China seemed destined for political upheaval. As the leadership broadened its experiments with capitalism and ever larger numbers of Chinese logged on to the Internet for the first time, plenty more voices warned that the regime was doomed.

Twenty years later, China has become the symbol of state capitalism's power, and it is China that will determine how long this trend survives. At the 2009 World Economic Forum in Davos, Premier Wen Jiabao blamed a "failure of financial supervision" in the United States for triggering the global recession. His implication, of course, was that Chinese-style state capitalism is the better system. To make his case, he could point to China's thirty years of double-digit growth or its $2.3 trillion in foreign-currency reserves, a sum that allows it to invest where others cannot. He could point to astronomical U.S. debt and his government's increasingly prominent role in financing it. He could highlight China's role in leading the global economy out of the worst recession since World War II. He could then set statistics aside and compare China's surging national pride with deepening American gloom.

No one can deny that China has benefited enormously from a shift in the world's economic center of gravity from West to East. In relative terms, the United States and Europe will continue to see a drop in their share of global wealth over the next several years. Emerging middle classes in countries like China, India, and Indonesia will gain as Western multinationals, mutual funds, and pension plans bet their investment dollars on higher returns in Asia. Fast-growing consumer demand throughout China will gradually lessen the dependence of its economy on exports to Europe and America. Asian countries will deepen commercial relations with one another, with China acting as regional commercial hub. Over time, they will diversify their holdings away from the dollar, undermining the resilience of the U.S. economy. The world can see America struggling to recover from a crisis generated by its own failure to regulate market activity—and can watch China rise as its government engineers continued high growth.

But at the same time, China's vulnerabilities are increasingly obvious. The Communist Party leadership believes it must create 10 to 12 million new jobs each year to maintain employment rates—and therefore social order. The World Bank estimated in 2008 that the country needed a growth rate of 9.5 percent simply to maintain a constant rate of employment.[7] Whatever the true tipping point, the economic efficiencies brought about by growth of the private sector and advanced technological investment in the state-owned sector are increasing worker productivity. That means more output from fewer workers, generally a good thing. But it also means that China will create fewer new jobs for each extra unit of growth. In other words, the treadmill is moving faster, and the leadership must run harder to remain in the same place—by continually accelerating the pace of growth to create the same number of jobs. China can't keep pace indefinitely. The leadership will have to reexamine assumptions about the capacity of government to generate long-term growth, stability, and prosperity—or accept the bulk of the blame when things go wrong.

The leadership's challenges don't stop there. It must continually satisfy demand for ever-higher levels of prosperity from new generations of Chinese consumers who aren't old enough to remember the deprivations of the 1960s and 1970s. It must grow rich before it grows old to create a vast social safety net for a country with a rapidly aging population.* It must continue to quell tens of thousands of large-scale

---

* As of 2009, fewer than 20 percent of Chinese workers can expect pensions. Just 14 percent have unemployment insurance. See House Committee on Small Business, Role of Small Business Suppliers and Manufacturers in the Domestic Auto Industry, Testimony of Chris Norch, president, Denison Industries, on Behalf of the American Foundry Society, May 13, 2009, http://www.house.gov/smbiz/hearings/hearing-5-13-09-auto-industry-suppliers/Norch.pdf, p. 7.

protests each year. It must engineer economic development that closes the increasing gap between the rich (primarily along the eastern and southern coasts) and the hundreds of millions of poor people throughout the interior. It must manage the effects—political, economic, and environmental—of thirty years of explosive growth on China's air and water. It must maintain order as millions travel between the countryside and the country's fast-growing cities. It must monitor the output of the 600 million Internet users that China can expect by 2012, and it must prevent political and social activists from using twenty-first-century communications tools to organize opposition to government plans—or to the government itself. It must also prevent these tools from becoming an amplifier of public demand that essentially tells the leadership what to do.

In the end, it's much more likely that the Chinese leadership will have to reconsider core assumptions about government's role in an economy than that the leaders in the United States will retreat fundamentally from free-market principles.

What Is to Be Done?

State capitalism was growing before the market meltdown of 2008, but the financial crisis and global recession have made it much more difficult for those who believe in free-market capitalism to make their case to those who don't. For at least the next several years, China's economy and its international influence will grow, and U.S. great-power advantages will continue to narrow. State capitalism may not be with us forever, but it's likely to be around for decades to come.

This trend will have three important and related implications: First, hopes that the increasingly free flow of ideas, information, people, money, goods, and services (globalization) can create a more prosperous and open global economy will face new skepticism, because the friction created by the collision of free-market and state-capitalist systems will drag on economic growth. Second, as governments focus increasingly on political challenges at home and in their immediate neighborhoods, states will invest more heavily in domestic markets and in ways that increase their leverage with states along their borders. That's a shift from the recent past when trade and investment flows reflected a desire for maximum efficiency and profitability by seeking opportunities anywhere in the world they could be found. Third, to take full advantage of globalization, companies and investors need access to global labor, capital, and consumer markets. Essential to their success is the freedom to hire workers and borrow money where they are least expensive and to sell in the fastest-growing markets—even if this implies simultaneous operations in dozens of countries. But as governments look increasingly to favor domestic companies and investors at the expense of their foreign competitors, privately owned Western companies will lose some of their access to all three. This has already happened to energy multinationals as state-owned oil companies become much more competitive. It's about to happen in many economic sectors at once. All these factors will make it more difficult in coming years for policy makers, corporate decision makers, and investors to accept the following policy recommendations. Yet active promotion of free-market capitalism and efforts to ensure that the United States remains an indispensable player in international politics and the global economy are essential if free markets are to prevail. This idea of "indispensability" is crucial.

The Private Sector

There are practical steps that private sector companies and investors can take to survive and thrive in the new order. They can adapt to better compete with state-owned enterprises and national champions. In many cases, private companies can't afford to go head-to-head with state players that are backed by generous government subsidies and their governments' political clout, but they can invest more heavily in areas where they still have a competitive edge. On many traditional exploration and production projects, ExxonMobil doesn't have the political clout to compete directly with the larger national oil companies. That's why ExxonMobil has gradually become more a natural gas and technology firm than an oil company. Some energy multinationals have the experience and expertise to take on projects that are too technologically difficult for state-owned firms—on projects where oil is buried in the seabed at extreme ocean depths, for example. ExxonMobil also has the experience and talent to manage complex projects more efficiently and at lower cost than its state-owned rivals. This allows ExxonMobil to remain indispensable to many energy-development projects and to partner with some of their state-run rivals.

The principle is the same outside the energy sector. Privately owned firms are more likely than their state-owned competitors to successfully adapt their business models as market circumstances change, and they're better at finding creative new ways to market their products. They tend to outperform in sectors that depend on personal relationships, advertising, marketing, and consulting. In short, private companies can extend their comparative advantages in every area in which entrepreneurs outperform political bureaucrats.

Speak Up for Free Markets

The immediate aftermath of a recession of historic depth, breadth, and duration might not seem the best time to champion an economic system widely blamed for so much upheaval. After all, the trouble began in the United States and was triggered by a failure of free-market capitalism. After hundreds of billions of dollars in Chinese state-directed stimulus spending put local producers back on their feet, the Chinese economy reemerged with a vengeance—even before its recession-ravaged customers in Europe, the United States, and Japan had recovered their balance. The global economic meltdown boosted state capitalism as a system that can give political leaders the tools they need to engineer short-term growth, put people back to work, and limit social unrest. That's precisely why now is the time to make the case that only genuinely free markets can generate broad, sustainable, long-term prosperity.

There are plenty of people who can answer this call. Left-of-center parties in the free-market world—America's Democrats, Britain's Labour Party, Germany's SPD, and others—tend to believe in greater government involvement in economies than their conservative counterparts do. But however overheated the domestic debate within these countries, their differences with domestic rivals over the role of government in the economy are relatively narrow. There is consensus in the West that the private sector is the only reliable long-term engine of robust and sustainable growth. No political figure in any of these countries would remain credible for long if he suggested a move toward state capitalism. Politicians will always disagree over how best to target taxes and spending and to reregulate markets as they undergo structural and technological changes. These debates take place within a free market of ideas. But spirited defense of marked-based capitalism is one of the very few issues on which members of both major U.S. political parties can wholeheartedly agree.

That said, Democrats can do more than Republicans to extol the virtues of markets, because they're the ones who mean to tighten regulation of them over the next several years. If they're able to work with Republicans to minimize the risk of another meltdown brought on by misplaced faith in the ability of markets to self-regulate, they will have done free-market capitalism an enormous favor. During his first year in office, President Obama missed an extraordinary opportunity. In fairness, he ran for the office just as heavyweight U.S. financial institutions had begun to implode and as the country began hemorrhaging jobs at an accelerated pace. As president, he inherited an economy in the depths of a two-year recession. But as both president of the United States and leader of a party associated (fairly or not) with protectionism, his renewed public commitment to free trade and open markets would make an important difference.

Unfortunately, Obama began his presidency by portraying large-scale government intervention in the U.S. economy more as an unwanted burden than a necessary evil. At the press conference that marked his hundredth day in office on April 29, 2009, he told reporters: "I don't want to run auto companies. I don't want to run banks. If you could tell me right now that, when I walked into this office that the banks were humming, that autos were selling, and that all you had to worry about was Iraq, Afghanistan, North Korea, getting health care passed, figuring out how to deal with energy independence, deal with Iran, and a pandemic flu, I would take that deal."[8] Instead of implying that political officials are simply too busy to run automakers and banks, he might have acknowledged that long-term commercial success depends on a private sector that moves for commercial reasons—not political officials who naturally factor politics into every decision. He might have said that a flourishing private sector is as core an American value as any constitutional principle. That kind of defense would grab headlines precisely because underregulated free markets have taken most of the blame for America's economic meltdown. Failure to properly regulate markets is not a failure of markets themselves, and President Obama should say so—more forcefully and more often.

Since the dawn of the industrial revolution, in all but the most extreme circumstances (like the onset of depression in the 1930s), wealth creation within the United States and other capitalist democracies has depended on government's willingness to allow free markets to flourish. Even the most severe economic downturns have served as commas, not periods, in a longer-term growth story. Over time, political power within industrialized democracies tends to alternate between center-left social-democratic parties that favor relatively more activist government and center-right conservative parties that favor a smaller, less interventionist model. Their acrimonious debates, particularly during election campaigns, hide the extent to which they agree on fundamental free-market principles. Growing public unease with globalization's progress and its effects on middle-class livelihoods leaves politicians of all stripes more willing to defend a free lunch than a free market—and more eager to build barriers meant to protect their constituents. Yet despite the global recession–induced bout of state interventionism throughout the developed world, markets there are generally freer than they were a generation ago.

That's even truer for Europe than for America, and leaders on both sides of the old East-West divide now have every reason to publicly extol the virtues of free-market capitalism. U.S. conservatives too often dismiss European states (especially France) with the word *socialist,* a term of derision for governments that are now only slightly more statist than their own. But over the longer term, it's the attraction of the free market that has brought Europe together as never before. The scale of this achievement is immense. Wars between major European powers, which plagued the continent for centuries, have become unthinkable. From the ashes of World War II, few could have imagined the prosperity that exists in most of today's Europe. Since 1980 in particular, governments in Western Europe have fueled growth by liberalizing (in some cases, privatizing) key industries. Governments throughout Eastern Europe have moved from Communism toward entry into a single European market.

Liberalization has far to go. The European Commission, the closest thing Europe has to a central government, should push to complete the single market—by extending it to cover all services, by preventing backsliding on state aid and budgetary rules, by eliminating competition among member states over tax rates, and by forcing tighter regulation of tax havens to prevent capital flight. The French and German governments will eventually have to find the political courage to accept gradual (but sharp) cuts in farming subsidies, payouts that now make up nearly half the EU budget via the Common Agricultural Policy. But the European Union and its commitment to free markets are already a success story worthy of emulation. Membership remains a powerful draw for many in Turkey, Croatia, Serbia, Ukraine, Georgia, and several other developing states on Europe's periphery. Holding open the possibility of accession for these states will provide a gravitational pull that helps them resist deeper economic dependence on ties with authoritarian, state-capitalist Russia. Nonmembers Iceland, Norway, and Switzerland now have wide-ranging free-trade agreements with the EU.

For many reasons, global protectionist pressures will likely increase over time. As Americans watch the gap continue to narrow between U.S. political, economic, and cultural influences and those of many other countries, they're liable to grow less confident that their children will enjoy an ever-rising standard of living. More forcefully than ever, they will call on their elected representatives to protect their jobs. Governments in Western Europe will have to welcome larger numbers of immigrants from Eastern Europe, Africa, and Asia to provide the tax revenue needed to support an aging workforce, feeding a xenophobic and protectionist backlash that has already begun in several countries. In China, more citizens will use the Internet to demand that their government favor Chinese companies at the expense of foreign competitors. To meet these pressures, political officials must find the courage to make the case for the prosperity that only openness to trade, investment, and immigration can produce.

Don't Close the Door on Trade

Governments that practice free-market capitalism will continue to need long-term access to labor, capital, and consumer markets within state-capitalist countries. To secure as much of that access as possible, they need state-capitalist governments to depend on their trade and investment. This is why U.S. and European policy makers should continue to make active trade promotion, particularly with state-capitalist governments, a core foreign-policy principle. If they genuinely believe in the power of free markets to create sustainable, broad-based prosperity, they should offer the concessions needed to complete the Doha Round of global trade talks as quickly as possible. Success will require compromise, including concessions from Washington and Brussels on subsidies designed to protect local farmers from competition from those in poorer countries. If they follow through, developing countries are more likely to lower barriers on imported industrial goods and remove obstacles to the entry of foreign firms into their financial markets.

In addition, many of the emerging-market countries that will account for an increasingly large share of global economic growth over the next several years have elements of both free-market and state-capitalist systems. Political officials and lawmakers in India, Brazil, Indonesia, South Korea, Turkey, South Africa, Nigeria, and other countries are watching to see if free-market champions stick to their principles— and whether opportunities to expand trade ties will offer them genuine opportunities for growth. If not, they will turn toward a more statist approach. The contest over these "hybrids" will determine how much further free markets can expand over the next several years—and by extension, how quickly the global economy can grow.

But if champions of free markets are to encourage the hybrids to liberalize, they must accept a gradualist approach. In any country where the state owns companies that employ large numbers of people, there are enormous risks associated with moving too quickly toward competitive markets. During the 1990s, Russia moved at lightning speed from a system of state control toward what U.S. State Department official Strobe Talbott once called "too much shock and not enough therapy." The social upheaval and fear these changes generated helped push the country toward state capitalism as large numbers of people decided to invest in security and the strongman (Vladimir Putin) who promised to provide it. Russia's vast resources of oil and natural gas helped fuel this project, but political officials everywhere have incentives to experiment with market liberalization only when they're confident they won't create chaos for which they will take the fall.

Never was the need for greater openness to trade more obvious than during the recession of 2008–2009. To minimize the risk that the slowdown would spark social unrest within their countries, governments around the world rolled out stimulus packages. In deciding where to spend the money, policy makers focused on efforts to spur short-term growth, keep workers in their jobs, and protect their personal political capital. Concerns for longer-term growth came second. Efforts to revive the global economy ran a distant third. But one government's subsidy is another's trade barrier. Worse, both the United States and China included provisions in their respective stimulus plans that mandated the purchase of domestically made products. Officials in Washington can't complain about "Buy Chinese" provisions in Beijing's spending plans until they remove the "Buy American" clause from their own.

Don't Close the Door on Investment

Like trade, foreign investment has played a crucial role in the expansion of the global economy of the past several years. Just as U.S. policy makers can resist the populist temptations of trade protectionism, they can also refuse to allow popular paranoia to block valuable foreign investment in U.S. assets. The Committee on Foreign Investment in the United States (CFIUS), an interagency government committee that reports to the president, is charged with ensuring that proposed foreign investments in U.S. assets do not compromise national security. CFIUS was created in 1975 to placate a Congress increasingly concerned about the rapid rise in investments in American portfolio assets, both government securities and corporate stocks and bonds, by newly wealthy Arab sheikhs with political goals in mind. Today, it's Chinese sovereign wealth funds that are generating much of the investment anxiety in Washington. Until the 9/11 terrorist attacks, few outside Washington had ever heard of CFIUS. But new security fears gave the committee a new mandate: Protect critical U.S. infrastructure. Two problems arose. First, lawmakers failed to clearly define what they meant by "critical infrastructure." Second, fears that an investment bid might generate unprecedented levels of public scrutiny discouraged many foreign companies and institutions from proposing deals in the first place. In short, CFIUS and changes in the foreign-investment review process have injected politics into commercial decisions in ways that defy common sense.

Two cases tell the story. In June 2005, the China National Offshore Oil Corporation (CNOOC) bid $18.5 billion to buy Unocal, a U.S.-owned oil company with substantial oil interests in Central Asia that complemented CNOOC's expansion plans. Eight days before a vote by Unocal shareholders, CNOOC withdrew the bid. Why did this happen? A politically diverse group of Democratic and Republican lawmakers argued that the bid did not represent a free-market transaction because the Chinese government had put up more than two thirds of the money. By denouncing the deal, they claimed to be defending the rights of U.S. companies, which were denied access to similar assets in China. Some even argued that foreign ownership of U.S. oil assets would compromise national security.

In February 2006, Dubai Ports World, a firm owned by the government of the United Arab Emirates, launched a bid to take over a British firm's operation of six major U.S. ports. Dozens of U.S. lawmakers, ignoring both expert testimony that the deal posed no security threat and a veto pledge from President George W. Bush, moved to try to kill the bid. In the end, DPW agreed to sell the port operations to an American company. In this overheated political environment, controversies then emerged involving U.S. telecom equipment maker Lucent Technologies and the French firm Alcatel, Israel's Check Point Software and the U.S. firm Sourcefire, and Japan's Toshiba and the U.S. company Westinghouse. Fortunately, the CNOOC-Unocal and DPW cases are still exceptions rather than the rule, but the willingness of a few politicians to score easy political points provoked lasting resentment in China and the United Arab Emirates and made life tougher for U.S. companies hoping to do business there. If the United States is to maintain its role as champion of free-market capitalism, U.S. lawmakers must resist temptations to play populist politics with foreign investment.

Don't Close the Door on Immigrants

Just as U.S. lawmakers should welcome trade and investment, they should also continue to welcome those willing to work for a better life in America. Immigration has always been a hot topic in the United States for reasons political, cultural, and ideological, but wave after wave of immigrants over more than two centuries have helped power American prosperity. In many cases, immigrants have also enriched the countries they come from by sending money home to family and friends or by returning with know-how drawn from the American free-market tradition. This phenomenon has also taken place in much of Europe. Unfortunately, every new generation of immigrants meets resistance from those who fear change, competition, or both. Fear of immigrants is never more visceral than following a national security crisis (like the outbreak of World War II or the 9/11 attacks) or during a period of economic hardship.

Globalization draws its power to create wealth from the cross-border flow not only of goods and services but of people. America continues to attract workers trying to escape poverty, but also skilled workers, entrepreneurs, inventors, scientists, and engineers who come from every region of the world in search of opportunity. In 2009, about 9.1 million people applied for the 50,000 green cards available in the State Department's annual global visa lottery.[9] For 2008 and 2009, U.S. employers had applied for all 65,000 of the regular H1-B visas and 20,000 available advanced-degree employment visas available each year within one week of the opening of the application process. The 2000 census suggested that immigrants made up nearly half of PhD scientists and engineers in the United States. A Harvard Business School study in 2008 identified a disproportionately high representation of immigrants among patent applicants in the United States.[10] Some of the most talented and industrious people in the world still want to come to the United States—and America still needs them.

U.S. lawmakers continue to send the wrong signals. As part of the 2009 stimulus bill, the so-called Grassley-Sanders Amendment sharply restricted the freedom of companies that received bailout money under the Troubled Asset Recovery Program (TARP) to hire highly skilled foreign workers. Supporters of the amendment, particularly within labor unions, insisted that American companies bailed out with U.S. taxpayer dollars should hire only American workers. But world-class foreign workers have enriched America, and these kinds of restrictions cost the country an important part of its competitive edge as a center of innovation, research, and entrepreneurial genius. America needs a global talent pool.

Pick the Right Fights

In managing the competition with state capitalism, U.S. officials should pick their fights with care. Over the past several years, the United States and China have developed the world's most important bilateral commercial relationship. Some in Washington charge that Beijing manipulates the value of its currency, the yuan. The U.S. dollar is freely traded around the world, and its value relative to those of other currencies floats freely. The yuan floats too, but within a narrow range managed by the Chinese government. By maintaining an artificially low value for the yuan, Beijing boosts Chinese exports by ensuring that foreign consumers pay relatively low prices for Chinese products while Chinese consumers pay relatively high prices for imports. In recent years, several U.S. lawmakers have threatened to retaliate against what they consider an unfair trade practice.

Yet many of the dollars that the Chinese government, America's largest creditor, earns through exports or via foreign-exchange markets are then invested in U.S. treasury bonds. Whenever a U.S. lawmaker threatens to draft legislation that would punish China over the currency issue, there's a risk that the price of U.S. treasuries will fall and yields will rise—undermining the government's ability to finance its deficits. Beijing has allowed the yuan to appreciate, though not as quickly as some in Washington would like. U.S. policy makers should continue to press the Chinese to gradually allow the yuan to float freely and to find its true market value, but explicit punitive threats, however politically satisfying, are a bad idea.

That's not to say that U.S. policy makers and regulators should avoid every conflict. Washington must enforce existing rules whenever unsafe Chinese goods make their way into the United States—whether children's toys covered in lead-based paint, tires that shred in highway driving, toothpaste laced with toxic chemicals, or any other dangerous consumer product. Given the media attention these incidents generate and the fear they produce, no issue could inflict greater immediate and lasting damage on U.S.-Chinese trade relations. John McCain, the most unapologetic advocate of free trade to run for president in 2008, said this on the issue: "If I were president of the United States, the next toy that came into this country from China that endangered the lives of our children, it would be the last toy that came into the United States [from China]."[11]

The U.S. government should also continue to press China to enforce rules protecting intellectual property rights (IPR), a proper regulatory role for the state in the promotion of free markets. More than half of U.S. exports rely on some form of IPR protection, compared to less than 10 percent a half century ago.[12] Mass-production factories churn out pirated CDs, games, and DVDs in Russia and Malaysia,[13] but China is by far the worst offender on IPR violations. Software makers complain that more than 80 percent of all video games used in China are pirated,[14] and some are then reproduced for export.

There is one important piece of good news. When China joined the World Trade Organization in 2001, it was not at all clear that Beijing would abide by the WTO's rules. But by channeling its trade complaints through the WTO, by responding within the organization to U.S. complaints, and by abiding by WTO rulings, the Chinese government has accepted the organization's legitimacy, a development that has so far ensured that Beijing fights its trade disputes in an arena with a neutral referee. That's a major reason why U.S.-Chinese trade relations continue to expand—and why public support in America for free trade remains relatively strong despite the recent slowdown in the U.S. economy and the job losses that came with it. In fact, a poll conducted by the Pew Research Center for the People & the Press found that U.S. public support for free trade jumped from 35 percent in April 2008 to 44 percent in April 2009. Over that same period, the percentage opposing free trade fell from 48 percent to 35 percent.[15] That's an especially remarkable statistic given the meltdown then under way in the U.S. economy.

Keep Investing in Hard Power

There are other ways Washington can ensure that the United States remains an indispensable international player. Just as ExxonMobil survives in a world increasingly dominated by state-owned energy giants by cultivating its comparative technological advantages, the U.S. government can extend its singular international influence for decades by working to preserve the country's *hard power.* Hard and soft power, terms popularized by Joseph Nye, refer, respectively, to the coercive potential of U.S. military and economic might and to the power of American ideas, values, and culture to "entice and attract." Soft power helped swing the Cold War in America's favor, and it will continue to play a crucial role in extending U.S. influence abroad. Polling suggests that the election of Barack Obama has generated more positive attitudes toward America and American culture in dozens of countries. But over the next several years, it is hard power that will ensure that the United States remains an essential component of the world's political and economic stability, whatever the power of state capitalism to undermine American influence in other areas.

The erosion of U.S. soft-power advantages has already begun as emerging states, foreign firms, and new ideas compete with American rivals for shelf space and screen time. Whatever their limitations, America's hard-power advantages are more durable. The United States now spends nearly as much on its military capacity as all its potential competitors combined. It continues to outspend China by nearly ten to one and Russia by about twenty-five to one. Even if defense spending were significantly reduced over the next several years, the United States would continue to hold a dominant military position for the foreseeable future, because it will be decades before any potential rival will prove both willing and able to accept the burdens that come with global leadership. China and Russia already carry enormous clout within their respective spheres of regional influence, but neither would profit from a challenge to American hard power outside them.

U.S. military strength will remain useful—and not just for Americans. The governments of energy-importing countries around the world will try to reduce dependence on hydrocarbon-based energy in coming years. But the transition toward oil and gas alternatives will take decades. In the meantime, the world's oil companies, whether state-owned or multinational, will rely increasingly on supplies from unstable (and potentially unstable) parts of the world—the Middle East, the Caspian Sea basin, and West Africa. Energy consumers will continue to turn to America, which has the world's only global naval presence, to ensure the free flow of oil and gas supplies on which their economic futures depend.

The U.S. provision of global public goods will also extend to new military challenges. As Iran masters uranium-enrichment technology, some of its Arab neighbors will rely even more heavily on Washington to guarantee their security and to help them avoid the costs that come with a nuclear arms race. As governments in Eastern Europe worry over threats of Russian expansionism—an anxiety heightened by dependence on Russia's natural gas, Moscow's demonstrated willingness to bully its neighbors by turning off the taps, and its conflict with Georgia in August 2008—they will increasingly turn to a U.S.-led NATO to ease their anxieties. Without U.S. leadership, NATO won't remain a viable force for security. The U.S. military will also remain an essential weapon in America's soft-power arsenal, by delivering relief to victims of natural disasters all over the world, for example. All of these advantages can help Washington maintain its international influence, even if state capitalism undermines the appeal of the U.S. free-market model for years to come.

Mutually Assured Economic Destruction

The growing gulf between free-market and state capitalism has created a high-stakes competition between economic models, one that distorts the performance of the global economy and creates friction in international politics. Though this isn't a new Cold War, that conflict offers a useful metaphor for how the battle for free markets can be managed. For decades, the United States and the Soviet Union amassed nuclear arsenals large enough to destroy Earth many times over. The resulting stalemate, which came to be known as mutually assured destruction, helped prevent catastrophic conflict. Today, there are no ties more important for the future of the free market than those that bind America and China—the world's most powerful advocate of free trade and open markets and the largest and most influential practitioner of state capitalism.

U.S. policy makers can't afford to simply ignore the many disputes that burden commercial relations between the two states. But neither can they ignore the *mutually assured economic destruction* that now threatens them. America will need China to finance its debt, and Chinese exporters will need access to U.S. consumers for many years to come. Ensuring that U.S. and Chinese policy makers and business leaders continue to develop profitable partnerships and avoid unnecessary confrontation is crucial for the economic health of both countries, for the global economy, and for the broader appeal of the free-market model. What's true for the U.S. approach to China is true for relations with other champions of state capitalism. Profiting from access to markets in Russia, the Persian Gulf, and elsewhere means welcoming investment from these places—even from state-owned companies.

Free markets will always move in cycles. Greed will fuel more booms, and fear will drive more busts. Each time a bubble bursts, someone will retell the story of the tulip mania of 1636, the South Sea bubble of 1720, and the dot-com bubble of the 1990s. But markets are not to blame when governments fail to properly regulate them. As Philip Stephens wrote in the *Financial Times* at the height of the crisis in March 2009, "Prominent among the causes of the financial crash was the failure of politics to keep up with economic integration. Global markets ran far ahead of the capacity of governments to oversee, even to understand, them."[16]

Severe as it was, this crisis cannot obscure what came before. Between 1980 and 2007, global GDP rose by nearly 150 percent. Already-prosperous countries saw significant increases in their standards of living. Hundreds of millions within developing states moved from poverty into the global marketplace. An economic slowdown has temporarily pushed huge numbers of people back toward poverty, but expectations have been created that, over the longer term, only free markets can fulfill. Even the most pessimistic forecasts for the final effects of the slowdown will not dramatically set back the overall growth trajectory of the past thirty years, and expectations will rise again as recovery picks up steam.

State capitalism deserves some of the credit for this expansion, especially within countries like China and Russia that have grown from a very low base. But the broader story of the past three decades is one of command economies embracing capitalism and of states loosening their grip on economic activity. The strength and durability of recovery will depend on the willingness of those who believe in free markets to learn from the failures that triggered a crisis, to practice the kind of capitalism they preach, and to renew their commitment to the principles that have helped them prosper.

AFTERWORD

On January 5, 2011, the *New York Post* ran a front-page story on President Barack Obama wearing flip-flops during a Hawaiian vacation. The article noted that "historians agreed it was the first time they could remember seeing the leader of the free world snapped in a public setting, wearing nothing more than a flimsy strip of rubber on his feet."[*] Two months later, thumbing through *The Wall Street Journal,* I came across a comment from former Minnesota governor (and 2012 presidential candidate) Tim Pawlenty. Attacking Obama for an alleged failure to confront Libyan strongman Muammar Qaddafi, Pawlenty said, "A known psychopath is gunning down his own people in the streets of Libya, and the leader of the free world is muted for the better part of a week."[†]

Footwear and Qaddafi aside, is the president of the United States really the leader of the free world these days? Are elected leaders in India, Brazil, and South Africa part of something we might still call the "free world"? If so, do they consider President Obama to be their leader in any sense? Did they think differently of George W. Bush? Partisan political rhetoric aside, and assuming that any U.S. president could ever really have passed this test, isn't the title "leader of the free world" an anachronism?

Even if the U.S. president is not leading the world's democracies, any defense of free-market capitalism will have to begin in America,

---

[*]   www.nypost.com/p/news/national/that_quite_first_flip_flop_feet_PsHtRNc7D35bmrz NdrATWP.

[†]   http://blogs.wsj.com/washwire/2011/03/02/pawlenty-hits-obama-over-libya/.

the country that used this system to build the strongest, most resilient economy in history. The hardcover edition of this book seems to have provoked a couple of unintended responses. The first, from one end of the political spectrum, is that Barack Obama has essentially already imposed state capitalism on America.[*] The second, from the other end, is that the financial crisis has fully and finally discredited American-style free-market capitalism.[†] I don't accept either of these arguments, but let's take a closer look at both.

State capitalism in America?

Barack Obama is not a state capitalist. History shows, and this book acknowledges, that Obama has presided over one of the largest government-led economic interventions in American history. Faced with a crisis of historic magnitude, he empowered the U.S. government to take ownership of large U.S. financial institutions and automakers. He dramatically increased government spending to try to restore confidence in the U.S. financial system, to limit the loss of jobs, to help create new jobs, and to stimulate economic growth. He also pushed to extend health-care coverage to tens of millions of uninsured Americans. In the process, his plans have launched the country's budget deficit to dizzying new heights.

Yet Obama has made no move to redesign the U.S. economic system to promote state dominance of markets. The financial crisis offered him a prime political opportunity to nationalize large U.S. banks. He refused. In rewriting rules for the financial sector, the White House and both parties in Congress have essentially agreed that the U.S. government should never bail out another company. Government did little to manage the firms in which it owned stakes, and the Treasury Department moved to sell off the last of its large stakes in Citibank and General Motors.

---

[*]   www.hoover.org/publications/policy-review/article/64571.

[†]   http://seekingalpha.com/article/210846-book-review-the-end-of-the-free-market.

This is the opposite of state capitalism. A president intent on building a system in which the state dominates markets would be increasing the government's stake in multiple economic sectors and working to establish effective operational control of the country's largest companies. A state capitalist would be drawing in more wealth, not holding corporate taxes as a percentage of GDP at levels lower than any seen since the 1950s.[*]

Markets don't buy the state capitalism charge either. If the Obama administration were genuinely determined to transfer private wealth into state hands or toward the Democratic Party's key constituents, the anxiety would play out in U.S. equity markets. Instead, the S&P 500 Index rose more than 59 percent over the first two years of the Obama presidency.[†] Markets will rise and fall with fluctuations in investor confidence, but more than two years after President Obama assumed office and inherited a financial crisis, there is no sign that market players genuinely believe that state capitalism has arrived in America.

Finally, the health-care reform plan President Obama signed into law in 2010 has transformed a large segment of the U.S. economy and sharply increased government spending on an already robust U.S. social safety net. Wisely or not, Obama resisted pressure from much of his political base for a "public option," a plan that would have allowed citizens to pull the state much deeper into the health-care sector. Again, look to the markets. The president's critics say he has socialized health care, but the Dow Jones U.S. Health Care Index rose nearly 45 percent between January 2009 and March 2011.[‡]

President Obama has not argued nearly forcefully enough that free-market capitalism is essential to America's future prosperity. Yet anyone who believes he's a state capitalist, or that any U.S. president has the political power to impose state capitalism on an unwitting American public, should look more closely at how growth and wealth are generated in the United States—and how they are generated in China.

---

[*] www.usnews.com/opinion/blogs/robert-schlesinger/2011/02/08/under-obama-taxes-reach-lowest-level-since-truman.html.

[†] www.bloomberg.com/apps/quote?ticker=SPX:IND.

[‡] www.djindexes.com/globalindexes/.

Free-market capitalism has not failed

Second is the idea that free-market capitalism has already failed. That's nonsense. As I argue in chapter six, this book is not championing some sort of Darwinian economic system in which the biggest and baddest must dominate and regulation is for communists. There's an important role for government to play in economic development and in establishing rules of the game that help build both a prosperous and a fair society. Pre-financial crisis America didn't meet that standard. In China, the state has captured corporations. In pre-crisis America, corporations were capturing the state. We shouldn't be surprised. Corporate decision makers aren't looking for fairness or a level playing field. They want the largest market share they can get. They want subsidies. They want the state to regulate only the competition. This is not because they're greedy, but because they're self-interested. They want to maximize profits for themselves and their shareholders, and they have money to spend to defend their interests. We expect them to be good citizens, but we also expect them to compete.

With so many lessons learned so quickly, so publicly, and with so much pain during the financial crisis, a strong political push for tighter regulation was inevitable—and entirely necessary. When the state fails to properly regulate market activity, it's all too easy for corporate decision-makers to try to maximize quarterly profits at the expense of a sound long-term growth strategy. As I asked in chapter five, why should a corporate executive deny shareholders the largest possible quarterly dividend payment when investment in the company's future will profit only his successor? Why should he ask the company's top performers to forgo bonuses when they might earn more by working for a competitor?

Goldman Sachs and other financial institutions made huge amounts of money on collateralized debt obligations (CDOs) with little regard for the collateral damage they were bound to inflict. At the same time, ratings agencies dozed as banks sold high-risk securities in low-risk packaging and lawmakers left banks to essentially regulate themselves. British Petroleum spent lots of money to maximize oil production in the Gulf of Mexico and virtually nothing to prepare for the day when its operations might spring a leak. But regulators at the Interior Department's Minerals Management Service had every opportunity to see the risk of a massive oil spill months in advance and did little to prevent it from happening. Government must be a strong, fair, and independent referee if free-market capitalism is to fulfill its promise. It won't be easy to restore intelligently regulated, free-market capitalism, particularly in an environment in which industry lobbyists and political rivals are quick to label opponents as defenders of "big government." It will require a degree of political courage all too rare in Washington. It will also require the common sense not to increase the power of the state too much by pushing regulation too far.

The biggest challenge

The biggest challenge in promoting the longer-term vitality of free-market capitalism in the future is in winning a series of games in which the world's state capitalists have so many advantages. Here again, government has a crucial role to play.

For most Americans, the idea of national security is limited mainly to soldiers, sailors, aircraft carriers, fighter jets, airport security, and terrorist surveillance. Yet in coming years, state-owned companies, banks, sovereign wealth funds, trade and currency policies, market access, and enforcement of intellectual property rights are the primary tools—in some cases, weapons—that some governments will use to promote national security and to pursue their foreign and domestic interests. That's why traditional American mistrust of state "interference" in commerce can be such a dangerous thing.

Washington must do a better job of protecting the public interest from the excesses of those who care mainly about today's profit, but it must also do what it can to enable innovation in American companies and do a much better job of promoting their interests abroad. China's authoritarian system allows for a degree of coordination among the architects of economic, financial, trade, energy, foreign, and defense policy that is not possible in the United States. Given America's form of government, that cannot and will not change. Recognizing this disadvantage, the White House and lawmakers of both parties must learn to think strategically about how best to ensure that these various agencies of government coordinate where possible to promote national goals by helping American firms compete more effectively with state-backed rivals.

The U.S. government should never make day-to-day strategic decisions for American companies. Market forces will always outperform political bureaucrats in valuing assets and allocating resources. But government can use policy and investment to set U.S. industrial goals and to encourage corporate behavior that serves the nation's long-term interests—through deeper investment, for example, in strategic economic sectors and industrial research and development. The Pentagon publishes a quadrennial defense review to give coherence to strategic thinking on national security. Why not a quadrennial review of U.S. industrial policy?

With or without more active support from their government, American companies must prepare for an intensifying conflict. When expectations of access to a massive new market drew Google into China, its leadership must have known that its corporate commitment to transparency and freedom of information would run headlong into the Great Firewall. But it should also have known that it would soon face local competition from companies that China's government has reason to promote and protect. In January 2010, Google complained that its proprietary source code and the personal Gmail accounts of Chinese human rights activists had been targeted in a sophisticated cyberattack originating from inside China. American media covered the story as if the conflict were primarily about censorship and state persecution of dissidents.

Those issues were important, but the battle was also about the market dominance of Baidu, Google's primary Chinese rival. Baidu already held a larger Chinese market share than Google, and its slice of the pie has only grown in the year since. Now we've seen the emergence of Renren, a Chinese version of Facebook, Sina Weibo, a Chinese microblog similar to Twitter, and Youku, a Chinese knock-off of YouTube. These firms are much less likely than their foreign competitors to resist state demands for censorship. In China, that's a pretty big commercial advantage.

Western firms are not the only victims of state-supported domestic competition within China. For years following the end of the Cold War, China spent billions of dollars on Russian-made weaponry from small arms to fighter jets. Chinese engineers have taken these products apart and put them back together, and Chinese manufacturers, who have since cloned everything from spare parts to a jet engine, now make them at home. According to a recent report in *The Wall Street Journal,* Beijing hasn't placed a single major order from Moscow in the past two years.* Chinese arms-makers are now competing with Russian companies in third countries.

These are the kinds of challenges that multinational companies from around the world can expect to face in state capitalist countries. To meet them, they'll have to return to the tried-and-true formula of focusing their resources to compete in areas where they maintain a competitive advantage, for example, in areas where technical innovation and superior branding can keep them a step ahead. But they must also accept the need to hedge their bets on individual markets and to develop the best possible exit strategy when they find themselves competing in a game that's been rigged.

The only certainty they face is that the intensifying confrontation between free market and state capitalism will be with us for many years to come.

Ian Bremmer

New York City

July 12, 2011

---

* http://online.wsj.com/article/SB10001424052748704679204575646472655698844.html.

ACKNOWLEDGMENTS

Events sometimes overtake a book. In this case, they caught up with one. I had been noodling for entirely too long with the idea of state capitalism, the growth in importance of the state as an economic actor that had been slowly but surely developing for decades. It was probably the challenge that initially grabbed my attention and persuaded me to apply political science to Wall Street and the private sector. But there's nothing like a global crisis to focus the mind—and to force a writer to get a move on.

I've incurred all sorts of debts while putting this book together, and many people were indispensable to *The End of the Free Market*. First there's my Eurasia Group cohort, a brilliant group of political scientists who cover every corner of the world. Our analysts answered each question with incisive commentary, reminding me yet again that I'm privileged to sit among them. I can't begin to express my thanks to Dan Alamariu, Erasto Almeida, Irmak Bademli, David Bender, Allyson Benton, Heather Berkman, Alex Brideau, Nick Consonery, Tanya Costello, Philippe de Pontet, Seema Desai, Patrick Esteruelas, Nancy Ferrante, Chris Garman, Bob Herrera-Lim, Jonas Horner, Kim Iskyan, Ana Jelenkovic, Robert Johnston, Daniel Kerner, Abraham Kim, David Kiu, Alexander Kliment, Cliff Kupchan, Maria Kuusisto, Jon Levy, Damien Ma, Kate Miller, Jun Okumura, Will Pearson, Wolfango Piccoli, Geoff Porter, Greg Priddy, Divya Reddy, Courtney Rickert, Scott Rosenstein, Hani Sabra, Ross Schaap, Sebastian Spio-Garbrah, Jenia

Ustinova, Sean West, and Valeria Zhavoronkina. Thanks also to Iku Fujimatsu and Laurel Donaldson for their talents and tirelessness.

Preston Keat and I have worked together for years, and we've co-authored a book on political risk. To keep us honest, we team-teach at Columbia. We work through these kinds of issues as a matter of course (as it were). John Green is intellectually well grounded and stubbornly opinionated—a combination I've come to truly appreciate. More to the point, he's always ready to pick over (and into) a tough argument. I've been bouncing ideas off David Gordon for more than a decade, and now I get to work with him full time. It's an honor and a privilege to partner with and learn from all three of them.

This book gave me the perfect excuse to collaborate with the esteemed (and now honorable) Jon Benjamin. We worked hand in glove on this project for the better part of a year, and I can't imagine having put it together without him. My principal sadness is that it couldn't have lasted longer—he has now become Britain's ambassador to Chile. My loss is the Queen's gain. Not quite so lucky is Willis Sparks, who has been working with me for five years (and three books!) now. He's an invaluable resource to me and to all my colleagues, with boundless enthusiasm for better understanding the world around us. Visiting him is a journey of about three steps. The remarkably resourceful Ksenia Tomilina provided plenty of crucial research support. Many thanks to her as well.

My friend Jim Hoge at *Foreign Affairs* immediately took up the argument and talked it up, providing me with a forum or three with some of the best analytical minds on global thinking to hone the eventual book.

As it took shape, I bounced my ideas and the ever-evolving manuscript off lots of friends. Thanks to Vint Cerf, Sam Di Piazza, Bill Emmott, Catherine Fieschi, David Fromkin, Ken Griffin, Harry Harding, Ho Ching, Adi Ignatius, Art Kleiner, Sallie Krawcheck, Scott Malcomson, Steve Mann, Maziar Minovi, Mary Pang, Niko Pfund, Juan

Pujadas, Joel Rosenthal, Nouriel Roubini, Kirsten Sandberg, Tad Sano, Marci Shore, Tom Stewart, Nick Thompson, Antoine van Agtmael, and Enzo Viscusi. George Will gave me some great input as well.

My colleagues at Portfolio are very much appreciated. Throughout the editing process I was blessed with a tremendous editor in Courtney Young. She's an exceptionally thoughtful foil, and virtually every suggestion she offered made the book better. My thanks to her. Adrian Zackheim and I have talked about doing books together for a good long while. He's very smart, no nonsense, and kind of quirky. He's also irascible, and I find that endearing.

To the folks in my office who know the business of making a book work, many thanks for their leadership: Mariah Kunkel, Alex Lloyd, Jenna Rosebery, and Jennifer Swetzoff. As I finish the acknowledgments, most of their hard work is just beginning.

Finally, much love to Ann Shuman, who generally puts up with my insufferable nature. And to my favorite brother, Robert Coolbrith. They're both brilliant, adorable, and would be in more paragraphs if good taste didn't dictate otherwise.

NOTES

CHAPTER ONE: The Rise of a New System

1. Francis Fukuyama's essay "The End of History" appeared in the *National Interest,* Summer 1989, and was expanded into the book *The End of History and the Last Man* (New York: Free Press, 1992).

2. According to the Economist Intelligence Unit's 2008 Democracy Index, "Democracy can be seen as a set of practices and principles that institutionalize and thus ultimately protect freedom. Even if a consensus on precise definitions has proved elusive, most observers today would agree that, at a minimum, the fundamental features of a democracy include government based on majority rule and the consent of the governed, the existence of free and fair elections, the protection of minority rights and respect for basic human rights. Democracy presupposes equality before the law, due process and political pluralism."

3. United Nations, *Human Development Report 1993* (New York: Oxford University Press).

4. Kenichi Ohmae, *The End of the Nation State: The Rise of Regional Economies* (New York: Simon & Schuster, 1995), 12.

5. Donald McIntyre, "North Korea: A Nation in the Dark," *Time,* http://www.time.com/time/world/article/0,8599,366219,00.html.

6. Some regional organizations have achieved more than others. The Caribbean Community (Caricom) and the Pacific Island Forum give a host of micro nation-states the chance to punch above their weight on the international stage on a few issues important to them. The Antarctic Treaty system has prevented military deployments and promoted scientific cooperation for forty years on the world's only uninhabited continent. The Gulf Cooperation Council en-

ables six Arab states to develop an effective common market for goods and services. But none of these organizations has eroded the sovereign power of its member states.

7. The best recent reports on China's system of censorship include Rebecca MacKinnon, "China's Censorship 2.0: How Companies Censor Bloggers," First Monday blog, vol. 14, no. 2-2 Feb. 2009; *Race to the Bottom: Corporate Complicity in Chinese Internet Censorship,* Human Rights Watch, Aug. 2006; and *Journey to the Heart of Internet Censorship,* Reporters Without Borders, Oct. 2007.

8. Naomi Klein, *No Logo* (Toronto: Knopf, 1999), xxiii.

9. Sarah Anderson and John Cavanagh, *The Top 200: The Rise of Corporate Global Power* (Washington, D.C.: Institute for Policy Studies, Dec. 2000), based on statistics from *Forbes* magazine.

10. Frances Maguire, "The New Masters of the Universe," *Banker,* Jan. 2, 2006.

11. United Nations Conference on Trade and Development (UNCTAD), *World Investment Report 2008: Transnational Corporations and the Infrastructure Challenge* (New York/Geneva).

12. These critics had plenty of vivid stories to make their charges stick: Union Carbide's chemical plant in Bhopal, India, which accidentally released tons of toxic gas in December 1984, killing several thousand people over a period of several years; the Exxon Valdez oil spill that badly damaged Alaska's Prince William Sound in March 1989; the reported use of poorly paid and treated workers, and even child labor, in footwear factories producing shoes for Nike, Puma, Reebok, and Adidas in countries like Pakistan, Bangladesh, Indonesia, and Vietnam; Philip Morris's allegedly aggressive marketing of carcinogenic cigarettes in developing countries; and the refusal of big pharmaceutical companies to allow patented HIV/AIDS drugs to be reproduced cheaply in the African countries that arguably needed them most. These and many other cases persuaded some companies to pay huge sums in compensation and to adopt new policies and practices.

13. See the UNCTAD *World Investment Report 2008;* and Peter F. Drucker, "Trading Places," *National Interest,* Spring 2005.

14. Antoine van Agtmael, *The Emerging Markets Century: How a New Breed of World-Class Companies Is Overtaking the World* (New York: Free Press, 2007).

15. From Bill Clinton's 1996 State of the Union Address, http://clinton4.nara.gov/WH/New/other/sotu.html.

16. *Forbes* magazine's Global 2000 list of companies for 2008.

CHAPTER TWO: A Brief History of Capitalism

1. Adam Smith, *The Wealth of Nations* (1776; New York: Modern Library, 1994), book 4, ch. 2, pp. 484–85.

2. Adam Smith, *The Theory of Moral Sentiments* (1759; Cambridge, UK: Cambridge University Press, 2002), Introduction.

3. During the savings-and-loan crisis of the 1980s (and early 1990s) more than a thousand savings-and-loan associates failed at a cost of at least $125 billion to the U.S. federal government.

4. The South Sea Company, founded in 1711, enjoyed a monopoly over British trade with Spanish South America and the Pacific region. Its share price rose 800 percent in little more than six months in 1720 when holders of government bonds were offered swap shares in the company at discounted rates. The shares then fell 90 percent in the remainder of 1720, ending the year at the January price but ruining many latecomers to the market in the process. In the same year, a similar Mississippi Bubble led to the collapse in value of the French-based Louisiana Company shares, which had risen 3,600 percent the year before. These two first stock-based bubbles were preceded nearly a century earlier by the Netherlands' tulip mania, in which tulip bulbs briefly became a commodity as valuable as gold before the price collapsed in February 1637. All three bubbles were first popularly summarized in Charles Mackay's *Extraordinary Popular Delusions and the Madness of Crowds* (1841; New York: Harmony Books, 1980).

5. The most accessible reference to Wilhelm Liebknecht's use of this phrase is at http://www.marxists.org/archive/liebknecht-w/1896/08/our-congress.htm.

6. Ludwig von Mises, *Socialism: An Economic and Sociological Analysis,* trans. J. Kahane (London: Jonathan Cape, 1936; rev. ed. New Haven, CT: Yale University Press, 1951).

7. Leon Trotsky, *The Revolution Betrayed: What Is the Soviet Union and Where Is It Going?* trans. Max Eastman (New York: Dover, 2004), ch. 9, http://www.marxists.org/archive/trotsky/1936/revbet/ch09.htm.

8. Murray N. Rothbard, "A Future of Peace and Capitalism," in *Modern Political Economy,* ed. James H. Weaver (Boston: Allyn & Bacon, 1973), ch. 28, pp. 419–30, http://mises.org/story/1559.

9. "Military-Industrial Complex Speech, Dwight D. Eisenhower, 1961," http://coursesa.matrix.msu.edu/~hst306/documents/indust.html.

10. A definition offered by Laura LaHaye, *Concise Encyclopedia of Economics,*

Library of Economics and Liberty, http://www.econlib.org/library/Enc/Mercantilism.html.

11. The Anglo-Spanish wars of 1585–1604 were clashes not only in English and Spanish ports or on the sea between them (most notably Sir Francis Drake's defeat of the Spanish Armada in 1588) but also in and around the present-day territories of Florida, Puerto Rico, the Dominican Republic, and Panama, where Drake died.

12. Mercantilism was an inherently protectionist system, but individual loyalty was an eminently tradable commodity. It was, after all, an Englishman, Henry Hudson, a protoglobal citizen working secretly for the Dutch, who sailed into New York harbor a little more than four hundred years ago and set in train the inclusion of what later became the United States into the early mercantilist imperial world.

13. There were other examples of the British crown or government giving privately owned joint-stock companies similar trade monopolies. For example, the Muscovy Company, perhaps the world's first joint-stock company (formed in 1555), had a monopoly on trade with Muscovy and on whaling; the Hudson Bay Company (1670) had a monopoly on the "Indian trade," mostly fur, in British Canada; and the South Sea Company (1711) had a monopoly on trade with Spanish South America.

14. "Defense of Great Britain depends very much upon the number of its sailors and shipping. The act of navigation, therefore, very properly endeavors to give the sailors and shipping of Great Britain the monopoly of the trade of their own country." Smith also stated, "It is of importance that the kingdom depends as little as possible upon its neighbors for the manufactures necessary for its defense." Adam Smith, *The Wealth of Nations* (1776; New York: Modern Library, 1994), bk. 4, ch. 2.24 and bk. 5, ch. 5.36.

15. Hume said that "where an open communication is preserved amongst nations, it is impossible but that the domestic industry of everyone must receive an increase from the improvements of others." David Hume, "The Jealousy of Trade," *The Philosophical Works of David Hume* (London: Tait, 1826), vol. 3, p. 369. Hume also described the "trade surplus good, deficit bad" approach of mercantilism as a "narrow and malignant opinion" that focused on producers, who benefited, rather than consumers, who suffered.

16. Alexander Hamilton explained his promercantilist philosophy in "The Report on Manufactures" presented to the U.S. Congress in December 1791.

17. Running for the Illinois State Assembly in 1832, Lincoln said: "My politics

are short and sweet . . . I am in favor of the internal improvement system and a high protective tariff." Norton Garfinkle, *The American Dream vs. the Gospel of Wealth: The Fight for a Productive Middle-Class Economy* (New Haven, CT: Yale University Press, 2007), p. 34. Lincoln was dubious about the utility of foreign trade for the economy, worrying about the "useless labor" involved in transporting goods from one country to another.

18. John Maynard Keynes, *The General Theory of Employment, Interest and Money* (Amherst, NY: Prometheus Books, 1997), ch. 23: "Notes on Mercantilism."

19. WTO Web site, http://www.wto.org/English/thewto_e/whatis_e/tif_e/fact3_e.htm.

20. World Trade Organization, *International Trade Statistics,* 2008.

21. By late 2009, 153 of the world's 194 independent countries were full members of the World Trade Organization. The largest nonmember economies were Russia, Iran, and Kazakhstan.

22. According to the European Commission, in 2008–2009, the EU Common Agricultural Policy (CAP) and associated rural-development projects still accounted for about 43 percent of the total EU budget (about 55 billion of a total of nearly 117 billion euros). This figure is, however, down from 75 percent of the total (though then much smaller) EU budget in 1980. Farmers in France, Spain, and Germany are the largest recipients in absolute terms, while Greece and Ireland are the largest recipients in per capita terms. Fewer than 5 percent of EU citizens now work in the agricultural sector, averaged out from a range from 18 percent in Poland to less than 2 percent in Sweden.

CHAPTER THREE: State Capitalism: What It Is and How It Happened

1. The French president was addressing an international conference, New World, New Capitalism, in Paris on January 8, 2009. This was a reversal of Sarkozy's previous message: He had been elected in May 2007 on a conservative platform of cutting taxes, bureaucracy, and state jobs.

2. MITI's functions were taken over by the newly created Ministry of Economy, Trade and Industry (METI) in 2001.

3. This movement from MITI to the premiership was known as *amakudari,* or "descending from heaven."

4. The Scandinavian countries regularly hold top places in the UN's annual Human Development Indexes, which measure per capita income, life expectancy and other

leading health indicators, literacy rates, educational enrollment, and other factors to tabulate scores of quality of life globally by country. Data are also drawn from the Gini Index, which assesses levels of economic inequality within countries.

5. Human Development Reports, http://hdr.undp.org/en/statistics.

6. The term *dirigisme* was coined by Jean-Baptiste Colbert as Louis XIV's finance minister in the second half of the seventeenth century. Colbert was a prominent advocate of the mercantilist system we examined in chapter two.

7. One example is the automaker Renault, one of the few large pre–World War II French industrial enterprises. Renault was nationalized in 1945, partly because its then owner, Louis Renault, was accused of being a Nazi collaborator. The company was privatized in 1994, though the French government is still the largest single shareholder with a 15 percent stock holding.

8. For example, from 1917 to 1995, Clause 4 of the British Labour Party's constitution included the following language: "To secure for the workers by hand or by brain the full fruits of their industry and the most equitable distribution thereof that may be possible upon the basis of the common ownership of the means of production, distribution and exchange, and the best obtainable system of popular administration and control of each industry or service." This was seen as a "slow boat to communism" commitment. Under Tony Blair, this clause was changed to a closer approximation of social democracy, rather than socialism, with a new Clause 4 referring to the need ". . . to create for each of us the means to realise our true potential and for all of us a community in which power, wealth and opportunity are in the hands of the many, not the few. . . ."

9. BBC News, "Q&A: Singapore Elections," May 5, 2006, http://news.bbc.co.uk/2/hi/asia-pacific/4976536.stm.

10. Major price fluctuations were not just the hallmark of the OPEC oil crisis. During the first Gulf War, the per-barrel oil price more than doubled between July and November 1990, before halving again by February 1991 (from $15 to $35 and back to under $18). The price nearly doubled between March 1994 and October 1996, but halved again by June 1998 (from $13 to over $25 and back to under $12), dipping below $10 in December 1998 before doubling to $20 by August 1999. Between September 2003 and July 2008, oil prices rose from $27 to $144 per barrel before falling back below $40 by December 2008. Figures taken from the Brent Crude price recorded by the U.S. federal government's Energy Information Agency (EIA).

11. These and the immediately following statistics are an amalgam of those published by the International Energy Agency, an intergovernmental organization,

and the EIA. These underlying figures in turn conflate estimates from British Petroleum, the *Oil and Gas Journal, World Oil* magazine, and CEDIGAZ.

12. *BP* magazine's annual *Statistical Review of World Energy,* June 2008.

13. Over fifty years of nuclear-fusion experiments have failed to generate an order of magnitude more power than they have consumed. The jury remains out on whether low-cost, sustainable, clean, and inexhaustible nuclear fusion is a real possibility for the middle of the twenty-first century or a permanent science-fiction chimera.

14. From PetroStrategies, Inc., quoting the *Oil and Gas Journal,* Sept. 15, 2008, www.petrostrategies.org/Links/Worlds_Largest_Oil_and_Gas_Compa nies_Sites.htm. These figures aggregate known oil and natural-gas reserves, of which most of these state-owned companies have both. The formula used is that 5.85 billion cubic feet of natural gas reserves are taken to equal 1 million barrels of oil.

15. Fariborz Ghadar, "Iran at the Crossroads," Center for Strategic & International Studies, July 10, 2009, http://csis.org/publication/iran-crossroads.

16. Roger Stern, "The Iranian Petroleum Crisis and United States National Security," *Proceedings of the National Academy of Sciences* 104, no. 1 (Jan. 2, 2007), 377–82. Stern concluded that the U.S. assumption that Iran did not need civilian nuclear power was wrong. Whether or not Iran's nuclear-power projects provide a cover for a weapons program, Stern found that Iran's oil and gas industry was in such serious decline that it would eventually not be able to meet even domestic demand.

17. According to the International Energy Agency, Venezuelan oil production fell from 2.56 million barrels per day in 2005 to 2.18 million barrels per day in early 2009.

18. This company was amalgamated in 2007 from the oil and gas assets previously managed separately by Statoil and Norsk Hydro.

19. Some Arab Persian Gulf state NOCs, like Saudi Aramco, the Abu Dhabi National Oil Company, and Kuwait Petroleum Corporation, can afford to focus on still enormous domestic reserves.

20. See Daniel Yergin's *The Prize: The Epic Quest for Oil, Money and Power* (New York: Simon & Schuster, 1991).

21. Bolivian Vice President Álvaro García Linera, in an interview with the *Christian Science Monitor,* Mar. 27, 2007.

22. Increasing resource nationalism at a time of high prices has been called the paradox of plenty. For examples, see Terry Lynn Karl, *The Paradox of Plenty: Oil Booms and Petro-States* (Berkeley: University of California Press, 1997).

23. Russia, Canada, Australia, Niger, and Namibia are the world's other major uranium producers. The Organisation for Economic Co-operation and Development (OECD) Nuclear Energy Agency and the International Atomic Energy Agency estimated in 2007 that, given known reserves and forecast consumption rates, the global supply of uranium should last for another century, significantly longer than most credible estimates for oil and gas.

24. Credit for coining the term *sovereign wealth fund* goes to Andrew Rozanov of State Street Global Advisors in his article "Who Controls the Wealth of Nations?" *Central Banking Journal* 15, no. 4 (Nov. 2005), 52–57.

25. "Fund Rankings," Sovereign Wealth Fund Institute, http://www.swfinstitute .org/funds.php.

26. The major SWF transparency index seems to bear this out. The Sovereign Wealth Fund Institute ranks SWFs according to the Linaberg-Maduell Transparency Index. Other evidence of the link between government and SWF transparency (or lack thereof) is in Edwin M. Truman's *Sovereign Wealth Funds: The Need for Greater Transparency and Accountability,* a policy brief for the Peterson Institute of International Economics, Washington, D.C., Aug. 2007.

27. According to the Sovereign Wealth Fund Institute and International Financial Services London, which follow the SWF world on a detailed and daily basis.

28. Emily Thornton and Stanley Reed, "Inside the Abu Dhabi Investment Authority," *BusinessWeek,* June 6, 2008, http://www.busnessweek.com/globalbiz/ content/jun2008/gb2008065_742165.htm.

29. ADIA bought 10 percent of Apollo Management and 20 percent of Ares Management in mid-2007. A second Abu Dhabi SWF, Mubadala, simultaneously bought 7.5 percent of Carlyle Group, while one of Dubai's two SWFs, International Capital, bought 10 percent of Och-Ziff.

30. International Working Group of Sovereign Wealth Funds, *Sovereign Wealth Funds: Generally Accepted Principles and Practices—"Santiago Principles,"* Oct. 2008, http://www.iwg-swf.org/pubs/eng/santiagoprinciples.pdf.

31. The ailing Western banks that received the largest SWF infusions included Citigroup, which received $6.8 billion from Singapore's GIC, $7.6 billion from Abu Dhabi, and $7.7 billion from Kuwait's Investment Authority (KIA)— cumulatively about 13.5 percent of the bank's market value at the time; Merrill Lynch, which received $5 billion from Singapore's Temasek, $3.4 billion from Kuwait's KIA, and $2 billion from South Korea's Investment Corporation, a total equivalent to a 22.5 percent stake; UBS, which received $9.8 billion from

Singapore's GIC and $1.8 billion from SAMA, the equivalent of a 10.6 percent stake; and Morgan Stanley, in which the China Investment Corporation invested $5 billion for a 9.9 percent stake. In total, SWFs injected over $60 billion into Western private financial institutions between March and June 2008.

32. The Council on Foreign Relations is at the lowest end of estimates for the value of the main UAE sovereign wealth funds. In early 2009, the CFR thought these funds might be worth less than half the most liberal estimates, in a range of $300–$500 billion rather than anything up to $950 billion. The CFR's thesis was that UAE funds were heavily invested on global stock markets and might therefore have lost up to 40 percent of their net worth during 2008. Brad Setser and Rachel Ziemba, *GCC Sovereign Funds: Reversal of Fortune,* Council on Foreign Relations Center for Geoeconomic Studies, Jan. 2009.

33. Russia's Ministry of Finance valued the Reserve Fund at $136 billion and the National Welfare Fund at $84 billion in late 2008.

34. Although this is a nominal social security fund, it is classified as an SWF because it holds foreign-currency assets mostly invested overseas with a degree of risk.

35. Figures from *Sovereign Wealth Funds: A Work Agenda,* International Monetary Fund, Feb. 2008. The IMF noted that total SWF funds had grown at an annual rate of nearly 25 percent during the period 2003–2007, but this included a surge of new start-up funds, and a boom in commodity and equity prices, which were then substantially rolled back.

36. OPEC had been formed in September 1960 at a conference in Baghdad among seven Arab oil producers and Iran, Ecuador, Indonesia, Nigeria, Angola, and Venezuela. It was born in part out of frustration that Western international oil companies effectively decided oil prices and production levels and out of a desire among oil-owning governments to control those mechanisms themselves.

37. The acronym BRIC was coined by Jim O'Neill in Goldman Sachs Global Economic Group paper no. 60, "Building Better Global Economic BRICs," Nov. 2001. Goldman's predictions for BRIC and other emerging markets' growth rates were revised upward by Dominic Wilson and Roopa Purushothaman in "Dreaming with BRICs: The Path to 2050," Global Economics Paper no. 99, Oct. 2003, and upward again in *BRICs and Beyond,* Nov. 2007, http://www2 .goldmansachs.com/ideas/brics/book/BRIC-Full.pdf.

38. Medvedev Confident in His Bank Accounts Despite Crisis: Report, Agence France Presse, Oct. 29, 2008, http://afp.google.com/article/ALeq M5jJGwiNtdVPcD3GapKrTdLV1AGdlw.

CHAPTER FOUR: State Capitalism Around the World

1. Andrew Hammond, "Saudi's Economic Cities Under Pressure to Deliver," Reuters, Aug. 20, 2008, http://www.reuters.com/article/inDepthNews/idUSL 1910285120080820?sp=true.

2. King Abdullah Economic City, http://www.kingabdullahcity.com/en/About KAEC/VisionOfTheCity.html.

3. "The World's Billionaires: #19 Prince Alwaleed Bin Talal Alsaud," Forbes, Mar. 5, 2008, http://www.forbes.com/lists/2008/10/billionaires08_Prince-Alwaleed-Bin-Talal-Alsaud_0RD0.html.

4. Frank Kane, "Dubai's New Energy Bodies Have Work Cut Out," UAE National, Sept. 1, 2009, http://www.thenational.ae/apps/pbcs.dll/article?AID=/20090901/BUSINESS/709019950/1058&template=columnists.

5. "New UAE Media Censorship Law Sparks Criticism," Press TV (Iranian news agency), Apr. 15, 2009, http://www.presstv.com/detail.aspx?id=91435& sectionid=351020205.

6. Lionel Laurent, "Beware an Abu Dhabi Exposé," Forbes, Aug. 27, 2009, http://www.forbes.com/2009/08/27/davidson-abu-dhabi-markets-econ-censor ship.html.

7. Catrina Stewart, "Russian Regional Governor Said ArcelorMittal Could Lose Coal Mines," Breaking News 24/7, July 10, 2009, http://blog.taragana.com/n/russian-regional-governor-said-arcelormittal-could-lose-coal-mines-105670.

8. Working Group on Privatization and Corporate Governance of State Owned Assets, "State Owned Enterprises in India: Reviewing the Evidence," Organisation for Economic Co-operation and Development, Jan. 26, 2009, based on work by Professor Ram Kumar Mishra.

9. Ibid, p. 6.

10. Fortune Global 500, 2009, http://money.cnn.com/magazines/fortune/global 500/2009/full_list.

11. Fareed Zakaria, "Meeting with World Leaders at the United Nations," CNN, Sept. 28, 2008, http://transcripts.cnn.com/TRANSCRIPTS/0809/28/fzgps.01.html.

12. David Lague, "China Corners Market in a High-Tech Necessity," New York Times, Jan. 22, 2006, http://www.nytimes.com/2006/01/22/business/world business/22iht-rare.html?_r=1&pagewanted=print.

13. Dan Levin, "In China, a Rocky Ascent for Basketball," New York Times, July

22, 2009, http://www.nytimes.com/2009/07/23/sports/basketball/23basketball
.html.

14. "Schott's Vocab: Guo Jin Min Tui," *New York Times,* Mar. 26, 2009, http://
schott.blogs.nytimes.com/2009/03/26/guo-jin-min-tui.

CHAPTER FIVE: The Challenge

1. Elaine Wu, "China's Presence Increasingly Important in Cooling the World's
Hot Spots," *US-China Today,* University of Southern California US-China
Institute, http://www.uschina.usc.edu/(X(1)A(S2G8hytzygEkAAAAN2E4O
WIxYTktNmQ1Mi00MGU2LWI4N2UtOGViMDE3OWVkMzFhkUeeeg
e3nS7H-7o_mq0t7O3XI8U1)S(avuz4p45gojo1p45wahedkfo))/ShowFeature.
aspx?articleID=2069&AspxAutoDetectCookieSupport=1.

2. The phrase "rise of the rest" was popularized by Fareed Zakaria in *The Post-
American World* (New York: Norton, 2008).

3. Karl-Heinz Büchemann, "The 'Dumbest Idea in the World': Jack Welch, the
Figurehead of Shareholder Value, Disowns His Doctrine," *Atlantic Times,* Apr.
2009, http://www.atlantic-times.com/archive_detail.php?recordID=1716.

4. Organisation for Economic Co-operation and Development, *Principles of Corporate Governance,* May 1999.

5. Welch rejected the approach in an interview with the *Financial Times,* Mar. 12,
2009: "Shareholder value is a result, not a strategy."

6. President Hoover was petitioned by more than a thousand leading U.S. economists of the time not to sign the Smoot-Hawley Act. Compared to the previous
1922 Tariff Act (which itself had led to dramatic increases in earlier levels), Smoot-
Hawley increased tariffs for 890 groups of goods while decreasing them for 235. By
1932, the average U.S. tariff in dutiable imports was 59 percent, a level surpassed
only once before, a century earlier. See "The Battle of Smoot-Hawley," *Economist,*
Dec. 18, 2008, available several places online, including http://www.people.fas
.harvard.edu/~hiscox/SmootHawley.pdf.

7. "What Is the World Trade Organization?" http://www.wto.org/english/
thewto_e/whatis_e/tif_e/fact1_e.htm.

8. The G20 communiqué, "London Summit—Leaders' Statement," is at http://
www.g20.org/Documents/g20_communique_020409.pdf

9. "Confidence in Obama Lifts U.S. Image Around the World," Global Attitudes Project, Pew Research Center, http://pewglobal.org/reports/display.php?
ReportID=264.

CHAPTER SIX: **Meeting the Challenge**

1. Murray N. Rothbard, "A Future of Peace and Capitalism," in *Modern Political Economy,* ed. James H. Weaver (Boston: Allyn & Bacon, 1973), ch. 28.

2. George Will, "Capitalism Goes Out of Tune," *Washington Post,* May 10, 2009, p. 2.

3. In fact, Schumpeter believed that capitalism would eventually give way to some form of socialism as economies fail to create enough jobs for those who want them and intellectuals seize on social discontent to create welfare states.

4. Roger Altman, "Globalization in Retreat," *Foreign Affairs,* July–Aug. 2009.

5. World Bank press release, Feb. 12, 2009, http://web.worldbank.org/WBSITE/ EXTERNAL/NEWS/0,,contentMDK:22067892~pagePK:64257043~piPK: 437376~theSitePK:4607,00.html.

6. Tom Biracree, "IHS Herold/Harrison Lovegrove Study Finds 2008 Global Up-stream Oil & Gas Transaction Value Fell 32%," *Source,* IHS (Information Handling Services), http://press.ihs.com/article_display.cfm?article_id=4004.

7. From various reports by Albert Park, Cai Fang, and Du Yang for the World Bank's *China Quarterly Update.* According to the bank, in the 1980s, each 1 percent of GDP growth in China led to a 0.3 percent rise in employment, whereas since 2000, each 1 percent of growth may have yielded on average only a 0.1 percent growth in jobs. "How High Is China's Jobless Rate?" *Economist,* Nov. 27, 2008, http://www.economist.com/businessfinance/displayStory .cfm?story_id=12677296.

8. News Conference by the President, Apr. 29, 2009, http://www.whitehouse .gov/the_press_office/News-Conference-by-the-President-4/29/2009.

9. http://travel.state.gov/visa/immigrants/types/types_4317.html. The green-card lottery is officially known as the Diversity Visa Lottery and is available to applicants from all countries other than the ten that are already the largest sources of immigration to the United States. This information is based on U.S. Citizenship and Immigration Services data for 2007 as quoted by the National Foundation for American Policy.

10. William Kerr and William Lincoln, *The Supply Side of Innovation: H1-B Visa Reform and US Ethnic Innovation,* Harvard Business School, working paper 09-005, Dec. 2008.

11. Edwin Chen, "McCain Vows to Halt China Toy Imports If Children Endangered," Bloomberg News, Apr. 22, 2008, http://www.bloomberg.com/apps/ news?pid=20601087&sid=atqFrDRnvz.I&refer=home.

12. Robert D. Atkinson, "The Rise of the New Mercantilism," *Globalist,* May 29, 2008, http://www.theglobalist.com/StoryId.aspx?StoryId=7026.

13. Ibid.

14. "China's Piracy Hurting Its Own Industries," part 4, Associated Press/ MSNBC, July 7, 2006, http://www.msnbc.msn.com/id/13617619.

15. "Support for Free Trade Recovers Despite Recession," Pew Research Center for the People & the Press, Apr. 28, 2009, http://people-press.org/report/511/ free-trade-support-recovers.

16. Philip Stephens, "Wanted: Global Politics to Rescue Global Capitalism," *Financial Times,* http://m.ftchinese.com/index.php/ft/story/001025286/en.

INDEX

INDEX

Coming in March 2012

G-ZERO

Confronting the
Global Power Vacuum

IAN BREMMER

Author of *The End of the Free Market*

ISBN 978-159184-468-6
U.S. $26.95 \ CAN. $31.00

Available wherever books are sold

Portfolio / Penguin
A member of Penguin Group (USA) Inc.
www.penguin.com